WHO'S WHO of LIVERPOOL 1892 - 1989

Doug Lamming

BREEDON BOOKS
PUBLISHING COMPANY

For two young friends,
DAVID NEAL and MATTHEW BANKS,
Liverpool FC *aficionados* both.

WHO'S WHO of LIVERPOOL 1892-1989

Doug Lamming

BREEDON BOOKS
PUBLISHING COMPANY

First published in Great Britain by
The Breedon Books Publishing Company Limited
45 Friar Gate, Derby DE1 1DA
1989

ISBN 0 907969 55 0

Printed by The Russell Press, Nottingham
Jacket designed by Graham Hales

Acknowledgements

I am especially grateful to Jim Creasy and a trio of Michaels (in alphabetical order, Braham, Davage and Featherstone) who have gone to inordinate trouble to shed light on the dark (pre-1900) ages of Liverpool FC history. Kit Bartlett, Nigel Bishop, Graham Blackwood, Malcolm Hartley, Keith Warsop and Alex Wilson have also provided many leads and details. Brendan Kerney and Sid Woodhead have helped with the reproduction of early and often tattered, illustrative material, as has Garth Dykes, who has also supplied some career details.

Photographic Acknowledgements

Photographs supplied from the Colorsport, Steve Hale, Doug Lamming Collection.

Foreword

IT IS a measure of Liverpool Football Club's greatness that they were able, after the Hillsborough tragedy on 15 April 1989, to eventually extend to 24 matches an unbeaten run that started on 3 January. In doing so they won the FA Cup and failed, only at the last gasp, to carry off a second double in three years. And this following the 1987-8 season when the League Championship was won in a canter and another double denied only by a single goal in the 1988 FA Cup Final.

Liverpool have dominated the English game for an unprecedented quarter of a century. During that time they have brought their total of League Championships to 17 (eight ahead of their nearest rivals), won the FA Cup four times and the League Cup in four successive years (1981-84) and lifted the European Cup on four occasions and the UEFA Cup twice.

This book has been particularly pleasurable to write. The Who's Who genre has its own peculiar difficulties when one considers the time-scale to be covered and the wealth of detail required. In this case, however, one has been swept along by the sheer volume of big names, past and present, that have adorned the Reds' history and, consequently, the pages of this book.

Douglas Lamming
May 1989

Notes on the text

General

The years following each player's name are those when he was on Liverpool's books. The appearances etc, quoted immediately below, are those he made in peacetime League matches for Liverpool, plus any made in season 1914-15, when a full peacetime League programme was maintained. 'League debut' is the date of the player's initial appearance in a peacetime League match for Liverpool.

Positions

Precise labelling in the classical 11-position — goalkeeper to outside-left — wording has been used where appropriate. However, the game of the past 20 years or so, necessitates the adoption of broader concepts (defender, midfielder, forward) for players of the 1970s and 1980s.

Nomenclature

Clubs are given the title in use when the transfer or other event took place. Leicester Fosse, for instance, became Leicester City after World War One and Birmingham added 'City' to its title in 1945. 'Bradford' denotes the defunct Park Avenue club.

Transfer Fees

Many of the fees quoted are known to be authentic. The rest have been taken from Press reports.

Honours

Those recorded include international appearances at all levels and inter-League matches. Also, at club level, appearances in domestic and European Cup Finals and qualifications for divisional championship medals (ie where the player has appeared in one-third or more of the matches). For continuities sake, sponsors' names have been ignored (eg the League/Milk/Littlewood's Cup is referred to as the Football League Cup throughout). Figures are up to and including the end of the 1988-9 season.

By the same Author:

A Century of English International Football, 1872-1972 (with Morley Farror)

A Who's Who of Hull City AFC, 1904-1984

A Who's Who of Grimsby Town AFC, 1890-1985

A Scottish Soccer Internationalists' Who's Who, 1872-1986

An English Soccer Internationalists' Who's Who, 1872-1988

Liverpool players parade the Milk Cup around Wembley after beating Manchester United in the 1983 Final.

Frantic goalmouth action at Wembley in the 1950 FA Cup Final. Goalkeeper Cyril Sidlow and defenders Phil Taylor (right) and Bill Lambert scramble clear an Arsenal attack.

Emlyn Hughes holds aloft the FA Cup after the Reds beat Newcastle United in the 1974 Final at Wembley.

ABLETT, Gary Ian **1983-**
Left-back. 54 (3) apps; 1 goal.
League debut: 20 December 1986.
Born: Liverpool, 19 November 1965.
6ft. 11st 4lbs.
Career: Junior football. LIVERPOOL apprentice, professional during 1983-4 (Derby County, loan, January-March 1985; Hull City, loan, September-October 1986).
International honours: England Under-21.
Club honours: Liverpool, Division One champions 1988. FA Cup winners 1989, runners-up 1988.
Gary Ablett was the first local player since Sammy Lee to be developed to senior status by Liverpool. A confident young defender, Ablett made his League debut while on loan to Derby County and also had a month on loan to Hull City before making his Reds' first-team bow. Hull wanted to sign him permanently but the £66,000 they offered was way below Liverpool's valuation.

A'COURT, Alan **1952-64**
Outside-left. 355 apps; 61 goals.
League debut: 7 February 1953.
Born: Rainhill, Lancs, 30 September 1934.
5ft 8¼ins. 10st 7lbs.
Career: Liverpool County Schools. Prescot Celtic. Prescot Cables. LIVERPOOL September 1952. Tranmere Rovers October 1964 (£4,500). Norwich City player-coach July 1966. Later appointments included

Chester assistant manager early 1969, Crewe Alexandra assistant manager-coach 1969, Stoke City coach during 1969-70, Ndola United (Zambia) coach May-July 1972 and a further spell as Crewe Alexandra's assistant manager.
International honours: England. England Under-23. Football League.
Club honours: Liverpool, Division Two champions 1962.
A direct and speedy winger with excellent ball-control and blistering shooting power, Alan A'Court averaged around 35 League appearances per season in a ten-year period as first choice, a testimony to his consistency. He came from a family of Rugby League enthusiasts, who were apparently put out by his 'conversion' to soccer.

AITKEN, Andrew Liddell **1930-31**
Goalkeeper. 1 app.
League debut: 27 December 1930.
Born: Newcastle-upon-Tyne, 25 August 1909. Died: October 1984.
5ft 9ins. 11st 2lbs.
Career: Wallsend. LIVERPOOL March 1930 to 1931.
Andrew Aitken followed Charlie Thompson to Anfield, ten months after Thompson left Wallsend. Aitken's League outing was at Ewood Park, when the Reds drew 3-3 with Blackburn Rovers in a Christmas fixture.

ALDRIDGE, John W. **1987-**

Forward. 69 (12) apps; 49 goals.
League debut: 21 February 1987 (sub).
Born: Liverpool, 18 September 1958.
5ft 11ins. 10st 4lbs.
Career: South Liverpool. Newport County April 1979. Oxford United March 1984 (£78,000). LIVERPOOL January 1987 (£750,000).
International honours: Republic of Ireland.
Club honours: Newport County, Welsh Cup winners 1980; Oxford United, Division Two champions 1985. League Cup winners 1986; Liverpool, Division One champions 1988. FA Cup winners 1989, runners-up 1988.
John Aldridge scored freely for Newport and even more so for Oxford, for whom he averaged 1.5 goals every two games. He succeeded Ian Rush in 1987-8 and played a major role in the Reds' runaway Championship success. When Rush returned from Italy at the start of 1988-9, Aldridge responded magnificently, scoring heavily in the opening games. He went on to play a vital role in Liverpool's quest for another double, scoring the opening goal of the FA Cup Final against Everton.

ALLAN, George Horsburgh **1895-97 & 1898-99**

Centre-forward. 83 apps; 53 goals.
League debut: 14 September 1895.
Born: Linlithgow Bridge, West Lothian, 23 August 1875. Died: 9 October 1899.
5ft 10ins. 12st 4lbs.
Career: Broxburn Shamrock. Bo'ness until 1894; Leith Athletic 1894-5. LIVERPOOL September 1895. Celtic May 1897. LIVERPOOL April 1898, retired through ill health cs 1899.
International honours: Scotland.
Club honours: Liverpool, Division Two champions 1896; Celtic, Scottish League champions 1898.
An outstanding figure in Liverpool's early days, George Allan was a dynamic attacker who scored 60 goals in 97 League and FA Cup matches for the Reds. One writer summed him up thus: "A model centre; of fine physique, great speed and absolutely no fear." Allan died of tuberculosis when only 24 years old.

ALLMAN, Messina Wilson **1908-09**

Right-half. 1 app.
League debut: 13 March 1909.
Born: Burslem, Staffs, 1883.
5ft 8½ins. 11st 7lbs.
Career: Junior football. Burslem Port Vale *c.*1903. Reading 1905. Portsmouth cs 1907. Plymouth Argyle during 1907-08. LIVERPOOL 1908. Grantham cs 1909.
Allman was 18 when he made his League debut for Port Vale, winning a regular first-team place in 1904-05. In two seasons with Reading he made 61 Southern League appearances and played once for Pompey and 20 times for Plymouth Argyle in the same competition. He made his early reputation as a centre-forward or inside-left, moving to the half-back line around 1907.

ANDERSON, Eric **1951-57**

Inside-forward. 73 apps; 21 goals.
League debut: 28 March 1953.
Born: Manchester, 12 March 1931.
5ft 8½ins. 9st 12lbs.
Career: Army football. LIVERPOOL amateur December 1951, professional January 1952. Barnsley July 1957 (£4,000).

Bournemouth & Boscombe Athletic June 1959 (£1,000). Macclesfield.
Eric Anderson was a lightly-built forward, at home in both inside berths. He made up for his slight build with good ball skills and could capitalize on scoring chances. He played nine times in Barnsley's League side (one goal) in 1957-8. These turned out to be his last League appearances and his stay at Bournemouth was brief.

ARMSTRONG, Thomas **1920**
Goalkeeper. 1 app.
League debut: 13 March 1920
Born: Preston, Lancs.
5ft 10ins. 12st.
Career: Army football. Preston junior football. LIVERPOOL amateur January 1920. Preston North End amateur cs 1920.
A fourth-choice goalkeeper pressed into service at Hillsborough, Tom Armstrong was understandably nervous and Sheffield Wednesday's two first-half goals 'were in the nature of gifts' according to one report. He kept a clean sheet after the interval, however, and the Reds snatched a point with goals in the 80th and 89th minutes. His chance came because Elisha Scott and Kenny Campbell were on opposite sides in the Scotland-Ireland international that day and the famous amateur, Howard Baker, was unavailable.

ARNELL, Alan Jack **1953-61**
Centre-/inside-forward. 69 apps; 33 goals.
League debut: 5 December 1953.
Born: Chichester, 25 November 1933.
6ft 1in. 12st 9lbs.
Career: Worthing. LIVERPOOL amateur 1953, professional March 1954. Tranmere Rovers February 1961. Halifax Town July 1963. Runcorn July 1964, retired cs 1966.
Arnell was ideally built for the striker's role, his commanding height giving him supremacy when the ball was in the air. He maintained a respectable scoring rate — averaging a goal every two games — without ever establishing a regular first-team place. A fine schoolboy player, he represented Sussex Youth when with Worthing FC.

ARNOLD, Stephen Frank **1970-73**
Half-back. 1 app.
League debut: 26 April 1971.
Born: Wembley, 5 January 1951.
6ft 1in. 12st.
Career: Junior football. Crewe Alexandra apprentice 1968, professional January 1969. LIVERPOOL September 1970 (£10,000), (Southport, loan, January-April 1972; Torquay United, loan, August-October 1972). Rochdale June 1973. Weymouth 1974-6. Out of football for about two years before assisting Connah's Quay Nomads and West Kirkby.
A strong player, Steve Arnold's solitary League appearance for Liverpool (a 2-2 draw at Maine Road) coincided with rare outings for Chris Fagan and Ray Evans. Arnold was only 23 when he left the League scene after 75 matches (six as substitute). Most of these were in Rochdale's colours as a central defender.

ARROWSMITH, Alfred W. **1960-68**
Centre-forward/inside-left. 43 (4) apps; 20 goals.
League debut: 7 October 1961.
Born: Manchester, 11 December 1942.
5ft 9½ins. 11st 10lbs.
Career: Ashton United. LIVERPOOL August 1960 (£1,250). Bury December 1968 (£25,000). Rochdale June 1970 (£5,000). Macclesfield cs 1972.
Club honours: Liverpool, Division One champions 1964.
Nearly half of Alf Arrowsmith's League appearances for Liverpool came in the Championship-winning season of 1963-4, when he took over the inside-left spot from Jimmy Melia, soon to be transferred to Wolves. A useful link man, Arrowsmith also totalled over 40 League appearances for each of his subsequent clubs, Bury and Rochdale.

ASHCROFT, Charles Thomas **1943-55**
Goalkeeper. 87 apps.
League debut: 7 September 1946.
Born: Chorley, Lancs, 3 July 1926.
6ft 2½ins. 13st 2lbs.
Career: Eccleston Juniors. LIVERPOOL December 1943. Ipswich Town June 1955. Coventry City June 1957. Chorley cs 1958.
International honours: England 'B'.
Charlie Ashcroft was discovered in wartime football but, when the League resumed, he had to contest the first-team goalkeeper's place with Sidlow and Crossley and, despite being at Anfield for 12 years, had only a couple of seasons as first choice (1951-3). He really deserved much more senior football but at Ipswich he was reserve to Roy Bailey and at Coventry he shared first-team duties. He was especially adept at coping with high balls.

BALMER, John **1935-52**
Inside-forward. 292 apps; 99 goals.
League debut: 21 September 1935.

Born: Liverpool, 6 February 1916. Died: 25 December 1984.
5ft 9¾ins. 10st 5lbs.
Career: Collegiate School, Liverpool. Collegiate Old Boys (Everton amateur). LIVERPOOL amateur May 1935, professional August 1935 (wartime guest for Brighton & Hove Albion and Newcastle United), retired cs 1952.
Club honours: Liverpool, Division One champions 1947.
It was Jack Balmer's form as a high-scoring centre-forward for his Old Boys' side — he also represented the Liverpool County FA — which first brought him to Liverpool's attention and he occasionally led the Reds' attack, even though he figured mostly at inside-forward. A thoughtful player and an England trialist, Balmer was by no means a confirmed favourite with the Anfield crowd — apparently they considered him middle class — despite long and loyal service to the club. In the space of seven League games in November-December 1946 he scored 15 goals, including three consecutive hat-tricks. His uncles, William and Robert Balmer, were a famous Everton full-back pairing in the early 1900s.

BAMBER, John **1915-24**
Right-half. 72 apps; 2 goals.
League debut: 13 September 1919.
Born: Peasley Cross, St Helens, 11 April 1895. Died: 1971.
5ft 9½ins. 11st 9lbs.
Career: St Helens Recreation. Heywood. LIVERPOOL December 1915. Leicester City February 1924. Tranmere Rovers July 1927. Prescot Cables August 1930.
International honours: England. Football League.
Club honours: Leicester City, Division Two champions 1925.
At the time of his England appearance, Jack Bamber was judged one of the best three right-halves in the country, a strong-tackling player who gave good support to his attack. Alas, he missed most of the 1921-2 and 1922-3 Championship-winning seasons through injury. The move to Leicester was beneficial and he won a Second Division championship medal at Filbert Street, maintaining a regular place at left-half until Sid Bishop's arrival. At Tranmere, Bamber turned out at centre-half. He played twice against South Africa during the FA tour in 1920.

BANKS, Alan **1956-61**
Centre-/inside-forward. 8 apps; 6 goals.
League debut: 3 September 1958.
Born: Liverpool, 5 October 1938.
5ft 8ins. 11st 2lbs.
Career: Rankin Boys. LIVERPOOL amateur 1956, professional May 1958; Cambridge City cs 1961. Exeter City October 1963 (£6,000, then Exeter's record fee: £3,000 to Cambridge City and £3,000 to Liverpool). Plymouth Argyle June 1966. Exeter City November 1967. Poole Town cs 1973. Tiverton Town 1975-6.
Alan Banks had few chances in Liverpool's first team but he was a prolific scorer in lower grades of football. In 1957-8 he scored ten goals in five Central League games for the Reds and netted over 100 in two seasons with Cambridge City (including a 23-match run when he scored in every game). His 106 League goals in two spells with Exeter established a record aggregate total for the Devon club.

BANKS, William **1913-19**
Inside-right. 26 apps; 6 goals.
League debut: 14 March 1914.
Born: Cramlington, Northumberland, 1893.
5ft 6½ins. 11st 6lbs.
Career: Ashington. LIVERPOOL during the 1912-13 season. Fulham (£600) December 1919 to 1921.
A man of squat build, Willie Banks was more a link man than an individualist. Although he missed Liverpool's 1914 FA Cup Final appearance, the Reds' inside-right berth was in some contention and he seemed to have gained a regular place when the League programme was replaced by wartime competitions. Banks played 40 Second Division games (12 goals) for Fulham until replaced by the England international, Danny Shea.

BARKAS, Henry Brown **1929-32**
Centre-forward. 5 apps.
League debut: 3 January 1931.
Born: Wardley Colliery, Northumberland, 21 January 1906. Died: 1974.
5ft 8½ins. 11st 7lbs.
Career: Spennymoor United. South Shields December 1929. LIVERPOOL December 1930 to 1932 (£1,500).
Harry Barkas had been on the League scene for only a short time before Liverpool snapped him up. Twenty-three goals in 40 Third Division North matches for South Shields (and Gateshead, which the club became in 1930) was the form which attracted the Reds. He was a member of the famous North-East footballing family that included, among others, Ned Barkas (Huddersfield Town) and Sam Barkas, the England full-back.

BARNES, John Charles Bryan **1987-**
Forward. 71 apps; 23 goals.
League debut: 15 August 1987.
Born: Kingston, Jamaica, 7 November 1963.
5ft 11ins. 12st.
Career: Sudbury Court. Watford July 1981. LIVERPOOL June 1987 (£900,000).
International honours: England. England Under-21.
Club honours: Watford, FA Cup runners-up 1984; Liverpool, Division One champions 1988. FA Cup winners 1989, runners-up 1988.

The fact that John Barnes was voted Player of the Year by both the Football Writers' Association and the PFA in 1988 illustrates perfectly the impact which he made in his first season at Anfield. Surrounded by outstanding players, his ability to run at defences and his ball-control, explosive shooting and feinting dribbles seemed to take on another dimension. The son of an army officer, he made his League debut two months after turning professional with Watford. Barnes won his 40th England cap in the 1988 European Championship Finals but sadly failed to reproduce his club form during the competition. In 1988-9, however, he was back to his best with the Reds.

BARON, Frederick John **1925-27**
Centre-forward/inside-left. 20 apps; 7 goals.
League debut: 16 March 1925.
Born: Prudhoe, Northumberland, 29 December 1901.
5ft 9ins. 11st 8lbs.
Career: Prudhoe Castle. Mid-Rhonnda. LIVERPOOL February 1925. Southend United March 1927 to 1932.
In one of those recurring surname coin-

cidences that can confuse football historians, Liverpool fielded two (seemingly) unrelated Barons and, in due course, transferred each to Southend United. The first, Fred, soon gained a run in the Reds' first team, leading the attack in nine of the last ten League games in 1924-5. The following term, however, found him unable to retain his place. In five years at Southend, Fred maintained a good scoring rate (41 goals in 62 League appearances). His best season was 1929-30 when he netted 21 in 25 matches.

BARON, Kevin Mark Patrick 1944-54
Inside-forward. 140 apps; 32 goals.
League debut: 8 September 1947.
Born: Preston, Lancs, 19 July 1926. Died: 5 June 1971.
5ft 6ins. 10st 7lbs.
Career: Preston schoolboy and junior football. Preston North End amateur. LIVERPOOL amateur 1944, professional August 1945. Southend United May 1954. Northampton Town September 1958. Gravesend & Northfleet 1959. Wisbech Town 1959-60. Aldershot July 1960. Cambridge City 1961. Bedford Town later in 1961. Maldon Town (Essex) player-coach cs 1962.
Club honours: Liverpool, FA Cup runners-up 1950.
Liverpool used Kevin Baron mostly at inside-right. On his day he was a grand little forward who combined foraging and dribbling skills with a useful eye for goals. A small frame contributed to his natural elusiveness. He was preferred to Jack Balmer for the 1950 FA Cup Final.

BARTON, Harold 1929-34
Outside-right. 101 apps; 25 goals.
League debut: 9 October 1929.
Born: Leigh, Lancs, 30 September 1911.
5ft 8ins. 10st 6lbs.
Career: Whitegate Juniors (Blackpool). LIVERPOOL November 1928. Sheffield United June 1934 (wartime guest for Bradford, Chesterfield, Lincoln City, Rotherham United and Sheffield Wednesday). Did not play any first-class football after the war.
Club honours: Sheffield United, FA Cup runners-up 1936
Harold Barton was a favourite winger whose speed, control and craft captivated the Anfield crowd. He scored four goals in an FA Cup match against Chesterfield in 1932 and his hat-trick which helped the Reds beat Everton 7-4 in February 1933 made him even more popular with Liverpool fans. Barton, a former butcher's boy, was a regular in Sheffield United's 1938-9 promotion side.

BARTROP, Wilfred **1914-18**
Outside-right. 3 apps.
League debut: 19 December 1914.
Born: Worksop, 1889. Killed in action 1918.
5ft 8ins. 12st.
Career: Worksop Town. Barnsley June 1909. LIVERPOOL May 1914.
Club honours: Barnsley, FA Cup winners 1912, runners-up 1910.
Wilf Bartrop, a skilful, orthodox winger, was a Barnsley regular for five years after joining them from Midland League Worksop. He arrived at Anfield as a veteran of 182 League and Cup games (17 goals) for the Colliers and was a member of their famous Cup-fighting teams of the late 1900's. He lost his life while serving as a gunner in the Royal Field Artillery.

BATTLES, Bernard ('Barney') **1896 & 1898**
Left-back/right-half. 6 apps.
League debut: 21 March 1896.
Born: Springburn, Glasgow, 13 January 1875. Died: 9 February 1905.
5ft 10½ins. 13st 10lbs.
Career: Linlithgow junior football. Broxburn. Bathgate. Heart of Midlothian 1894. Celtic 1895. LIVERPOOL 1896. Celtic cs 1896. Dundee May 1897. LIVERPOOL 1898. Celtic October 1898. Dundee *c.*1903. Kilmarnock cs 1904.
International honours: Scotland. Scottish League.
Club honours: Hearts, Scottish League champions 1895; Celtic, Scottish League champions 1896. Scottish Cup winners 1899, 1900, runners-up 1901, 1902.
Barney Battles lived up to his name, a big, bustling Scottish celebrity who assisted Liverpool late in the 1895-6 season (including three 'Test matches') and played a solitary League game for the Reds in March 1898. He was ponderous but his lack of speed was compensated for by excellent anticipation. His son, also named Barney, played for Hearts & Scotland.

BEADLES, G(eorge) Harold **1921-24**
Centre-forward/inside-left. 17 apps; 6 goals.
League debut: 24 September 1921.
Born: Llanllwehaiarn, Newtown, Mont, 28 September 1897. Died: 29 August 1958.
5ft 7½ins. 11st 2lbs.
Career: Newtown FC. Army football. LIVERPOOL amateur cs 1920 (Grayson's FC, Garston, 1920-21), professional June 1921, Cardiff City May 1924. Sheffield Wednesday November 1925. Southport August 1926. Dundalk player-coach July 1929.

International honours: Wales.
Club honours: Cardiff City, FA Cup runners-up 1925.
Harry Beadles played mainly as an inside-left. He was a good header of the ball, created plenty of chances for others and was no mean goal-getter, scoring 61 in 92 Third Division North matches for Southport. He was a Liverpool licensee after leaving football.

BEARDSLEY, Peter Andrew **1987-**
Forward. 69 (6) apps; 25 goals.
League debut: 15 August 1987.
Born: Longbenton, Newcastle-upon-Tyne, 18 January 1961.
5ft 8ins. 11st 7lbs.
Career: Wallsend Boys Club. Carlisle United August 1979. Vancouver Whitecaps, Canada 1981 (£27,500). Manchester United September 1982 (£250,000). Vancouver Whitecaps 1983. Newcastle United September 1983 (£120,000). LIVERPOOL July 1987 (£1.8m, a British record).

International honours: England.
Club honours: Liverpool, Division One champions 1988. FA Cup runners-up 1988.
Peter Beardsley first achieved prominence as Newcastle United's greatest asset and then in a fine partnership with Gary Lineker in the England team. Beardsley is able to find his way through most defences, aided by fine ball-control and dribbling skills. He was a vital cog in the Reds' 1988 Championship side but disappointed for England in the European Championships.

BECTON, Francis **1895-98**
Inside-left. 74 apps; 37 goals.
League debut: 25 March 1895.
Born: Preston, Lancs, 1873. Died: 6 November 1909.
5ft 6½ins. 10st 2lbs.
Career: Preston junior football. Fishwick Ramblers. Preston North End *c.*1891. LIVERPOOL March 1895 (£100). Sheffield United October 1898. Bedminster June 1899. Preston North End September 1900. Swindon Town cs 1901. Ashton Town cs 1903. New Brighton Tower for a spell before retiring because of ill health.
International honours: England. Football League.
Club honours: Liverpool, Division Two champions 1896.
Frank Becton was a creative inside-forward who brought the best out of many wingers, especially Harry Bradshaw during his Liverpool association. Becton was the best-known member of a prominent soccer family. He died from tuberculosis at an early age, as did so many players in the Victorian and Edwardian eras.

BEEBY, Augustus Richard **1909-11**
Goalkeeper. 16 apps.
League debut: 27 December 1909.
Born: Ashbourne, Derbys, 1889.
Career: Osmaston FC (Ashbourne & District League). LIVERPOOL 1909. Manchester City May 1911 to cs 1912.
Beeby understudied the great Sam Hardy for a couple of seasons and proved a capable deputy. He made 11 appearances for Manchester City, all of them First Division matches.

BEGLIN, James M. **1983-89**
Left-back. 64 apps; 2 goals.
League debut: 10 November 1984.
Born: Waterford, 29 July 1963.
5ft 11ins. 11st.
Career: Shamrock Rovers; LIVERPOOL May 1983; Leeds United June 1989.
International honours: Republic of Ireland.
Club honours: Liverpool, Division One champions 1986. European Cup runners-up 1985. FA Cup winners 1986.
A fine defender, Beglin's intelligent use of the ball has been a hallmark of his performances. He fitted admirably into the Liverpool scheme of things until a broken leg sustained early in 1987 sidelined him for the remainder of that season and the whole of the next campaign. Unable to regain his place in 1988-9, he was given a free transfer.

BENNETT, Thomas Samuel **1916-20**
Inside-right. 1 app.
League debut: 11 October 1919.
Born: Walton, Liverpool, 1891. Died: 11 January 1923.
5ft 7½ins. 10st 11lbs.
Career: Merseyside junior football. LIVERPOOL 1916, retired because of ill health.
Tommy Bennett had a marvellous goalscoring record in wartime soccer. Playing mostly at centre-forward, he netted 77 in 70 matches, including 48 in 35 games during 1917-18 when he was playing part-time and working as a plumber in a shipyard. A consumptive, he died at the age of 31.

BERRY, Arthur **1907-09 & 1912-13**
Forward. 4 apps.
League debut: 11 April 1908.
Born: Liverpool, 3 January 1888. Died: 15 March 1953.
5ft 8½ins. 11st 6lbs.
Career: Oxford University (Blue 1908, 1909). LIVERPOOL 1907. Fulham September 1909. Everton season 1909-10. LIVERPOOL June 1912 (also assisted Oxford City, Wrexham and Northern Nomads) retired 1913.
International honours: England. England amateur.
Club honours: Oxford City, FA Amateur Cup runners-up 1913.
Arthur Berry was a leading amateur — he made 32 appearances for England at that status — whose talents were enjoyed by several clubs. Unpretentious, direct and precise, Berry won Olympic gold medals in the 1908 and 1912 soccer tournaments. A barrister by profession (called to the Bar 1913), he was the son of a Liverpool FC director, who was chairman from 1904 to 1909.

BIMPSON, J(ames) Louis **1953-59**
Centre-forward/inside-right. 94 apps; 39 goals.
League debut: 7 March 1953.
Born: Rainford, Lancs, 14 May 1929.
6ft 1in. 12st 5lbs.
Career: Burscough. LIVERPOOL January 1953. Blackburn Rovers November 1959 (£6-7,000). Bournemouth & Boscombe Athletic February 1961. Rochdale August 1961. Wigan Athletic July 1963.
Club honours: Blackburn Rovers, FA Cup runners-up 1960; Rochdale, Football League Cup runners-up 1962.
Despite doubts about Louis Bimpson's ability to perform well in Division One,

his tally of goals was a respectable one and he certainly did not lack commitment. He was at outside-right for Blackburn in the 1960 FA Cup Final and there can have been few Cup Final wingers as hefty as him.

BLANTHORNE, Robert **1907**

Inside-right/centre-forward. 2 apps.
League debut: 13 March 1907.
Born: Birkenhead, 8 January 1884. Died: 1965.
6ft 1in. 12st 2lbs.
Career: Rock Ferry (four seasons). Birkenhead FC (one season). LIVERPOOL 1907. Grimsby Town later in 1907. Newcastle United May 1908 (£350). Hartlepools United December 1910.

Bob Blanthorne was a centre-half during his Rock Ferry days, later developing into a stylish forward who usually led the attack. Newcastle paid what was then a sizeable fee for him to succeed another ex-Mariner, 'Cockles' Appleyard, but Blanthorne appeared in only one League match for the Magpies, breaking his leg against Bradford City in the opening game of 1908-09. He was never the same player again.

BLENKINSOP, Ernest **1934-37**

Left-back. 71 apps.
League debut: 17 March 1934.
Born: Cudworth, Yorks, 20 April 1902.
Died: 24 April 1969.
5ft 9ins. 11st 5lbs.
Career: Cudworth United Methodists. Hull City October 1921 (£100). Sheffield Wednesday January 1923 ('four-figure fee'). LIVERPOOL March 1934 (about £5,000). Cardiff City November 1937. Buxton August 1939. Wartime guest for Halifax Town, Bradford and Hurst before retiring.
International honours: England. Football League.
Club honours: Sheffield Wednesday, Division One champions 1929, 1930. Division Two champions 1926.

A prodigious talent, Ernie Blenkinsop was one of the finest full-backs England has produced. He was polished and a master of positional tactics. At Anfield he complemented his England partner, Tommy Cooper. Perennially young-looking, Blenkinsop was a Sheffield licensee at the time of his death.

BLORE, Reginald **1957-60**
Outside-right. 1 app.
League debut: 17 October 1959.
Born: Wrexham, 18 March 1942.
5ft 9ins. 11st.
Career: Liverpool Schools. LIVERPOOL groundstaff, professional May 1959. Southport July 1960. Blackburn Rovers November 1963 (£6,000). Oldham Athletic December 1965 (£8,500). Bangor City cs 1971. Ellesmere Port Town 1971-2.
International honours: Wales Under-23.
Reg Blore's reputation was made as a lively centre-forward who became Southport's first representative player in some 30 years. Later in his career he played in midfield. He won the PFA's golf championship in 1968. After leaving football he was employed by an insurance company at Maghull.

BOERSMA, Philip **1965-75**
Forward. 73 (9) apps; 17 goals.
League debut: 27 September 1969.
Born: Kirkby, Liverpool, 24 September 1949.
5ft 10½ins. 11st 7lbs.
Career: Junior football. LIVERPOOL amateur 1965, professional September 1968 (Wrexham, loan, March 1970). Middlesbrough December 1975 (£72,000). Luton Town July 1977 (£35,000). Swansea City September 1978 (£35,000, then a Swansea record), retired April 1981. Remained in football as Rangers' physiotherapist.
Club honours: Liverpool, UEFA Cup winners 1973 (sub, 2nd leg). Division One champions 1973.
Phil Boersma's chance came in 1972-3 when John Toshack was sidelined. Competition for places was intense, however, and Boersma was always on the edge of selection. With his other clubs he totalled 94 League appearances (plus 12 as substitute) and 12 goals.

BOVILL, John McKeown **1911-14**
Inside-right. 27 apps; 7 goals.
League debut: 4 September 1911.
Born: Rutherglen, Lanarks, 21 March 1886.
5ft 7ins. 11st 3lbs.
Career: Junior football. Rangers. Blackburn Rovers April 1908. Chesterfield Town. LIVERPOOL April 1911. Linfield cs 1914.
Club honours: Linfield, Irish Cup winners 1915, 1916.
'A tricky inside-forward . . .he shows excellent control of the ball and is a good shot,' wrote a local reporter at the conclusion of John Bovill's first, and most successful, Liverpool season (23 League games and seven goals). He could play in all the inside positions and was inside-left in the 1915 Irish Cup Final, as well as leading the attack in the following year's Final.

BOWEN, George **1901-02**
Outside-right. 2 apps.
League debut: 14 September 1901.
Born: Walsall.
Career: Bridgetown Amateurs, Staffs, (Walsall League). Wolverhampton Wanderers cs 1899. LIVERPOOL May 1901 to 1902.
George Bowen, who joined Liverpool in

company with the seasoned George Fleming, was, in the words of the *Athletic News*, 'a young and speedy outside-right'. According to the writer of a Wolves' history he had been 'transformed into a first-class and saleable asset'. Indeed, straight from junior soccer he scored 12 goals in 48 First Division games during his two years at Molineux. At Anfield he was a candidate for either flank and his second League game for Liverpool was at outside-left, but John Cox, Tom Robertson and newly-signed Arthur Goddard monopolized the wing positions.

BOWYER, Samuel **1907-12**
Forward. 45 apps; 14 goals.
League debut: 7 September 1907.
Born: Northwich, 12 October 1887. Died: 11 April 1961.
5ft 7ins. 10st 5lbs.
Career: Earlestown (Lancashire Combination). LIVERPOOL cs 1907 to 1912.
Sam Bowyer was signed from a strong Earlestown side which, as runners-up, had just won promotion to Division One of the Lancashire Combination. He soon made his League debut, playing in the second game of his first Anfield season. He proved a versatile player who appeared in all five forward positions and also had one League outing at left-half. The remaining 44 were divided thus: outside-right (1), inside-right (9), centre-forward (8), inside-left (16) and outside-left (10).

BRADLEY, James Edwin **1905-11**
Left-half. 169 apps; 5 goals.
League debut: 23 September 1905.
Born: Goldenhill, Staffs, 1881. Died: 12 March 1954.
5ft 10ins. 11st 7lbs.
Career: Potteries junior football. Stoke 1898. LIVERPOOL September 1905. Reading cs 1911. Stoke cs 1913 to 1915.
Representative honours: Football League.
Club honours: Liverpool, Division One champions 1906; Stoke, Southern League Division Two champions 1915.
Jim Bradley was a model of consistency and a regular first-teamer for Stoke from the age of 17. At his peak he was in the running for an England cap and the *Liverpool Echo* reckoned him unlucky when passed over in favour of R.M.Hawkes of Luton Town. His younger brother, Martin, played for Grimsby Town, Sheffield Wednesday and Bristol Rovers before World War One.

BRADSHAW, Thomas ('Tiny') **1930-38**
Centre-half. 277 apps; 3 goals.
League debut: 25 January 1930.
Born: Bishopton, Renfrewshire, 7 February 1904. Died: 22 February 1986.
6ft 1¾ins. 13st 13lbs.
Career: Woodside Juniors (North-West Lanarkshire League). Bury July 1922. LIVERPOOL January 1930 (£8,000). Third Lanark September 1938. South Liverpool February 1939. Subsequently Norwich City's chief scout following an appointment at Preston with an insurance company.
International honours: Scotland.
'Tiny' Bradshaw possessed a surprisingly delicate touch for someone so well-built and he was strong in defence and attack. He won only one Scottish cap — as a member of the famous 1928 'Wembley Wizards' line-up — but he was unlucky in being a contemporary of the long-serving David Meiklejohn. Bradshaw was extremely consistent, totalling nearly 500 League appearances in 17 seasons.

BRADSHAW, T(homas) Henry 1893-97
Outside-left. 124 apps; 49 goals.
League debut: 28 October 1893.
Born: Liverpool, 24 August 1873. Died: 25 December 1899.
Career: Northwich Victoria. LIVERPOOL October 1893. Tottenham Hotspur May 1898. Thames Ironworks cs 1899.
International honours: England. Football League.
Club honours: Liverpool, Division Two champions 1894, 1896.
Harry Bradshaw spent nearly two seasons at Anfield playing at either centre-forward or inside-left before switching to what proved to be his best position, on the left wing. As an inside man he had scored at the rate of a goal every two games. He later proved a speedy partner to the scheming Becton. He was only 26 when he died.

BRATLEY, Philip Wright 1914-15
Centre-half. 13 apps.
League debut: 3 October 1914.
Born: Rawmarsh, Yorks, 26 December 1880. Died: 1962.
5ft 10½ins. 11st 5lbs.
Career: Rotherham County. Barnsley May 1910. LIVERPOOL May 1914 to 1915.
Club honours: Barnsley, FA Cup winners 1912.
Phil Bratley was a latecomer to the League scene but he proved a worthy successor at Barnsley to the redoubtable England pivot, Tommy Boyle, and made a vital contribution to the Colliers' 1912 Cup Final triumph. Besides his defensive heroics he scored the only goal of the semi-final. Bratley joined the Reds, together with Wilf Bartop, a few months before the outbreak of World War One.

BRIERLEY, Kenneth 1948-53
Inside-/outside-left. 58 apps; 8 goals.
League debut: 6 March 1948.
Born: Ashton-under-Lyne, 3 April 1926.
5ft 8ins. 10st 10lbs.
Career: Range Boilers FC (Oldham). Oldham Athletic April 1945. LIVERPOOL February 1948 (£7,000). Oldham Athletic March 1953 (£2,750). Stalybridge Celtic cs 1955. Mossley August 1956.
Ken Brierley could also give a fair performance at left-half. He had excellent ball-control and vision and was, as one critic described him, 'strong and willing'. In his two spells at Boundary Park he totalled 125 League games and scored ten goals.

BROMILOW, Thomas George 1919-30
Left-half. 341 apps; 11 goals.
League debut: 25 October 1919.
Born: Liverpool, 7 October 1894. Died: 4 March 1959.

5ft 9ins. 11st 2lbs.
Career: Fonthill Road School. West Dingle (Liverpool & District League). Army football. United West Dingle Presbyterians. LIVERPOOL 1919, retired May 1930. Coach in Amsterdam cs 1931. Burnley manager October 1932. Crystal Palace manager July 1935-June 1936 and again from December 1936. Leicester City manager July 1939-May 1945. Leicester City scout July 1950 to his death.
International honours: England. Football League.
Club honours: Liverpool, Division One champions 1922, 1923.
Invalided out of the Army because of septic poisoning, Tommy Bromilow asked for a trial at Anfield and two seasons later had blossomed into an England player. He was a constructive player and a crisp tackler. Brother-in-law of Theo Kelly, Everton's long-serving secretary and their manager from 1939 to 1948.

BROUGH, Joseph **1910-12**
Inside-right. 10 apps; 3 goals.
League debut: 10 September 1910.
Born: Burslem, Staffs, 10 May 1886.
5ft 7ins. 11st 2lbs.
Career: Potteries junior football. Burslem Port Vale *c.*1906. Stoke cs 1907. Tottenham Hotspur July 1908. Burslem Port Vale. LIVERPOOL cs 1910. Bristol City 1911 to 1913. Port Vale to 1922.
Joe Brough was a stocky raider who could score goals as well as create them for others. For Bristol City he netted 11 in 22 appearances. As a veteran he played 61 matches after Port Vale were recalled to the Second Division as replacement club for the expelled Leeds City in 1919-20.

BROWNBILL, Derek A. **1972-74**
Forward. 1 app.
League debut: 15 September 1973.
Born: Liverpool, 4 February 1954.
5ft 9ins. 10st 10lbs.
Career: Junior football. LIVERPOOL February 1972. Port Vale February 1975 (£6,000). Wigan Athletic September 1978 to 1980.
Derek Brownbill's solitary League outing for the Reds was in a 1-1 draw at St Andrew's, Birmingham. He had more opportunities at Port Vale, making 92 League appearances (eight as substitute) and scoring 13 goals. He made 48 Fourth Division appearances (16 as sub) and netted eight goals for Wigan Athletic.

BROWNING, John **1934-39**
Left-half. 19 apps.
League debut: 20 April 1935.
Born: Alexandria, Dunbartonshire, 27 January 1915. Died: August 1971.
5ft 9ins. 11st 5lbs.
Career: Bridgton Waverley. Dunoon Athletic. LIVERPOOL March 1934 to 1939.
John Browning was a versatile performer. Four of his League games were at right-half and one at inside-left. He was a useful stand-in for Jimmy McDougall and later, Jimmy McInnes. His father, John senior, was a Scottish international winger who played for Celtic and Chelsea.

BRUTON, Leslie Hector Ronald **1932-33**
Inside-left. 7 apps; 1 goal.
League debut: 20 February 1932.
Born: Coventry, 1 April 1903.
5ft 10ins. 11st 7lbs.
Career: Peterborough & Fletton United. Southampton cs 1923. Peterborough & Fletton United 1926. Raith Rovers November 1928. Blackburn Rovers May 1929. LIVERPOOL February 1932. Leamington Town August 1933. Later on Coventry City's training staff.
Les Bruton could play in any of the inside-forward positions and scored freely during his brief time in the Scottish League, as well as netting 23 goals in 38 League games for Blackburn. In Scotland he was described as 'a human tank' and in 1931 it was observed, '. . .he plays with intelligence and can stand punishment from opposing defenders. Astutely supplied with passes, he is a dangerous marksman.'

BUCK, Frederick Richard **1903-04**
Inside-right. 13 apps; 1 goal.
League debut: 5 September 1903.
Born: Newcastle-under-Lyme, Staffs, 1879. Died: June 1952.
5ft 6½ins. 10st 5lbs.
Career: Newcastle-under-Lyme Schools. Stafford Wesleyans. Stafford Rangers. West Bromwich Albion November 1900. LIVERPOOL May 1903. Plymouth Argyle early 1904. West Bromwich Albion April 1906. Swansea Town May 1914, retired 1917.
Representative honours: Football League. Club honours: West Bromwich Albion, Division Two champions 1911. FA Cup runners-up 1912.
Fred Buck was quite a celebrity with West Brom but spent only a brief time at Anfield. Fast and dangerous, he could be brilliant on his day. In 1912 he was switched to centre-half and was soon judged to be among the best pivots in the country. He played at centre-half in the 1912 Cup Final.

BULL, B. **1895-96**
Outside-right. 1 app; 1 goal.
League debut: 25 January 1896.
Bull was a reserve forward who had the satisfaction of scoring a goal in his only League game. It was the Reds' second goal in a 6-1 rout of Lincoln City at Anfield.

BURKINSHAW, Keith H. **1953-57**
Centre-half. 1 app.
League debut: 11 April 1955.
Born: Higham, Barnsley, 23 June 1935.
5ft 11ins. 11st 12lbs.
Career: Denaby United (Wolverhampton Wanderers amateur). LIVERPOOL November 1953. Workington December 1957 (£2,500) (player-manager November 1964-March 1965). Scunthorpe United June 1965, retired cs 1968. Newcastle United assistant coach 1968 and first-team coach 1971-May 1975. Tottenham Hotspur chief coach June 1975, manager July 1976-May 1984. Bahrain national team coach June 1984. Gillingham manager October 1988-April 1989.
Apart from his Liverpool debut, Keith Burkinshaw's entire playing career was spent in the lower divisions of the Football League. A workmanlike wing-half, he totalled some 400 League appearances but became better known as a coach and manager, particularly at Tottenham.

BURROWS, David **1988-**
Defender. 16 (4) apps.
League debut: 22 October 1988.
Born: Dudley, Worcs, 25 October 1968.
5ft 8ins. 11st.
Career: Midlands junior football to West

Bromwich Albion as an apprentice, turning professional 1986-7. LIVERPOOL October 1988 (£500,000).
International honours: England Under-21.
David Burrows commanded a large fee after only a moderate number of Second Division games in an Albion shirt. He is a sturdy youngster, resolute with his tackling and a positive runner when engaged on an overlap.

BUSBY, (Sir) Matthew CBE 1936-45
Right-half. 118 apps; 3 goals.
League debut: 14 March 1936.
Born: Orbiston nr Bellshill, Lanarks, 26 May 1909.
5ft 10ins. 11st 9lbs.
Career: Alpine Villa. Denny Hibernian. Manchester City February 1928. LIVERPOOL March 1936 (£8,000) (wartime guest with Chelsea, Middlesbrough, Reading, Brentford, Bournemouth & Boscombe Athletic and Hibernian), retired October 1945. Manchester United manager February 1945 (taking up post October 1945), administrative manager June 1969; acting team manager December 1970-July 1971, director October 1971, president March 1980. Football League management committee member June 1973, League vice-president in February-July 1982. Resigned his Manchester United directorship August 1982 but remained president.
International honours: Scotland. Scotland wartime.

Club honours: Manchester City, FA Cup winners 1934, runners-up 1933.
Originally a moderate inside-forward, Matt Busby was moved to right-half late in 1930 and never looked back. He had all the skills and used the ball immaculately. Sir Matt became a major post-war figure, moulding Manchester United into one of the great clubs and surviving the Munich air crash to re-build a decimated team. He was Scotland's team manager 1958-9 and was awarded the freedom of Manchester in 1967.

BUSH, W(illiam) Thomas 1933-47
Centre-/left-half. 64 apps; 1 goal.
League debut: 30 December 1933.
Born: Hodnet, Salop, 22 February 1914.
Died: 20 December 1969.
6ft 1½ins. 13st.
Career: Shrewsbury Amateurs. LIVERPOOL March 1933 (wartime guest for Brighton & Hove Albion, Leeds United and Fulham), retired 1947. Coached in Holland. Later worked on Liverpool's coaching and office staff.
A long-time Liverpool servant on and off the field, Tom Bush had the fairly unusual experience of waiting three years for his second League appearance. He had the misfortune to play in the era of 'Tiny' Bradshaw and Jimmy McDougall. He also appeared at left-back and possessed an ideal physique for the centre-half position. Bush was one of many players whose careers were ended by war.

BYRNE, Gerald **1955-69**
Right-/left-back. 273 (1) apps; 2 goals.
League debut: 28 September 1957.
Born: Liverpool, 29 August 1938.
5ft 10ins. 12st 6lbs.
Career: Liverpool Schools. LIVERPOOL amateur, professional August 1955, retired through injury December 1969. Later on club's coaching staff.
International honours: England. England Under-23.
Club honours: Liverpool, European Cup-winners' Cup runners-up 1966. Division One champions 1964, 1966. Division Two champions 1962. FA Cup winners 1965.
Gerry Byrne is well remembered for his bravery in playing 117 minutes of the 1965 FA Cup Final with a broken collarbone when the Reds won the trophy after extra-time. He was a solid, 'give-nothing-away' defender who complemented his partner, the more attacking Chris Lawler.

CADDEN, Joseph Y. **1948-52**
Centre-half. 4 apps.
League debut: 23 September 1950.
Born: Glasgow, 13 April 1920.
6ft. 13st.
Career: Brooklyn Wanderers, USA. LIVERPOOL June 1948. Grimsby Town June 1952. Accrington Stanley June 1953 to 1954. New Brighton early in 1955.
Joe Cadden was a big Scot who took a circuitous route to League football. He went to the United States after being demobbed from military service and impressed the Anfield management during Liverpool's 1948 tour to the USA. He made five senior appearances (four League and one FA Cup) prior to a season spent mostly in Grimsby Town's reserve side with only one League outing. Cadden enjoyed far more first-team football at Accrington before going into non-League soccer.

CALLAGHAN, Ian Robert MBE **1957-78**
Outside-right, later midfield. 636 (4) apps; 49 goals.
League debut: 16 April 1960.
Born: Liverpool, 10 April 1942.
5ft 7ins. 10st 11lbs.
Career: Liverpool Schools. LIVERPOOL

groundstaff 1957, professional March 1960. Swansea City September 1978-January 1981. Later that season assisted Cork United and Soudifjord (Norway). Crewe Alexandra October 1981-February 1982.
International honours: England. England Under-23. Football League.
Club honours: Liverpool, European Cup winners 1977. European Cup-winners' Cup runners-up 1966. UEFA Cup winners 1973, 1976. Division One champions 1964, 1966, 1973, 1976, 1977. Division Two champions 1962. FA Cup winners 1965, 1974, runners-up 1971, 1977 (sub). Football League Cup runners-up 1978.
Ian Callaghan holds the Reds' appearances record and enjoyed a remarkably long League career. He was thoughtful, efficient and never committed a mean act. The Football Writers' Player of the Year 1974 and awarded the MBE in 1975. Became a restauranteur in 1981.

CAMERON, J. 1894-95
Left-back/half-back. 4 apps.
League debut: 6 October 1894.
Born: probably in Glasgow.
Career: Linthouse. Rangers August 1893. LIVERPOOL June 1894 to 1895.
Cameron was a Scot who spent a season at Anfield. By way of coincidence, he also made four first-team appearances for Rangers (all friendlies), two at full-back and two in the half-back line. The pattern was repeated with Liverpool. He played a couple of games at left-back and two as a half-back (one centre-half and one left-half).

CAMPBELL, Donald 1950-58
Left-half. 47 apps; 3 goals.
League debut: 14 November 1953.
Born: Bootle, 19 October 1932.
5ft 7½ins. 10st 10lbs.
Career: Bootle Schools. LIVERPOOL November 1950. Crewe Alexandra July 1958 (£4,000). Gillingham September 1962 (after two-month trial). Folkestone Town August 1964.
International honours: England Youth.
An adaptable player, Don Campbell made his League debut at inside-right and was also a useful right-half and centre-half. However, he was unable to establish a regular first-team place at Anfield, his best season being his last (27 League games). He was a regular at Crewe, averaging 37 League appearances per season.

CAMPBELL, Kenneth 1911-20
Goalkeeper. 125 apps.
League debut: 10 February 1912.
Born: Glasgow, 6 September 1892. Died: 28 April 1977.
5ft 11ins. 11st 9lbs.
Career: Rutherglen Glencairn. Cambuslang Rovers. LIVERPOOL May 1911. Partick Thistle April 1920 (£1,750). New Brighton June 1922. Stoke March 1923. Leicester City November 1925. New Brighton November 1929, retired cs 1931.
International honours: Scotland. Scottish League.
Club honours: Liverpool, FA Cup runners-up 1914; Partick Thistle, Scottish Cup winners 1921.
Kenny Campbell's name figures prominently in the list of Liverpool's international goalkeepers. He was a cool, consistent 'keeper, universally liked because of an unassuming and friendly character. In October 1922 he opened a sports outfitter's shop at Wallasey and the business is still going strong today.

CAMPBELL, Robert J. **1954-61**
Wing-half. 14 apps; 1 goal.
League debut: 5 September 1959.
Born: Liverpool, 23 April 1937.
5ft 9ins. 11st 9lbs.
Career: Liverpool Schools. LIVERPOOL amateur, professional May 1954. Wigan Athletic cs 1961. Portsmouth November 1961 (£1,000 paid to Liverpool). Aldershot July 1966, retired through injury 1967. Portsmouth coach. Queen's Park Rangers coach 1972 to 1974. Arsenal coach 1974 to 1976. Fulham coach cs 1976, manager December 1976-October 1980. Portsmouth coach, manager March 1982-May 1984. Arsenal assistant manager. Queen's Park Rangers reserve-team coach. Chelsea coach February 1988, caretaker manager March 1988, manager May 1988.
International honours: England Youth.
Bobby Campbell was a reserve at Liverpool. A powerful wing-half, he played 60 League games (plus one as substitute) for Pompey in his longest spell with one club. Campbell is better known as a coach and manager.

CARLIN, John **1902-07**
Inside-forward. 31 apps; 8 goals.
League debut: 17 January 1903.
Born: Liverpool.
5ft 7½ins. 11st 2lbs.
Career: Merseyside junior football. LIVERPOOL 1902. Preston North End cs 1907 to 1909.
Club honours: Liverpool, Division One champions 1906.
When he joined Liverpool, John Carlin was described as 'a local player of considerable promise'. Carlin certainly impressed with his resolute and dashing style. Almost half his League appearances for the Reds were in 1905-06, which meant he qualified for a Championship medal. At Preston he made 32 League appearances (five goals) before fading from the scene. Even the omnipotent *Athletic News* confessed ignorance of his whereabouts.

CARLIN, William **1958-62**
Inside-forward. 1 app.
League debut: 10 October 1959.
Born: Liverpool, 6 October 1940.
5ft 6ins. 9st 7lbs.
Career: Liverpool Schools. LIVERPOOL amateur, professional May 1958. Halifax Town August 1962 (£1,500). Carlisle United October 1964 (£10,000). Sheffield United November 1967 (£40,000). Derby County August 1968 (£63,000, Derby record). Leicester City October 1970 (£35,000). Notts County September 1971 (£18,000). Cardiff City November 1973 (originally on loan), retired May 1974.

International honours: England Schoolboy. England Youth.
Club honours: Carlisle United, Division Three champions 1965; Derby County, Division Two champions 1969; Leicester City, Division Two champions 1971.
Willie Carlin was considered too small by the Liverpool management but he gave fine service to several clubs, attracted significant fees and collected three championship medals. A tenacious schemer, he totalled 442 League matches (plus three as substitute) and scored 74 goals. After retiring, he ran a newsagent's shop near Derby before going to live in Majorca.

CARNEY, Leonard F. **1939-48**
Inside-forward. 6 apps; 1 goal.
League debut: 31 August 1946.
Born: Liverpool, 30 May 1915.
Career: Collegiate Old Boys (Liverpool). LIVERPOOL amateur.
Len Carney was a product of the same Merseyside club which launched Jack Balmer on his way. He played a fair amount of wartime soccer for the Reds, from 1939-40 onwards, and partnered Billy Liddell in the first two League fixtures after normal football resumed. Carney, a graduate of Liverpool University, taught history at Oldham Grammar School.

CARR, Leslie L. ('Lance') **1933-36**
Outside-left. 31 apps; 8 goals.
League debut: 16 December 1933.
Born: Johannesburg, 18 February 1910.
5ft 9ins. 11st 11lbs.
Career: Johannesburg Calies. Boksburg FC (South Africa). LIVERPOOL August 1933. Newport County October 1936. South Liverpool August 1937. Newport County 1938 (wartime guest with Bristol City, Swindon Town and Aldershot). Bristol Rovers August 1946 to 1947.
Club honours: Newport County, Division Three South champions 1939.
Lance Carr joined Liverpool as an inside-left around the same time as fellow South African, Berry Nieuwenhuys. He played his first two League games in that position before switching to the flank in 1934-5. It was at outside-left that he starred in Newport's promotion line-up, in the last pre-war season. Carr, the son of a professional runner, had exceptional speed and this was his most obvious quality.

CASE, James Robert **1973-81**
Forward. 170 (16) apps; 23 goals.
League debut: 26 April 1975.
Born: Liverpool, 18 May 1954.
5ft 9ins. 11st 7lbs.
Career: South Liverpool amateur (LIVERPOOL amateur 1972 to 1973), professional. LIVERPOOL May 1973 (£500). Brighton & Hove Albion August 1981 (£350,000). Southampton March 1985 (£25,000).
International honours: England Under-23.
Club honours: Liverpool, European Cup winners 1977, 1978, 1981 (sub). UEFA Cup winners 1976. Division One champions 1976, 1977, 1979, 1980. FA Cup runners-up 1977. Football League Cup winners 1981, runners-up 1978; Brighton & Hove Albion, FA Cup runners-up 1983.
'A ball winner who goes in hard,' was one scribe's pithy summing-up of Jimmy Case, who also possessed one of the hardest shots in football. A thoroughly wholehearted performer, Case served his apprenticeship as an electrician before taking up full-time professional football.

CHADBURN, John **1903-04**
Right-back. 2 apps.
League debut: 5 September 1903.
Born: Mansfield, 1873. Died: 31 December 1924.
5ft 8ins. 11st 10lbs.
Career: Mansfield junior football. Lincoln City 1892. Notts County cs 1894. Wolverhampton Wanderers 1897. West Bromwich Albion January 1900. LIVERPOOL May 1903. Plymouth Argyle cs 1904. Swindon Town 1906. Mansfield Town *c.*1907, retiring soon afterwards.
John Chadburn played in the two opening League fixtures of 1903-04 and that was the extent of his senior career with Liverpool. He was fast and was said to have a volatile nature. He also appeared at outside-right.

CHADWICK, Edgar Wallace **1902-04**
Inside-forward. 43 apps; 7 goals.
League debut: 6 September 1902.
Born: Blackburn, 14 June 1869. Died: 14 February 1942.
5ft 7ins. 11st.
Career: Little Dots FC. Blackburn Olympic 1886-87. Blackburn Rovers cs 1887. Everton July 1888. Burnley cs 1899. Southampton August 1900. LIVERPOOL cs 1902. Blackpool May 1904. Glossop cs 1905. Darwen cs 1906, retired 1908. Coached in Germany and Holland.
International honours: England. Football League.
Club honours: Everton, Division One champions 1891. FA Cup runners-up 1893, 1897; Southampton, Southern League champions 1901. FA Cup runners-up 1902.
A football celebrity of the 1890s, Edgar Chadwick formed a legendary left-wing partnership with Alf Milward during his long Everton career. One critic described him as 'a plodding, straightforward player who passed well', but that did him scant justice and he was generally admired for his all-action style. His cousin, Arthur Chadwick, played for several clubs including Southampton and Portsmouth, and won two England caps. Edgar was a baker by trade.

CHALMERS, William Green **1923-25**
Outside-left. 2 apps.
League debut: 29 November 1924.
Born: Aberdeen, 3 April 1901.
5ft 10ins. 11st 7lbs.
Career: Old Aberdeen FC. LIVERPOOL cs 1923. Tranmere Rovers June 1925 to 1926.
Billy Chalmers, who was tall for a winger, impressed Liverpool in the trials which preceded the 1923-4 season but did not make his League bow until 15 months later. He was in the shadow of Fred Hopkin at Anfield and had more scope at Prenton Park, making 23 League appearances for Tranmere and scoring three goals.

CHAMBERS, Henry ('Smiler') **1915-28**
Centre-/inside-forward. 310 apps; 135 goals.
League debut: 30 August 1919.
Born: Willington Quay, Northumberland, 17 November 1896. Died: 29 June 1949.
5ft 9½ins. 13st 2lbs.
Career: Tynemouth Schools. Willington United Methodists. North Shields Athletic. LIVERPOOL April 1915 (wartime guest

with Belfast Distillery and Glentoran). West Bromwich Albion March 1928. Oakengates Town player-manager July 1929. Hereford United January 1933.
International honours: England. Football League.
Club honours: Liverpool, Division One champions 1922, 1923; Glentoran, Irish Cup runners-up 1919.
Harry Chambers is one of the great names of Liverpool's early story. Despite his hefty frame he showed delightful touches and possessed a fierce left-foot shot. Perhaps best at inside-left, he moved to centre-half after joining West Brom. A shipyard worker by trade.

CHARLTON, John Browell **1929-32**
Left-back. 3 apps.
League debut: 10 October 1931.
Born: Leadgate, Co Durham, 23 March 1908. Died: 1969.
5ft 8ins. 11st 9lbs.
Career: Wallsend. Bradford City June 1928. LIVERPOOL October 1929 to 1932.
John Charlton did not appear in Bradford City's League team and he did not play in Liverpool's until his last season at Anfield, when he deputized for Tommy Lucas on three occasions. He could also play on the right flank and did well in the Central League.

CHECKLAND, Francis Joseph **1919-23**
Right-half. 5 apps.
League debut: 10 September 1921.
Born: Seaforth, Liverpool, 31 July 1895. Died: 19 June 1960.
5ft 7½ins. 11st 2lbs.
Career: Junior football. LIVERPOOL during 1918-19 season. Tranmere Rovers October 1923 to cs 1925.
Originally on Liverpool's books as an amateur, Frank Checkland was described as 'a young local player of possibilities' in a 1922 annual publication. However, he did not have much opportunity to blossom in the shadows of McNab, Bamber and Bromilow. His League appearances came in successive fixtures (10 September-8 October 1921). A schoolmaster, he taught at St Xavier's College, Liverpool.

CHILDS, Albert R. **1953-54**
Right-back. 2 apps.
League debut: 19 September 1953.
Born: Liverpool, 25 September 1930.
Career: Northern Nomads for several seasons. LIVERPOOL amateur 1953. Bishop Auckland.
International honours: England Amateur.
Club honours: Bishop Auckland, FA Amateur Cup winners 1957.
Bert Childs played in successive League fixtures for the Reds, against Burnley (home) and Charlton Athletic (away) in September 1953. The results were a 4-0 win and a 6-0 defeat respectively. Childs won his cap the following season and played left-back in the 1957 FA Amateur Cup Final.

CHISNALL, J(ohn) Philip **1964-67**
Centre-forward. 6 apps; 1 goal.
League debut: 22 August 1964.
Born: Manchester, 27 October 1942.
5ft 8ins. 11st.
Career: Stretford Schools. Manchester United amateur 1958, professional November 1959. LIVERPOOL April 1964 (£25,000). Southend United August 1967 (£12,000). Stockport County September 1971 to cs 1972.
International honours: England Schoolboys. England Under-23.

Phil Chisnall was a schoolboy star who won six England caps and was quickly snapped up by Manchester United. It was the era of Law and Charlton and he managed only 35 League appearances for United. He was also a reserve at Anfield but found regular first-team football with Southend and Stockport, boosting his League appearances total to more than 200.

CHORLTON, Thomas **1904-12**
Utility player. 118 apps; 8 goals.
League debut: 24 September 1904.

Born: Huyton, Liverpool.
5ft 8ins. 11st 9lbs.
Career: Accrington Stanley. LIVERPOOL cs 1904 to 1912.
Tom Chorlton was a versatile defender who also made occasional appearances in the forward line. Most of his League games were at full-back (51 on the right flank and 36 on the left) and 27 were at wing-half (18 and 9 respectively).

CHRISTIE, Frank **1949-51**
Left-half. 4 apps.
League debut: 15 March 1950.
Born: Scone, Perthshire, 17 February 1927.
6ft. 12st 4lbs.
Career: Scone Juniors. LIVERPOOL March 1949. East Fife January 1951

(around £8,000), retired 1958. Forfar Athletic trainer-coach.
Club honours: East Fife, Scottish League Cup winners 1954.
Frank Christie played on the right flank for East Fife and was a pillar of the Methil club in the 1950s. He was described as 'a grand tackling wing half-back who gets the ball through with intelligence'. His League debut, though, for the Reds against Manchester United at Old Trafford, was at inside-left.

CLARK, J(ohn) Robert **1928-31**
Forward. 40 apps; 11 goals.
League debut: 4 February 1928.
Born: Newburn, Newcastle-upon-Tyne, 6 February 1903. Died: 1977.
6ft. 14st.
Career: Spencer's Welfare. Hawthorn Leslie. Newburn Grange. Newburn FC. Prudhoe Castle. Newcastle United February 1923 (£130). LIVERPOOL January 1928 (£3,000). Nottingham Forest July 1931-May 1932. Later in the 1930s had a spell as North Shields player-coach.
Club honours: Newcastle United, Division One champions 1927.
Regarded as an inside-right at Newcastle, Bob Clark played in all three inside positions and at outside-left while at Anfield. He was immensely popular at St James' Park and 'built like an elephant', according to a local historian. Clark carried a block-busting shot but, although quite skilful, was on the slow side and rarely excelled in the air. He scored 17 goals in 76 League games for Newcastle.

CLEGHORN, Thomas **1896-99**
Left-half. 60 apps.
League debut: 21 March 1896.
Born: Leith, Edinburgh, 1871.
Career: Leith Athletic. Blackburn Rovers 1894. LIVERPOOL early 1896. Portsmouth 1899 to 1902.
Club honours: Portsmouth, Southern League champions 1901.
Tom Cleghorn was enthused over by Charles Francis, an early Blackburn Rovers historian who described him as 'a great little player who never knew when he was beaten. He worked like a demon, tackled effectively and headed the ball with wonderful skill. His value was enhanced by the judgement he displayed in feeding the forwards. On many occasions Cleghorn roused crowds to a frenzy of enthusiasm.'

CLELAND, James W. **1895**
Inside-left. 1 app (Test match).
League debut: 27 April 1895.
Born: probably in Lanarkshire.
Career: Minerva FC. Royal Albert (Larkhall). Edinburgh St Bernard's December 1894. LIVERPOOL for the above Test match only).
International honours: Scotland.
Club honours: St Bernard's, Scottish Cup winners 1895.
It was acceptable to recruit players just to play in the Tests that decided relegation in the 1890s and Liverpool fielded Jimmy Cleland against Bury at Blackburn. The Reds lost and were relegated. He was one of three Clelands in the Royal Albert team of the period and the most distinguished, being the club's only full cap. He was also a member of the Minerva team which won the Scottish Junior Cup in 1891-2. He played inside-left for Liverpool but was described as a left winger 'who could control the ball and swing it in from the touch-line right into goal with some pith.' Cleland was employed as a clerk in Glasgow.

CLEMENCE, Raymond Neal MBE **1967-81**

Goalkeeper. 470 apps.
League debut: 31 January 1970.
Born: Skegness, Lincs, 5 August 1948.
5ft 11½ins. 12st.
Career: Skegness schools football. Skegness Youth Club (Notts County amateur). Scunthorpe United August 1965. LIVERPOOL June 1967 (£18,000). Tottenham Hotspur August 1981 (£300,000), retired April 1988. Tottenham Hotspur Reserves coach June 1989.
International honours: England. England Under-23. Football League.
Club honours: Liverpool, European Cup winners 1977, 1978, 1981. UEFA Cup winners 1973, 1976. Division One champions 1973, 1976, 1977, 1979, 1980. FA Cup winner 1974, runners-up 1971, 1977. Football League Cup winners 1981, runners-up 1978; Tottenham Hotspur, FA Cup winners 1982, runners-up 1987. Football League Cup runners-up 1982.
Ray Clemence graduated from being a deck-chair attendant on Skegness beach to a world-class goalkeeper whose total of 61 full England caps would have been even greater but for the presence of Peter Shilton. Clemence had the full range of goalkeeping skills and was very much the master of his own penalty area.

COCKBURN, William Old **1924-28**

Centre-half. 63 apps.
League debut: 20 September 1924.
Born: Willington Quay, Northumberland, 1899. Died: 27 December 1958.
6ft 0¼in. 12st.
Career: Rosehill FC (Newcastle). Stockport County cs 1921. LIVERPOOL May 1924. Queen's Park Rangers July 1928. Swindon Town July 1930, retired cs 1931.
The first of two centre-halves — Norman Low was the other — to play for Liverpool between the wars, having been produced by the Newcastle-on-Tyne junior club, Rosehill. Cockburn made his first 12 appearances for the Reds at right-half and took over the centre-half spot in 1926-7, after Watty Wadsworth's departure. The following season he lost his place to Jimmy Jackson.

COHEN, Abraham ('Avi') **1979-81**

Left-back. 16 (2) apps; 1 goal.
League debut: 15 September 1979.
Born: Cairo, 14 November 1956.
5ft 11½ins. 11st 11lbs.
Career: Macabbi (Tel Aviv). LIVERPOOL trial February 1979, permanently May 1979 (£200,000). Macabbi (Tel Aviv) November 1981 (£100,000). Rangers May 1987.
International honours: Israel.

Avi Cohen was already an Israeli international when he arrived at Anfield. He proved both brave and resolute, qualities that probably induced his Anfield contemporary, Graeme Souness, to sign him for Rangers.

COLLINS, James Henry **1936-37**
Inside-forward/outside-left. 7 apps.
League debut: 1 February 1936.
Born: London, 30 January 1911. Died: 10 July 1983.
5ft 8ins. 12st 3lbs.
Career: Tooting & Mitcham. Queen's Park Rangers 1931-2 season. Tunbridge Wells Rangers July 1933. Rochdale September 1933. Stockport County cs 1934. Walsall cs 1935. LIVERPOOL January 1936. Cardiff City May 1937 (wartime guest for Swindon Town and Aberamen).
Club honours: Cardiff City, Welsh Cup runners-up 1939.
Jimmy Collins was a strongly-built, adaptable forward who travelled around the League circuit during the 1930s. Latterly he seemed to relish the Third Division and scored 14 goals in 22 League outings with Walsall, then 45 in 78 matches for Cardiff before the outbreak of war.

COLVIN, Robert **1897-98**
Outside-right. 3 apps.
League debut: 8 January 1898.
Born: Kirkconnel, Dumfries, 5 December 1876.
5ft 4½ins. 10st.
Career: Junior football. LIVERPOOL 1897. Glossop North End cs 1898. New Brighton Tower cs 1899. Luton Town cs 1901. Queen's Park Rangers cs 1902. Swindon Town cs 1903 to 1904.
Bobby Colvin was a tiny footballer who proved a skilful and elusive performer. Apparently he suffered ill health and in 1903 it was reported that Colvin 'has been given his papers by QPR and is at present recovering in Scotland.' He recovered sufficiently to join Swindon. Colvin's best season was 1901-02 when he made 28 Southern League appearances for Luton. He made 34 League appearances in his two years with New Brighton Tower.

COOPER, Thomas **1934-39**
Right-back. 150 apps.
League debut: 8 December 1934.
Born: Fenton, Stoke-on-Trent, 9 April 1904. Died: 25 June 1940.
5ft 9½ins. 12st 2lbs.
Career: Trentham (Cheshire League). Port Vale August 1924 (£20). Derby County March 1926 (£2,000). LIVERPOOL December 1934 (£7,500) (wartime guest player for Wrexham in 1939-40).
International honours: England. Football League.
A star of the inter-war period, Tommy Cooper was a skilful and polished defender whose only alleged weakness was heading. He captained Derby and England and became Liverpool's skipper, lining up at Anfield with his international full-back partner, Ernie Blenkinsop. Cooper lost his life in a motor-cycle accident while serving with the Military Police.

CORMACK, Peter Barr **1972-76**
Midfield. 119 (6) apps; 21 goals.
League debut: 2 September 1972.
Born: Granton, Edinburgh, 17 July 1946.
5ft 8ins. 10st 12lbs.
Career: Tynecastle Boys Club. Heart of Midlothian groundstaff. Hibernian 1962. Nottingham Forest March 1970 (£80,000). LIVERPOOL July 1972 (£110,000). Bristol City November 1976 (£50,000). Hibernian February 1980, retired December 1980. Partick Thistle manager December 1980-May 1984. Anartosi FC, Cyprus, manager. Botswana's national coach August 1986
International honours: Scotland. Scotland Under-23. Scotland Amateur. Scottish League.
Club honours: Hibernian, Scottish League Cup runners-up 1969; Liverpool, European Cup winners 1973. UEFA Cup winners 1973. Division One champions 1973, 1976. FA Cup winners 1974.
Peter Cormack started as an 'old-style' inside-forward and, as tactics changed, became known as an attacking midfielder (he wore the Liverpool number-five shirt from February 1974). Cormack had a penchant for nipping in on the blind side and was a fine header, and accurate passer, of the ball.

COTTON, Charles **1903-04**
Goalkeeper. 12 apps.
League debut: 1 January 1904.
Born: Plymouth, 1878.
5ft 8ins. 10st 9lbs.
Career: Sheppey United. Reading 1900. West Ham United cs 1903. LIVERPOOL late 1903. West Ham United 1904-1906. Southend United.
Apart from his short time at Liverpool, Charlie Cotton spent his senior career in the Southern League. A sound 'keeper, he was ever-present for three seasons at Reading. He began as first choice at West Ham, too, but then had to settle for understudying, in turn, Fred Griffiths (Wales), Matt Kingsley (England) and George Kitchen (an inter-League 'cap').

COX, John **1898-1909**
Outside-right/outside-left. 327 apps; 72 goals.
League debut: 12 March 1898.
Born: Blackpool, 21 November 1876.
5ft 9½ins. 12st 6lbs.
Career: South Shore Standard (Blackpool). South Shore FC. Blackpool cs 1897. LIVERPOOL February 1898. Blackpool player-manager cs 1909, retired cs 1911.
International honours: England. Football League.
Club honours: Liverpool, Division One champions 1901, 1906. Division Two champions 1905.

Jack Cox played for four seasons on the Reds' right flank before moving to the left, where he won his honours. He was an extremely fast goalscoring winger, although some critics felt that he tended to overdo the trickery. Cox was a noted athlete who won several handicap races. Also, in the mid-1920s, he was successful in bowls competitions.

CRAIK, H.C. 1903-04
Left-half. 1 app.
League debut: 26 September 1903.
Born: Scotland.
5ft 10ins. 10st 10lbs.
Career: Morton. LIVERPOOL cs 1903 to 1904.
Craik was given a run out in the fourth fixture of 1903-04, a 3-1 win over West Bromwich Albion at Anfield.

CRAWFORD, Edmund 1932-33
Centre-forward/inside-left. 7 apps; 4 goals.
League debut: 27 August 1932.
Born: Filey, Yorks, 31 October 1906. Died: 1977.
5ft 11ins. 12st.
Career: Filey FC. Halifax Town cs 1931. LIVERPOOL cs 1932. Clapton Orient July 1933 (wartime guest for Watford and Brighton & Hove Albion).
Ted Crawford's 21 goals in 30 matches for Halifax during his League debut season made him a hot property. At Anfield, however, he played in only the first few games of 1932-3, his four goals coming in his first three appearances. Apparently the management doubted his potential for top-flight football. Back in Division Three he led Clapton Orient's attack for six seasons, scoring 68 goals in 199 League games.

CRAWFORD, Robert Stuart 1909-15
Right-/left-back. 108 apps; 1 goal.
League debut: 13 February 1909.
Born: Blythswood, Renfrews, 4 July 1886.
5ft 8½ins. 11st.
Career: Arthurlie. LIVERPOOL January 1909 to 1915.
Bob Crawford was given his League baptism less than a month after moving from Arthurlie, the Barrhead club which went on to finish bottom of the Scottish League Division Two that season. A local scribe wrote about Ferguson on that occasion that his 'tackling was superb and general display satisfactory, but his clearances needed much to be desired'. He developed into a competent full-back but a recurring injury marred his late career and, by 1912, the emerging Longworth and newly-signed Bob Pursell monopolized the full-back positions.

CROSSLEY, Russell 1947-54
Goalkeeper. 68 apps.
League debut: 21 October 1950.
Born: Hebden Bridge, Yorks, 25 June 1927.
5ft 10ins. 11st 5lbs.
Career: Army football. LIVERPOOL June 1947. Shrewsbury Town July 1954. Kettering Town November 1959.
'Daring almost to the point of recklessness,' was one critic's reaction to this courageous player. Crossley was signed on the recommendation of Cyril Sidlow and was one of four 'keepers on the books all capable of holding a senior place. The others were Sidlow, Ashcroft and Minshull. An elder brother, Roy, assisted Halifax Town from 1948-51. Russell Crossley was first choice throughout his time at Shrewsbury.

CUNLIFFE, Daniel **1897-98**
Centre-forward. 14 apps; 6 goals.
League debut: 4 September 1897.
Born: Bolton, 1875. Died: 28 December 1937.
5ft 8ins. 11st 7lbs.
Career: Little Lever. Middleton Borough. Oldham County. LIVERPOOL cs 1897. New Brighton Tower cs 1898. Portsmouth cs 1899. New Brighton Tower May 1900. Portsmouth May 1901. New Brompton May 1906. Millwall Athletic cs 1907. Heywood September 1909 to April 1912. Rochdale cs 1912 to 1914.
International honours: England.
Club honours: Portsmouth, Southern League champions 1902.
Dan Cunliffe was generally recognized as an inside-right but 13 of his 14 League matches in a Liverpool shirt were at centre-forward. Difficult to dispossess, his dogged perseverence created many goals for colleagues as well as himself.

CUNNINGHAM, William **1920-24**
Half-back/forward. 3 apps.
League debut: 12 March 1921.
Born: Radcliffe, Lancs, 27 October 1899.
5ft 6ins. 10st 4lbs.
Career: Blyth Spartans. LIVERPOOL May 1920 (£50). Barrow January 1924. Mid-Rhondda September 1924.
Willie Cunningham occupied a different position in each of his League appearances for Liverpool — on the right and left wings and at left-half. He had 39 League outings for Barrow before returning to the non-League scene.

CURRAN, John **1894-96**
Right-back. 21 apps.
League debut: 3 November 1894.
Born: Scotland (probably in Glasgow).
Career: Glasgow Benburb. Celtic. LIVERPOOL late 1894. Motherwell January 1896. Celtic.
Club honours: Celtic, Scottish League champions 1893, 1894. Scottish Cup runners-up 1894.
John Curran was a product of Celtic's then nursery club, Benburb. Celtic regarded him as a wing-half but he did well at full-back for Liverpool, despite arriving during the disastrous 1894-5 season. He was succeeded by Archie Goldie.

DABBS, Benjamin Edward **1932-38**
Right-/left-back. 54 apps.
League debut: 26 August 1933.
Born: Oakengates, Salop, 17 April 1909.
5ft 10½ins. 12st.
Career: Oakengates Town (Birmingham League). LIVERPOOL June 1932. Watford June 1938 to 1941.
Ben Dabbs' best Anfield season was 1936-7 (32 appearances) when he took over from Ernie Blenkinsop at left-back. Strangely, he did not gain a regular first-team place with Watford and had played only five Third Division South matches when war was declared.

DALGLISH, Kenneth Mathieson MBE **1977-**
Forward. 342 (12); 118 goals.
League debut: 20 August 1977.
Born: Dalmarnock, Glasgow, 4 March 1951.
5ft 8ins. 11st 13lbs.
Career: Glasgow Schools. Drumchapel Amateurs. Glasgow United. Celtic August 1967 (played with Cumbernauld United for a spell). LIVERPOOL August 1977 (£440,000, record fee between British clubs), player-manager June 1985.
International honours: Scotland. Scotland Under-23. Scotland Youth. Scotland Schoolboys.
Club honours: Celtic, Scottish League

champions 1972, 1973, 1974, 1977. Scottish Cup winners 1972, 1974, 1975, 1977, runners-up 1973. Scottish League Cup winners 1975, runners-up 1972, 1973, 1974, 1977; Liverpool, European Cup winners 1978, 1981, 1984, runners-up 1985. Division One champions 1979, 1980, 1982, 1983, 1984, 1986. FA Cup winners 1986. Football League Cup winners 1981, 1982, 1983, 1984, runners-up 1978.

Kenny Dalglish, the holder of a record 102 full Scottish caps, is among the greatest British forward talents of all time. He accomplished the rare feat of scoring over 100 goals in both the Football League and Scottish League. He is a Freeman of Glasgow and was the Football Writers' Footballer of the Year in 1979, as well as being voted Manager of the Year in 1986 and 1988. Liverpool's first player-manager, Dalglish took them to the League and FA Cup double in his first season in charge.

DAVIDSON, David Leighton 1928-30

Centre-half. 58 apps; 2 goals.
League debut: 25 August 1928.
Born: Aberdeen, 4 June 1905. Died: June 1969.
5ft 11ins. 11st.
Career: Garthdee FC. Aberdeen Argyle. Forfar Athletic. LIVERPOOL July 1928. Newcastle United January 1930 (£4,000). Hartlepools United June 1937 (£50). Gateshead October 1937, retired cs 1938. Whitley Bay manager 1945. Ashington manager for approximately 12 years to cs 1963.
Club honours: Newcastle United, FA Cup winners 1932.

A rugged stopper who gave little away, Davidson was first choice at Anfield until the arrival of 'Tiny' Bradshaw. He made 144 League and Cup appearances during seven and a half seasons with Newcastle. After the war he moulded Whitley Bay and Ashington into formidable non-League sides.

DAVIES, J. 1900-03
Forward. 9 apps.
League debut: 9 March 1901.
Career: LIVERPOOL season 1900-01. Blackpool cs 1903.
A utility player, Davies occupied four forward positions in ten senior games for Liverpool (one in the FA Cup). He did not play in the League for Blackpool.

DAWSON, James Maxwell 1913-16
Inside-right. 13 apps; 3 goals.
League debut: 1 November 1913.
Born: Edinburgh, 13 August 1890.
Career: Junior football. LIVERPOOL in 1912-13 to 1916.
Jimmy Dawson was a clever ball-playing footballer. Two of his League games for the Reds were at outside-right and, in the 1915-16 wartime season, all his appearances were at outside-left. Of his debut in November 1913, at Old Trafford, one report said Dawson was 'artistic but needed to infuse more devil into his work at close quarters'.

DEVLIN, William Alexander 1927
Centre-forward. 19 apps; 15 goals.
League debut: 7 May 1927.
Born: Bellshill, Lanarks, 30 July 1899. Died: July 1972.
5ft 9ins. 11st 1lb.
Career: Junior football. Clyde *c.*1921 (King's Park, loan, 1921-2). Cowdenbeath 1923. Huddersfield Town February 1926 (£4,200). LIVERPOOL May 1927. Heart of Midlothian December 1927. Macclesfield November 1928.

Cowdenbeath June 1929. Mansfield Town June 1930. Burton Town March 1931. Shelbourne June 1931. Bangor City August 1932. Boston United August 1933. Also Ashton National and Olympique Marseilles (France).
Ninety-nine goals in the Scottish League for Cowdenbeath between 1923 and 1926 earned Bill Devlin the nickname of 'Demon' and tempted Huddersfield Town to part with a big fee. The remainder of his career yielded 46 goals in 86 League outings. At Mansfield he was reputedly on a record non-League salary.

DEWHURST, Gerald Powys 1894
Centre-forward. 1 app.
League debut: 24 March 1894.
Born: London, 14 February 1872. Died: 29 March 1956.
Career: Repton School (1st XI 1889-90). Cambridge University (Blue 1892-3-4). Liverpool Ramblers. LIVERPOOL amateur 1893-4. Corinthians 1892 to 1895.
International honours: England.
Dewhurst's League debut caused some interest because he was a distinguished amateur, but he did not have a happy beginning and in the second-half moved to inside-right where his game improved. Although well built he was fast, but tended to hold on to the ball too long. A cotton merchant based in Liverpool, he lived near Wrexham during the 1930s.

DICK, Douglas C. **1893-94**
Outside-/inside-right. 10 apps; 2 goals.
League debut: 28 October 1893.
Born: Scotland.
Career: Morton. Rangers 1893. LIVERPOOL late 1893. Third Lanark 1894. Kilmarnock FC director, chairman 1930-32.
'Fearless, dribbled and centred well,' was how a local reporter described Douglas Dick. The player had done well with Morton and played two senior games (one goal) for Rangers. Dick scored the first penalty in a Scottish League match 'with a low, swift shot' for Morton against Celtic on 4 August 1891. The penalty-kick had been introduced a couple of months earlier, on 2 June 1891.

DICKSON, Joseph J. **1952-58**
Inside-forward. 6 apps; 3 goals.
League debut: 29 February 1956.
Born: Liverpool, 31 January 1934.
5ft 6½ins. 10st 7lbs.
Career: Liverpool Schools. Merseyside junior football. LIVERPOOL professional June 1952-8.
International honours: England Youth.
Joe Dickson's League appearances were all made in 1955-6. His debut was at outside-left but he then played twice at inside-right and three times at inside-left.

DINES, Joseph **1912-13**
Left-half. 1 app.
League debut: 9 September 1912.
Born: King's Lynn, 12 April 1886. Killed in action, 27 September 1918.
Career: Schoolboy and junior football. King's Lynn FC. Ilford from 1911. LIVERPOOL amateur cs 1912. Also Millwall Athletic amateur.
International honours: England Amateur
Joe Dines played in 27 Amateur internationals and won a soccer gold medal in the 1912 Olympic Games. According to one account he was known as 'the smiling footballer, this thoughtful young man, a commanding half-back and master of the art of dribbling.' Son of a blacksmith, and a schoolmaster by profession, Dines served in the Ordnance Corps and other units before being commissioned and transferred to the Liverpool Regiment. He was serving with them when he was killed on the Western Front.

DOIG, J(ohn) Edward **1904-08**
Goalkeeper. 51 apps.
League debut: 1 September 1904.
Born: Letham, Forfarshire, 29 October 1866. Died: 7 November 1919.
5ft 9¾ins. 12st 9lbs.
Career: St Helens FC (Arbroath). Arbroath 1883 (one appearance for Blackburn Rovers November 1889). Sunderland September 1890. LIVERPOOL August 1904 to 1908. St Helens Recreation.
International honours: Scotland.
Club honours: Sunderland, Division One champions 1892, 1893, 1895, 1902; Liverpool, Division Two champions 1905.
The first of the Reds' long line of international goalkeepers, Ned Doig was cool, resourceful and extraordinarily consistent. During his time with Sunderland he set a record for the number of consecutive seasons with one club. Doig retired in 1908 but came back to play for St Helens Recreation in his 43rd year.

DONE, Cyril Charles **1938-52**

Centre-forward/inside-left. 94 apps; 33 goals.
League debut: 12 October 1946.
Born: Liverpool, 21 October 1920.
6ft 0½ins. 13 st.
Career: Bootle Boys Brigade. LIVERPOOL January 1938. Tranmere Rovers May 1952. Port Vale December 1954. Winsford United cs 1957.
Club honours: Liverpool, Division One champions 1947.
Cyril Done actually made his first League appearance in the abandoned 1939-40 season, scoring the only goal of the game against Chelsea at Anfield. He scored a lot of goals for the Reds in wartime football and although not a 'pretty' player, a burly frame, industrious approach and a strong shot in his left foot made him a forward to be feared.

DONE, Robert **1926-35**

Right-/left-back. 147 apps; 13 goals.
League debut: 1 January 1927.
Born: Runcorn, 27 April 1904. Died: September 1982.
5ft 9ins. 11st 3lbs.
Career: Runcorn FC. LIVERPOOL April 1926. Reading May 1935. Chester June 1937. Accrington Stanley cs 1938 to 1939.
Although regarded as a left-back, Bob Done made several of his Liverpool appearances on the right flank. In the days before defenders were encouraged to go forward he liked to attack and he became the Reds' penalty-taker. Done was a railway worker before turning professional.

DONNELLY, W. **1896-98**

Goalkeeper. 6 apps.
League debut: 26 December 1896.
Born: Scotland.
Career: Hibernian. Clyde. LIVERPOOL May 1896. Clyde June 1898.
Although a reliable deputy for Harry Storer, Donnelly's eight consecutive senior appearances (including two in the FA Cup) were concentrated in the period December 1896 to February 1897. His run included five wins and a draw but the defeats were substantial and the Reds went down 4-1 and 6-1.

DRUMMOND, John **1894-95**

Outside-left. 15 apps.
League debut: 1 September 1894.
Born: Edinburgh.
Career: Partick Thistle. Preston North End late-1880s. Sheffield United cs 1891. LIVERPOOL cs 1894 to 1895.
Preston gave John Drummond his first chance in the League (11 appearances in 1890-91) before he became a regular with Sheffield United, where most of his games were at outside-right. He was not related to the celebrated Preston 'Invincible', Geordie Drummond.

DUNLOP, William **1895-1909**
Left-back. 322 apps; 2 goals.
League debut: 25 March 1895.
Born: Kilmarnock, 14 July 1871.
5ft 9½ins. 12st.
Career: Sandyford. Hurlford. Annbank. Kilmarnock. Abercorn 1893. LIVERPOOL January 1895 (£35) to 1909. Sunderland assistant trainer from January 1922.
International honours: Scotland.
Club honours: Liverpool, Division One champions 1901, 1906. Division Two champions 1896, 1905.
Billy Dunlop was a great Liverpool servant, who enjoyed 15 years at Anfield. A contemporary writer said that he 'carried good weight, as goalkeepers can testify. Very fast'. A younger brother joined Liverpool from Hurlford in the summer of 1909 but did not appear in the first team.

EASDALE, John **1937-48**
Centre-half. 2 apps.
League debut: 25 December 1946.
Born: Dumbarton, 16 January 1919.
Career: Junior football. LIVERPOOL February 1937 (wartime guest for Brighton & Hove Albion). Stockport County September 1948 to 1949.
Like so many pre-war hopefuls, John Easdale's League debut was considerably delayed. In Easdale's case there were further problems and in 1946-7, Liverpool could call on internationals Laurie Hughes and Bill Jones, as well as Tom Bush who was still around. Easdale made six Third Division North appearances for Stockport.

EASTHAM, Henry **1936-48**
Utility forward. 63 apps; 3 goals.
League debut: 31 October 1936.
Born: Blackpool, 30 June 1917.
5ft 7ins. 11st 3lbs.
Career: Junior football. Blackpool amateur 1934-5. LIVERPOOL February 1936 (wartime guest for New Brighton, Southport, Brighton & Hove Albion, Bolton Wanderers, Leeds United, Newcastle United and Blackpool). Tranmere Rovers May 1948. Accrington Stanley July 1953 to 1954.
Club honours: Liverpool, Division One champions 1947.
Harry Eastham was outside-right in the 1946-7 Championship side but could play anywhere in the attack. His brother was George Eastham senior and he was thus the uncle of George junior, the man who took on the football establishment over the retain and transfer system. Harry was a polished player, perhaps too much of an individualist for Liverpool's liking.

EDMED, Richard Alfred **1926-32**
Outside-right. 160 apps; 44 goals.
League debut: 28 August 1926.
Born: Gillingham, Kent, 14 February 1904.
Died: 1983.
5ft 9½ins. 11st.
Career: Chatham Centrals (New Brompton & District League). Rochester FC. Gillingham late-1923. LIVERPOOL January 1926 (£1,800). Bolton Wanderers May 1932, retired through injury 1932-3. Gillingham assistant trainer for many years.
Dick Edmed's speed, shooting and direct style soon brought First Division scouts to Gillingham. He was equally successful in the top flight, forging a much praised partnership with Gordon Hodgson at Liverpool that was ended by Edmed's cartilage trouble. It was that injury which forced his eventual retirement, but not before he had scored in an 8-1 Bolton victory over Liverpool. Originally he worked as a fitter's mate at Chatham Dockyard.

ENGLISH, Samuel **1933-35**
Centre-forward. 47 apps; 25 goals.
League debut: 26 August 1933.
Born: Coleraine, County Derry, 1910.
Died: April 1967.
5ft 9½ins. 12st 3lbs.
Career: Yoker Athletic. Rangers July 1931. LIVERPOOL August 1933 (about £8,000).

Queen of the South July 1935 (£1,700). Hartlepools United July 1936, retired 1938. Duntocher Hibs and Yoker Athletic coach in 1950s.
International honours: Northern Ireland.
Club honours: Rangers, Scottish League champions 1933. Scottish Cup winners 1932.
Sam English is best remembered as the player whose accidental collision with Celtic goalkeeper, John Thomson, resulted in the latter's death. The event cast a cloud over the career of a hard-working, free-scoring centre-forward. English set a Rangers' scoring record in 1931-2 with 53 League and Cup goals. Outside the game he was a shipyard worker.

EVANS, Alun W. **1968-72**
Inside-right/centre-forward. 77 (2) apps; 21 goals.
League debut: 21 September 1968.
Born: Bewdley, Worcs, 30 April 1949.
5ft 9ins. 11st.
Career: Mid-Worcester Schools. Birmingham Schools. Wolverhampton Wanderers apprentice cs 1965, professional October 1966. LIVERPOOL September 1968 (£100,000, then a record for a teenage player). Aston Villa June 1972 (£70,000). Walsall December 1975 (£3,000). Hellas FC (Melbourne) July 1978 (£10,000).
International honours: England Schoolboy. England Youth. England Under-23 international.
Club honours: Liverpool, FA Cup runners-up 1971.

Son of a former West Bromwich Albion professional, Alun Evans showed outstanding promise as a youngster and developed into a clever, strong and fast striker. His progress at Anfield, however, was marred by a much-publicized night club incident, which left him facially scarred, and a by cartilage operation. He was a player who never lived up to the potential he showed as a teenager.

EVANS, John William **1953-57**

Inside-left. 96 apps; 49 goals.
League debut: 26 December 1953.
Born: Tilbury, Essex, 28 August 1929.
5ft 11ins. 10st 11lbs.
Career: Bata Sports. Tilbury FC. Charlton Athletic amateur May 1949, professional July 1950. LIVERPOOL December 1953 (£12,500). Colchester United November 1957 (£4,000). Romford July 1960.
International honours: Football League.
John Evans played in all three inside-forward positions. He scored all five goals in the Reds' win over Bristol Rovers on 15 September 1954, the first time in over half a century that a Liverpool player had netted so many in one game. He went to Anfield along with Charlton's Frank Lock. The Reds' manager, Don Welsh, was a former Charlton player.

EVANS, Roy Q. **1965-74**

Left-back. 9 apps.
League debut: 16 March 1970.
Born: Bootle, 4 October 1948.
5ft 7ins. 11st.
Career: Bootle Schools. LIVERPOOL apprentice, professional October 1965, retired August 1974 upon appointment as LIVERPOOL reserve-team trainer.
International honours: England Schoolboys.
Roy Evans was a prominent schoolboy player but made only 11 senior appearances before retiring at the age of 25. As coach to the Reserves, Evans masterminded a series of Central League championships, including three in his first three seasons.

FAGAN, Christopher J. **1970-71**
Right-back. 1 app.
League debut: 26 April 1971.
Born: Manchester, 5 June 1950.
6ft. 11st 7lbs.
Career: Junior football. LIVERPOOL July 1970. Tranmere Rovers July 1971. Bangor City May 1975.
Chris Fagan was a tall, slim defender whose only senior outing for the Reds was in his native Manchester, in a 2-2 draw at Maine Road. He made 77 League appearances (plus seven as substitute) for Tranmere before leaving on a free transfer.

FAGAN, William **1937-52**
Centre-forward/inside-left. 161 apps; 47 goals.
League debut: 23 October 1937.
Born: Musselburgh, Midlothian, 20 February 1917.
5ft 10ins. 11st 6lbs.
Career: Junior football. Celtic mid-1930s. Preston North End October 1936 (nearly £7,000). LIVERPOOL October 1937 (wartime guest for Aldershot, Leicester City, Northampton Town, Newcastle United, Chelsea, Millwall, Reading and Crystal Palace). Belfast Distillery January 1952. Weymouth player-manager July 1952-55.
International honours: Scotland Wartime.
Club honours: Preston North End, FA Cup runners-up 1937; Liverpool, Division One champions 1947. FA Cup runners-up 1950.
Willie Fagan cost Preston a then sizeable fee when he joined them as an immensely promising 19-year-old from Celtic. He gave Liverpool good service either side of the war, playing in all the forward positions and at half-back. He worked as a Borstal officer after leaving the game.

FAIRCLOUGH, David **1974-82**
Forward. 64 (36) apps; 34 goals.
League debut: 1 November 1975.
Born: Liverpool, 5 January 1957.
5ft 9ins. 11st.
Career: Schoolboy football. LIVERPOOL on 'S' form, apprentice, professional January 1974. Toronto Blizzard, Canada, April 1982 (£150,000). LIVERPOOL. Lucerne FC, Switzerland July 1983. Norwich City March 1985. Oldham Athletic August 1985. Beveren SK, Belgium, August 1986.
International honours: England Under-21.
Club honours: Liverpool, European Cup winners 1978. UEFA Cup winners 1976. Football League Cup runners-up 1978 (sub), 1983 (sub).
A knack of entering the later stages of important matches and obliging with vital goals earned David Fairclough the 'super sub' tag which he was said to dislike. Fairclough was sometimes criticized for 'fading' during matches but his pace and marksmanship were always likely to turn the scales and he was certainly a crowd-pleaser on his day.

FAIRFOUL, Thomas **1913-15**
Right-half. 62 apps.
League debut: 1 September 1913.
Born: West Calder, Midlothian, 16 January 1881. Died: 1952.
5ft 9½ins. 11st 10lbs.
Career: Junior football. Kilmarnock. Third Lanark cs 1906. LIVERPOOL cs 1913 to 1915.
Representative honours: Scottish League.
Club honours: Liverpool, FA Cup runners-up 1914.
A seasoned campaigner by the time he reached Anfield, Tom Fairfoul proved a splendid signing. He had all-round ability for the wing-half position, tackling well and distributing accurately. Later, he was a taxi proprietor in Liverpool.

FERGUSON, Robert **1912-15**
Centre-/left-half. 92 apps; 2 goals.
League debut: 4 September 1912.
Born: Cleland, Lanarks, *c.*1886.
5ft 10½ins. 11st 5½lbs.
Career: Junior football. Third Lanark 1906. LIVERPOOL cs 1912 to 1915.
Club honours: Liverpool, FA Cup runners-up 1914.
Bob Ferguson arrived at Anfield with the reputation of being one of the best half-backs in Scotland, 'an energetic player of the hustling type'. He was an 'ever-present' in 1912-13 and moved to the left flank the following season to accommodate Harry Lowe. He reverted to pivot for the 1914 FA Cup Final because of Lowe's injury.

Ferguson emigrated to the United States and in the mid-1930s was reported to be living in Seranton, Philadelphia.

FERNS, Philip **1961-65**
Full-back/left-half. 27 apps; 1 goal.
League debut: 29 August 1962.
Born: Liverpool, 14 November 1937.
5ft 10ins. 11st 11lbs.
Career: Merseyside junior football. LIVERPOOL August 1961. Bournemouth & Boscombe Athletic August 1965. Mansfield Town August 1966. Rhyl cs 1968.
Club honours: Liverpool, Division One champions 1964.
Phil Ferns was a rugged, enthusiastic player whose best position was left-half. He totalled 101 League appearances for Bournemouth and Mansfield.

FINNERHAN, Patrick **1897-98**
Centre-forward. 5 apps; 1 goal.
League debut: 11 September 1897.
Born: Northwich, Cheshire, 1872.
Career: Northwich Victoria. Manchester City June 1894. LIVERPOOL March 1897 to 1898.
Representative honours: Football League.
Pat Finnerhan partnered the legendary Billy Meredith for both Northwich Victoria and Manchester City. All but one of his 85 League outings for City were at inside-right and he was ever-present in 1894-5 and 1895-6 (when he won his inter-League medal). All his League appearances for Liverpool were at centre-forward but he played inside-right in three FA Cup games in 1897-8.

FITZPATRICK, Harold J. **1907-08**
Inside-left. 4 apps; 2 goals.
League debut: 12 October 1907.
Born: Scotland.
5ft 8ins. 11st 12lbs.
Career: Scottish football. Luton Town 1906. LIVERPOOL cs 1907. Chesterfield Town cs 1908.
Harry Fitzpatrick was signed after scoring seven goals in 20 Southern League matches for Luton Town. His contribution to Chesterfield's last pre-war League season (1908-09) — they returned as founder members of Division Three North in 1921 — was one goal in 17 Second Division games.

FITZSIMMONS, Matthew John 1936-39
Centre-half. 1 app.
League debut: 14 September 1938.
Born: Toxteth Park, Liverpool, 10 December 1913.
Career: Mather United (Liverpool). LIVERPOOL October 1936. Ipswich Town June 1938 (wartime guest with York City), retired during war.
Matt Fitzsimmons played at full-back for his junior club but his only League appearance was at centre-half when he deputized for Fred Rogers in a 3-1 defeat at Burnden Park. He did not play in the League for Ipswich.

FLEMING, George **1901-06**
Left-half. 79 apps; 5 goals.
League debut: 21 September 1901.
Born: Bannockburn, Stirlings, *c.*1869.
Career: East Stirlingshire. Wolverhampton Wanderers cs 1894. LIVERPOOL May 1901 to 1906, later assistant trainer.
Club honours: Liverpool, Division Two champions 1905.
George Fleming was a fine utility player, turning out at full-back, half-back and in the forward line during his career. In his last four seasons with Wolves he missed only one League game. He had a benefit at Molineux when Wolves played the Corinthians in December 1899. One of six Scots on Wolves' books in 1894, his departure left them without any.

FORSHAW, Richard **1919-27**
Inside-right/centre-forward. 266 apps; 117 goals.
League debut: 8 September 1919.
Born: Preston, Lancs, 20 August 1895.
5ft 10ins. 11st 10lbs.
Career: Gateshead schools football. St George's Church Lads' Brigade (Gateshead). Gateshead St Vincent's. Army football (wartime guest with Nottingham Forest and Middlesbrough). LIVERPOOL cs 1919. Everton March 1927. Wolverhampton Wanderers August 1929. Hednesford Town August 1930. Rhyl Athletic October 1930.
Club honours: Liverpool, Division One champions 1922, 1923; Everton, Division One champions 1928.
Dick Forshaw was ever-present in both Liverpool's Championship-winning teams

of the 1920s, scoring 36 goals in the process. His move to Everton was a surprise but it soon brought him a third Championship medal.

FOXALL, Abraham **1899-1900**
Centre-forward. 1 app.
League debut: 7 October 1899.
Born: Sheffield, 1874.
Career: Sheffield junior football. Gainsborough Trinity cs 1897. LIVERPOOL cs 1899. Queen's Park Rangers cs 1900. Gainsborough Trinity August 1903 to 1906.
Abe Foxall was really an outside-left and a first-teamer for his other senior clubs. His only League appearance for Liverpool was against Derby County at Anfield, the Rams winning 2-0.

FURNELL, James **1962-63**
Goalkeeper. 28 apps.
League debut: 3 March 1962.
Born: Clitheroe, Lancs, 23 November 1937.
6ft 1in. 13st 5lbs.
Career: Schoolboy football. Burnley, professional November 1954. LIVERPOOL February 1962 (£18,000). Arsenal November 1963 (£15,000). Rotherham United September 1968 (£9,000). Plymouth Argyle December 1970, retired May 1976 and joined Plymouth's training staff. Blackburn Rovers assistant manager June 1981.
Club honours: Liverpool, Division Two champions 1962; Arsenal, Football League Cup runners-up 1968.
Jim Furnell signed amateur forms for Burnley at 16 but made only a couple of senior appearances in eight years due to the brilliance of international 'keepers, Colin McDonald and Adam Blacklaw. The move from Turf Moor saw his career take off and he went on to make an aggregate 430 League appearances over 20 years.

GARDNER, Thomas **1928-31**
Right-half. 5 apps.
League debut: 25 January 1930.
Born: Huyton, Liverpool, 28 May 1910.
Died: May 1970.
5ft 8ins. 10st 3lbs.
Career: Orrell FC (Liverpool). LIVERPOOL amateur 1928, professional 1929. Grimsby Town May 1931. Hull City May 1932. Aston Villa February 1934 (£4,500). Burnley April 1938 (wartime guest with Blackburn Rovers, Preston North End, Blackpool, Manchester United and Southport). Wrexham December 1945. Wellington Town August 1947. Oswestry Town player-manager, player-coach January 1952. Chester assistant trainer cs 1954 to May 1967.
International honours: England.
Club honours: Hull City, Division Three North champions 1933.
Tommy Gardner gained publicity in the early 1930s for his long throw-ins and in 1932 won a competition by throwing a football the notable distance of 32yds 2ins. When the ball was at his feet, however, he liked to keep it on the ground. Gardner played outside-right for Wrexham. He later worked as a club steward in Chester.

GARNER, James Albert **1922-26**
Right-/left-back. 5 apps.
League debut: 15 December 1924.
Born: Pendlebury, Manchester, 18 July 1895. Died: 9 April 1975.
5ft 8½ins. 11st.
Career: Army football. LIVERPOOL 1922. Southport cs 1926. New Brighton August 1927 to 1928.
Jim Garner, a capable reserve for Liverpool, was first choice at Southport, making 26 League appearances, but did not appear in the League for New Brighton.

GARSIDE, James Arthur **1904-06**
Outside-left. 5 apps.
League debut: 21 January 1905.
Born: Manchester, 1885.
5ft 9ins. 11st.
Career: Junior football. Preston North End 1900s. Accrington Stanley. LIVERPOOL cs 1904. Accrington Stanley cs 1906. Exeter City cs 1909 to 1913.
Representative honours: Southern League.
Jimmy Garside understudied international Jack Cox for a couple of years before returning to Lancashire Combination soccer. He made 99 Southern League appearances for Exeter and once scored a hat-trick for them.

GAYLE, Howard **1977-83**
Midfield. 3 (1) apps; 1 goal.
League debut: 4 October 1980 (sub).
Born: Liverpool, 18 May 1958.
5ft 10½ins. 10st 9lbs.
Career: Merseyside Sunday football. LIVERPOOL November 1977 (Fulham, loan, January-April 1980; Newcastle United, loan, November 1982-January 1983). Birmingham City January 1983 (£75,000). Sunderland August 1984 (£75,000). Dallas Sidekicks (American Indoor League) cs 1986. Stoke City April 1987 (originally on trial). Blackburn Rovers cs 1987.
International honours: England Under-21.
Club honours: Sunderland, Football League Cup runners-up 1985 (sub).
Howard Gayle won his England Under-21 caps while with Birmingham City and that was perhaps his best period. He was fast and would probably have operated at outside-right in the old formation.

GEARY, Fred **1895-99**
Forward. 40 apps; 14 goals.
League debut: 7 September 1895.
Born: Hyson Green, Nottingham, 23 January 1868. Died: 8 January 1955.
Career: Notts schoolboy football. Balmoral FC. Notts Rangers (three spells). Grimsby Town 1887. Notts County. Everton cs 1889. LIVERPOOL May 1895 (£60), retired 1899.
International honours: England. Football League.
Club honours: Everton, Division One champions 1891; Liverpool, Division Two champions 1896.
Fred Geary made his reputation at Everton as a tricky centre-forward with a powerful shot in the days of the celebrated Chadwick-Milward wing partnership. He arrived at Anfield as a veteran and played in other forward positions. A Liverpool licensee before retiring in 1946, Geary was reported to be a teetotaller in 1925. He represented Lancashire at bowls.

GERHARDI, Hugh **1952-53**
Inside-forward. 6 apps.
League debut: 7 February 1953.
Born: in South Africa, 5 May 1933.
6ft 4ins. 13st 7lbs.
Career: Thistle FC (Johannesburg). LIVERPOOL August 1952, returned to South Africa in 1953.

Hugh Gerhardi's physique seemed more appropriate for goalkeeping or central defenders's duties. Indeed, he was something of a versatile performer and of his six games for Liverpool, four were at inside-left, one at inside-right and the last at left-back.

GILHESPY, T(homas) W(illiam) Cyril 1921-25

Outside-right. 19 apps; 3 goals.
League debut: 4 March 1922.
Born: Fence Houses, Co Durham, 18 February 1898.
5ft 8½ins. 11st 2lbs.
Career: Chester-le-Street. Sunderland August 1920. LIVERPOOL August 1921. Bristol City cs 1925. Blackburn Rovers June 1929. Reading June 1930. Mansfield Town August 1931. Crewe Alexandra cs 1932 to 1933.
Club honours: Bristol City, Division Three South champions 1927.
According to a 1929 Lancashire football annual, Cyril Gilhespy arrived at Blackburn 'with a reputation as a fast winger who has developed both physically and as a player'. The most successful period of his career was at Bristol and he was a vital part of City's 1926-7 promotion line-up, missing only two League games and scoring eight goals. He made 16 First Division appearances for Sunderland before understudying Sheldon, Lacey and Rawlings in turn.

GILLESPIE, Gary Thompson 1983-

Defender. 111 (2) apps; 9 goals.
League debut: 12 October 1984 (sub).
Born: Stirling, 5 July 1960.
6ft 2ins. 12st 7lbs.
Career: Schools football. Falkirk 1977. Coventry City March 1978 (£75,000). LIVERPOOL July 1983 (£325,000).
International honours: Scotland. Scotland Under-21. Scotland Youth.
Club honours: Liverpool, European Cup runners-up 1985. Division One champions 1986, 1988. FA Cup runners-up 1988. Football League Cup runners-up 1987.
Originally a midfielder, Gary Gillespie showed exceptional promise as a youngster, captaining Falkirk when only 17 (after only 22 games) and he brought them a significant fee before reaching his 18th birthday. Although he played a lot of First Division football for Coventry, Gillespie had to wait for his Reds League debut. Tall and commanding, he won his first full Scotland cap late in 1987.

GILLIGAN, Samual A. 1910-13

Inside-forward. 41 apps; 16 goals.
League debut: 24 September 1910.
Born: Dundee, 1882.
5ft 9½ins. 12st.
Career: Belmont Athletic (Dundee). Dundee *c.*1902. Celtic 1903. Bristol City cs 1904. LIVERPOOL cs 1910. Gillingham player-manager cs 1913 to World War One.
Club honours: Bristol City, Division Two champions 1906. FA Cup runners-up 1909.
Sam Gilligan could also play centre-forward and that was his position in Bristol City's 1909 Cup Final line-up. He was a great favourite at Ashton Gate, a lively attacker who made 188 appearances and scored 78 goals for City. In his two years at Gillingham he played in 65 Southern League games, scoring 15 goals. In 1969 he was reported to be living in Vancouver, Canada.

GIVENS, J. 1893-95

Centre-forward/inside-left. 10 apps; 3 goals.
League debut: 17 March 1894.
Born: Scotland.
Career: Dalry FC (Ayrshire). LIVERPOOL during 1893-4. Abercorn cs 1895.
Givens played half his League matches at inside-left and then began 1894-5 at centre-forward. An adaptable performer, he figured at half-back for the Paisley club, Abercorn.

GLASSEY, Robert John 1934-37

Inside-left. 9 apps; 4 goals.
League debut: 7 December 1935.
Born: Chester-le-Street, 13 August 1914.
Died: July 1984.
5ft 10ins. 10st 9lbs.
Career: Horden Colliery. LIVERPOOL 1933-4. Stoke City 1937-8. Mansfield Town cs 1939 (wartime guest for Hartlepools United and Newcastle United).
Bob Glassey showed much promise with Liverpool but at Stoke his activities were wholly devoted to the Central League side. He appeared in three Third Division South games for Mansfield Town (scoring one goal) before war was declared and he did

not resume his career when peacetime football was restored.

GLOVER, John William 1900-03

Right-back. 59 apps; 1 goal.
League debut: 20 October 1900.
Born: West Bromwich, 22 October 1876.
5ft 8ins. 12st.
Career: Junior football. West Bromwich Albion. Blackburn Rovers cs 1897. New Brompton 1899. LIVERPOOL cs 1900. Small Heath 1903 to 1908.
Representative honours: Football League.
John Glover did not progress beyond West Brom's reserve team and it was Blackburn who gave him his first taste of League football. Then followed 24 Southern League games for New Brompton. Two of his 11 appearances in Liverpool's 1901 League Championship side were at left-back.

GODDARD, Arthur M. 1902-14

Outside-right. 388 apps; 75 goals.
League debut: 8 March 1902.
Born: Heaton Norris, Stockport.
5ft 9½ins. 11st 7lbs.
Career: Heaton Norris Albion. Stockport County. Glossop North End November 1899 (£250). LIVERPOOL March 1902. Cardiff City cs 1914 to 1920.
Representative honours: Football League.
Club honours: Liverpool, Division One champions 1906. Division Two champions 1905.

Arthur Goddard gave Liverpool a dozen years of sterling endeavour and skippered the side, rather unusually, from outside-right. He was known as 'Graceful Arthur', a tribute to his fast, fluent style. He went into business in Liverpool.

GOLDIE, Archibald 1895-1900
Right-back. 130 apps; 1 goal.
League debut: 28 September 1895.
Born: Hurlford, Ayrshire, 5 January 1874.
Career: Clyde. LIVERPOOL June 1895. New Brighton Tower cs 1900. Small Heath cs 1901 to 1904.
Club honour: Liverpool, Division Two champions 1896.

Archie Goldie was the elder brother of W.G.Goldie and they were members of a noted Ayrshire footballing family. Archie was a recognized first teamer at Anfield for the bulk of his time there. At Small Heath — soon to be renamed Birmingham FC — he was succeeded at right-back by another former Liverpudlian, John Glover.

GOLDIE, William Glover 1898-1904
Left-half. 158 apps; 6 goals.
League debut: 2 April 1898.
Born: Hurlford, Ayrshire, 22 January 1878.
5ft 7½ins. 11st 4lbs.
Career: Hurlford Thistle 1895. Clyde 1897. LIVERPOOL early 1898. Fulham January 1904. Leicester Fosse cs 1908, retired 1911.
Club honours: Liverpool, Division One champions 1901; Fulham, Southern League champions 1906, 1907.
Bill Goldie was a 'left-half who uses his brains to good purpose,' according to a Midlands writer in 1908. Brother Archie played alongside him at Liverpool and another brother, John, joined Fulham a few weeks after Bill was transferred to Leicester Fosse. Bill Goldie eventually became a licensee.

GOODE, Bertram John **1908-10**
Inside-forward. 7 apps; 1 goal.
League debut: 7 November 1908.
Born: Chester, 1886.
5ft 7ins. 10st 12lbs.
Career: Chester. Wrexham. LIVERPOOL 1908. Aston Villa 1910 (£250). Wrexham 1911. Hull City May 1912 (£300). Wrexham May 1913 (£225) to 1926.
Club honours: Chester, Welsh Cup winners 1908; Wrexham, Welsh Cup winners 1911, 1914, 1915, 1921, 1925, runners-up 1920.
Bert Goode's long association with Welsh club Wrexham took in that club's initial Football League seasons in the Third Division North. He possessed plenty of craft and later in his career was more of a schemer, although earlier he had been a noted goalscorer, netting 46 times for Aston Villa Reserves to help them win the Birmingham League championship. He did not figure in the first team at Villa Park.

GORDON, Patrick **1893-94**
Outside-right. 27 apps; 8 goals.
League debut: 2 September 1893.
Born: Scotland.
Career: Renton. Everton 1890. LIVERPOOL cs 1893. Blackburn Rovers late-1894 to 1895.
Club honours: Everton, FA Cup runners-up 1893; Liverpool, Division Two champions 1894.
Paddy Gordon was a speedy right winger who was equally effective at inside-forward, his position for the 1893 FA Cup Final when Everton lost to Wolves at Fallowfield, Manchester. He was a reserve at Renton, then a major force in Scottish soccer, understudying several international forwards. He managed only 23 League and Cup appearances during his three years at Goodison, although one of those was in an FA Cup Final.

GORMAN, James **1904-08**
Centre-half. 19 apps.
League debut: 21 April 1906.
Born: Middlesbrough, 1882.
5ft 8½ins. 11st 9lbs.
Career: St Mary's FC (Middlesbrough). Newport Celtic (South Bank & District League). South Bank FC (Northern League). Darlington St Augustine's. LIVERPOOL 1904. Leicester Fosse May 1908 to 1910.
Jimmy Gorman began his career at right-half but, with South Bank, played in every forward and both wing-half positions. He found his best position as Darlington's centre-half in North-East non-League football and Liverpool signed him following a trial. He went on to prove a sound deputy for the celebrated Alec Raisbeck, 'being zealous and untiring and placing well to his forwards'.

GRACIE, Thomas **1912-14**
Centre-/inside-forward. 32 apps; 5 goals.
League debut: 24 February 1912.
Born: Glasgow, 12 June 1889. Died: 23 October 1915.
5ft 8½ins. 12st.
Career: Junior football. Morton. Everton March 1911. LIVERPOOL February 1912 (with Billy Lacey, for Harold Uren). Heart of Midlothian 1914.
Representative honours: Scottish League.
Tom Gracie played mostly at inside-left for the Reds, although in 1912 one newspaper report said that he had 'played wonderfully well for Morton and selected as reserve centre-forward for Scotland'. He had a thin time at Goodison — one goal in 13 League matches as centre-forward. He died in Glasgow, while serving as a corporal in the Royal Scots, aged only 26.

GRAHAM, Robert **1960-72**
Forward. 96 (5) apps; 31 goals.
League debut: 26 September 1964.
Born: Motherwell, 22 November 1944.
5ft 8ins. 10st 5lbs.
Career: Schools football. LIVERPOOL

apprentice 1960, professional November 1961. Coventry City March 1972 (£70,000) (Tranmere Rovers on loan January-March 1973). Motherwell September 1973 (£20,000). Hamilton Academical (£18,000, Accies' record) August 1977 to 1981.

Bobby Graham was a utility forward who played mostly at centre-forward. His League outings with the Reds were somewhat unevenly spread, almost half of them coming in the year from April 1969 (he was an ever-present in 1969-70). He netted a hat-trick on his debut — in a 5-1 win over Aston Villa on 26 September 1964 — and scored in the next game, too, but was eventually crowded out by big-money signings at Anfield.

GRAY, W(illiam) James **1926-30**

Left-back. 1 app.

League debut: 5 September 1928.

Born: Glasgow, 16 September 1900. Died: 10 May 1978.

5ft 8½ins. 12st.

Career: South African football. LIVERPOOL during 1926-7. Exeter City January 1930, retired cs 1936.

International honours: South Africa.

Jimmy Gray was the third member of the 1924 South African touring party to join the Liverpool staff, the others being Arthur Riley and Gordon Hodgson. Unlike those notable players, however, Jimmy did not win a regular place in the Reds' League team. At Exeter City, though, he was part of a full-back pairing with Charlie Miller, reckoned to be the best in the Third Division South. He was dashing, quick to recover and quite fearless.

GRAYER, Frank **1912-15**

Right-back. 1 app.

League debut: 15 April 1914.

Born: Southampton, February 1890. Died: 21 January 1961.

6ft. 12st.

Career: Fazeley. St Mary's Athletic (Southampton). Southampton 1908. LIVERPOOL cs 1912 (£100).

Frank Grayer had only six Southern League games to his name when Liverpool signed him. Indeed, he had to wait patiently for three years in the Saints' reserve team before making his first appearance for them at senior level. He joined the Army early in World War One, but was badly wounded at Ypres and his career as a professional footballer thus ended. His one First Division game came in a 2-1 defeat by Manchester United at Anfield. After the war he found employment in Southampton and remained there until he retired.

GREEN, Thomas **1901-03**

Inside-forward. 7 apps; 1 goal.

League debut: 1 February 1902.

Born: Rock Ferry, Cheshire, 1881.

5ft 8ins. 11st 7lbs.

Career: Junior football. LIVERPOOL in 1901-02. Swindon Town cs 1903. Stockport County cs 1904. Middlesbrough February 1905 (£300). Queen's Park Rangers cs 1906. Stockport County cs 1907. Exeter City cs 1909. Preston North End cs 1910 to 1911.

Tommy Green's favourite positions, although not apparently at Liverpool, were outside-right and centre-forward. He was a regular first-teamer with all his clubs until reaching Preston. Green's first Stockport County spell saw him help them to the Lancashire Combination championship in 1904-05.

GRIFFIN, Michael **1907-09**

Inside-forward/outside-left. 4 apps.

League debut: 15 February 1908.

Born: Middlesbrough, *c.*1887.

5ft 8¾ins. 11st 7lbs.

Career: Darlington St Augustine's. LIVERPOOL cs 1907. Crystal Palace May 1909. Hartlepools United 1910. Barnsley cs 1912 to 1915.

Mick Griffin was a reserve with Liverpool but made 34 Southern League appearances for Crystal Palace in the season they finished seventh in the First Division of the Southern League. After non-League soccer with Hartlepools United, who were then in their formative years as a senior club, he returned to League football and went on to become a regular at Oakwell. In his three years there, Barnsley were a successful Second Division club. Griffin's career ended when League football was suspended for the duration of the war.

GRIFFITHS, Harold **1905-08**
Right-/left-back. 6 apps.
League debut: 14 October 1905.
Born: Middlesbrough, 1886.
5ft 10½ins. 12st 7lbs.
Career: Junior football. LIVERPOOL mid-1900s. Chesterfield Town cs 1908. Partick Thistle May 1909.
Harry Griffiths was a useful reserve. He linked up again with old Liverpool colleagues Alec Raisbeck and Maurice Parry at Partick Thistle. The Reds have had several links with Thistle down the years, including such players as Kenny Campbell, Jim McDougall and, more recently, Alan Hansen.

GROBBELAAR, Bruce David **1981-**
Goalkeeper. 300 apps.
League debut: 29 August 1981.
Born: Durban, South Africa, 6 October 1957.
6ft. 13st.
Career: Vancouver Whitecaps (Crewe Alexandra, loan, in 1979-80). LIVERPOOL March 1981 (£250,000).
International honours: Rhodesia/Zimbabwe. Football League.
Club honours: Liverpool, European Cup winners 1984, runners-up 1985. Division One champions 1982, 1983, 1984, 1986, 1988. FA Cup winners 1986, 1989, runners-up 1988. Football League Cup winners 1982, 1983, 1984, runners-up 1987.
Bruce Grobbelaar, one of the game's great entertainers, is also one of its finest goalkeepers. Quick to spot danger,

Grobbelaar will often venture well outside his penalty area to clear the ball. His handling is clean and his reflexes superb. Ironically, his surname is said to derive from a Dutch word meaning 'clumsy', a charge that could never be levelled against him. He recovered from meningitis to regain his place in 1988-9.

GUNSON, J(oseph) Gordon **1930-34**
Outside-left. 81 apps; 24 goals.
League debut: 15 March 1930.
Born: Chester, 1 July 1904.
5ft 9¾ins. 11st 4lbs.
Career: Chester schoolboy football. Brickfields FC (Chester). Nelson amateur 1923-4, later professional. Wrexham 1926. Sunderland June 1929 (£1,500). LIVERPOOL March 1930. Swindon Town June 1934. Wrexham May 1935-6. Bangor City's manager before ending his playing career. Crewe Alexandra trainer post-war. Flint Town manager. Welshpool manager. Dolgellau FC manager for a spell from cs 1964.
Gordon Gunson was a fast, goalscoring winger who was ever-present for Liverpool in 1931-2. He looked like succeeding Fred Hopkin for some time but a cartilage injury troubled him for the rest of his playing days. A few of his Liverpool appearances were at outside-right. He finished his League career with 69 goals from 272 matches.

HAFEKOST, Charles Henry **1914-15**
Right-half. 1 app.
League debut: 14 November 1914.
Born: Sunderland, 22 March 1890. Died: 1967.
5ft 11½ins. 11st 12lbs.
Career: Sunderland Royal Rovers. Gillingham cs 1912. LIVERPOOL cs 1914 to 1915.
Charlie Hafekost topped Gillingham's scoring list in 1913-14 and was signed by the Reds, who were perhaps tipped off by their former player Sam Gilligan, then Gillingham player-manager. In his two seasons with the Kent club, Hafekost made 50 Southern League appearances, scoring 14 goals. He was a product of the North-Eastern League club, Sunderland Royal Rovers, who sent several good players to senior clubs in the early years of the century.

HAIGH, Jack **1949-52**
Inside-forward. 11 apps; 3 goals.
League debut: 26 December 1950.
Born: Rotherham, 10 September 1928.
5ft 10ins. 10st 9lbs.
Career: Gainsborough Trinity. LIVERPOOL October 1949. Scunthorpe United August 1952 (about £4,000). Doncaster Rovers July 1960 (about £5,000) to 1962.
Club honours: Scunthorpe United, Division Three North champions 1958.
A key figure in Scunthorpe's championship line-up, Jack Haigh formed a telling left wing with another ex-Liverpudlian, Mervyn Jones. He gave splendid service during eight seasons at the Old Showground, grossing 329 League appearances and 65 goals.

HALL, Brian W. **1968-76**
Midfield. 140 (13) apps; 15 goals.
League debut: 7 April 1969 (sub).
Born: Glasgow, 22 January 1946.
5ft 7ins. 10st 6lbs.
Career: Lancashire schoolboy football (trials for Blackburn Rovers, Bolton Wanderers and Preston North End). Manchester University. LIVERPOOL July 1968. Plymouth Argyle July 1976 (£35,000). Burnley November 1977

(£25,000) to 1980. Subsequently played in non-League soccer.
Club honours: Liverpool, UEFA Cup winners 1973 (sub, 1st leg). Division One champions 1973. FA Cup winners 1974, runners-up 1971.
Brian Hall was an energetic little player, a favourite wherever he played because of his total commitment. He had to wait three years before establishing himself in the first team at Anfield but then shared in some of the Reds' successes before eventually losing his place to Jimmy Case. After leaving full-time professional soccer, Hall, a BSc, became a schoolmaster.

HANCOCK, Edmund **1931-33**
Inside-forward. 9 apps; 2 goals.
League debut: 28 March 1932.
Born: Rotherham, 29 March 1907.
5ft 8ins. 11st 8lbs.
Career: Denaby United. Gainsborough Trinity. LIVERPOOL January 1931. Burnley February 1933. Luton Town November 1936. Lincoln City July 1938 to 1939.
Club honours: Luton Town, Division Three South champions 1937.
Ted Hancock, a former miner, had 'good ball control, an excellent shot and is forceful ' according to a writer in 1934. He played quite a few games at outside-right and that was his position in Luton's 1937 promotion side. His longest spell with one club was at Burnley, where he scored 24 goals in 111 League games.

HANNAH, Andrew **1893-95**
Right-back. 41 apps; 1 goal.
League debut: 2 September 1893.
Born: Renton, Dunbartonshire, 17 September 1864. Died: June 1940.
Career: Renton FC. Everton 1890. Renton 1891. LIVERPOOL cs 1892. Rob Roy October 1895.
International honours: Scotland. Scottish League.
Club honours: Renton, Scottish Cup winners 1885, 1888, runners-up 1886; Everton, Division One champions 1891; Liverpool, Division Two champions 1894.
Andrew Hannah was a notable Victorian footballer and played for Liverpool in their very first season, in the Lancashire League. He was apparently quite a fearsome opponent, with a daunting physical presence, and an all-round athlete who won prizes at the Highland Games.

HANNAH, David **1894-97**
Inside-left. 31 apps; 12 goals.
League debut: 10 November 1894.
Born: Raffrey, Co Down, 28 April 1867.
5ft 6ins. 11st 3lbs.
Career: Renton. Sunderland cs 1889. LIVERPOOL November 1894. Dundee cs 1897. Woolwich Arsenal October 1897 to 1899.
Club honours: Sunderland, Division One champions 1892, 1893; Liverpool, Division Two champions 1896.
David Hannah moved to Renton when a boy and worked in the local dye works from the age of 13, eventually joining the local club as a young reserve. He was equally at home at inside-right and also played on both wings for Liverpool. No relationship between David and Andrew (*qv*) has been proven but it is possible they were cousins as the latter's father was also an Irishman.

HANSEN, Alan David **1977-**
Central defender. 403 apps; 8 goals.
League debut: 24 September 1977.
Born: Sauchie, Clackmannanshire, 13 June 1955.
6ft 1in. 13st.
Career: Sauchie Juniors. Partick Thistle provisional forms July 1973, permanently late-1973. LIVERPOOL May 1977 (£100,000).
International honours: Scotland. Scotland Under-23. Football League.
Club honours: Partick Thistle, Scottish League Division One champions 1976; Liverpool, European Cup winners 1978, 1981, 1984, runners-up 1985. Division One

champions 1979, 1980, 1982, 1983, 1984, 1986, 1988. FA Cup winners 1986, 1989, runners-up 1988. Football League Cup winners 1981, 1983, 1984, runners-up 1987.
Alan Hansen earned himself a reputation as one of the best central defenders in Europe, yet showed enough close control to create plenty of attacking moves. Despite captaining Liverpool to the double in 1985-6, he was surprisingly left out of Scotland's party for that summer's World Cup Finals. He suffered a serious injury on the eve of the 1988-9 season — at which point there was speculation that he might be taken on to Liverpool's coaching staff when his playing days ended — but recovered to figure in the hectic ending to the season. An all-round games player, Hansen represented Scotland at basket-ball, golf, volleyball and squash as a youngster. Younger brother of John Hansen (Partick Thistle & Scotland).

HANSON, Adolph Jonathan ('Alf') 1931-38

Outside-left. 166 apps; 50 goals.
League debut: 21 January 1933.
Born: Bootle, 27 February 1912.
5ft 8½ins. 10st 10lbs.
Career: Bootle JOC (trial with Everton). LIVERPOOL November 1931. Chelsea July 1938 (£7,500) (wartime guest with Liverpool, New Brighton, Chester, Wrexham, Manchester City, Bolton Wanderers, Crewe Alexandra, Rochdale, Tranmere Rovers and Southport). South Liverpool player-manager post-war. Shelbourne United player-manager.

Ellesmere Port Town player-manager February 1949.
International honours: England Wartime.
Alf Hanson was fast and renowned for his pinpoint accuracy when centering the ball. In his Liverpool days this resulted in many goals for Berry Nieuwenhuys, coming in from the opposite wing, and for the inside men. Hanson, a plumber by trade, was the elder brother of Stan Hanson, who kept goal for Bolton Wanderers from 1935 to 1956.

HARDY, Sam 1905-12

Goalkeeper. 219 apps.
League debut: 21 October 1905.
Born: Newbold, Chesterfield, 26 August 1883. Died: 24 October 1966.
5ft 9½ins. 12st.
Career: Newbold White Star. Chesterfield Town April 1903. LIVERPOOL May 1905 (£500). Aston Villa May 1912 (wartime guest for Nottingham Forest). Nottingham Forest August 1921, retired cs 1925.
International honours: England. England Victory. Football League.
Club honours: Liverpool, Division One champions 1906; Villa, FA Cup winners 1913, 1920; Nottingham Forest, Division Two champions 1922.
Sam Hardy was arguably the greatest of all the Reds' fine goalkeepers over the years. No spectacular showman, his virtues lay in remarkable anticipation and consistency. His first-class career encompassed 22 years. He always lived in Chesterfield and was a hotel proprietor there.

HARLEY, James **1934-49**
Right-/left-back. 117 apps.
League debut: 28 September 1935.
Born: Methil, Fife, 21 February 1917.
Career: Hearts o' Beath. LIVERPOOL April 1934, retired through injury 1948-9.
International honours: Scotland Wartime.
Club honours: Liverpool, Division One champions 1947.
Jim Harley was a powerful tackler with good positional sense, but his greatest asset was his speed. As an 18-year-old he won the famous Powderhall Sprint, using the pseudonym of 'A B Mitchell'. He served in the Royal Navy during World War Two but managed a few appearances for the Reds in most of the wartime seasons.

HARRINGTON, J(ames) Christopher **1920-21**
Outside-right/outside-left. 4 apps.
League debut: 5 February 1921.
Born: Liverpool 25 December 1896. Died: 6 May 1978.
5ft 10½ins. 11st 11lbs.
Career: South Liverpool. LIVERPOOL 1920-21. Wigan Borough 1921. Southport January 1923. Crewe Alexandra May 1923 to 1924. Mold. New York Giants.
Chris Harrington, who was tall for a winger, played two games on the left wing for Liverpool and two on the right. For Wigan, Southport and Crewe, Harrington grossed 48 Third Division North appearances and nine goals. Like McKinney and McMullan, he went to the USA to play for New York Giants.

HARROP, James **1907-12**
Centre-half. 133 apps; 4 goals.
League debut: 18 January 1908.
Born: Sheffield, 1884.
5ft 9½ins. 11st 10lbs.
Career: Junior football. Sheffield Wednesday 1904. Denaby United 1906. Rotherham Town 1907. LIVERPOOL 1907-08. Aston Villa cs 1912. Sheffield United March 1921 to cs 1922.
Representative honours: Football League.
Club honours: Aston Villa, FA Cup winners 1913.
A contemporary wrote that Jimmy Harrop was 'among the brainiest of half-backs, bringing intelligence to bear in both feeding and tackling'. He could also play at wing-half. He was Villa's skipper when they reached the 1920 FA Cup Final but missed the game through injury. During World War One he worked in the manufacture of agricultural implements.

HARROWER, James **1958-61**
Inside-forward. 96 apps; 21 goals.
League debut: 11 January 1958.
Born: Alva, Clackmannanshire, 18 August 1935.
5ft 9ins. 12st 4lbs.
Career: Sauchie Juveniles. Kilsyth Rangers. Sauchie Juveniles. Bo'ness

United. Hibernian, provisionally cs 1954, permanently 1955. LIVERPOOL January 1958 (£11,000). Newcastle United March 1961 (£15,000). Falkirk January 1962 (£3,115). St Johnstone cs 1963. Albion Rovers 1965.
International honours: Scotland Under-23. Scotland Youth.
Jimmy Harrower possessed excellent ball skills and the ability to make defence-splitting passes, but he lacked speed and consistency. He did, however, have an unusual gift in being able to glance in one direction and shoot accurately towards the other. His father and grandfather both played for St Mirren.

HARSTON, Edwin **1937-39**
Centre-forward. 5 apps; 3 goals.
League debut: 28 August 1937.
Born: Monk Bretton, Barnsley, 27 February 1907.
5ft 9ins. 11st 12lbs.
Career: Cudworth Village FC. Sheffield Wednesday 1928-9. Barnsley May 1930. Reading cs 1931. Bristol City cs 1934. Mansfield Town October 1935. LIVERPOOL June 1937 to 1939.
Ted Harston's phenomenal record at Mansfield (81 goals in 70 League games) made him a promising acquisition, even at the age of 30 and with no top-flight experience. 'Speed belies his sturdy build, and apart from his deadly shooting, can work the ball well and feed his wings', said a 1936 handbook. According to a later writer, though, 'he found First Division soccer beyond him,' despite scoring three goals in five games. His overall League record was 132 matches and 118 goals.

HARTILL, William John **1936**
Centre-forward. 5 apps.
League debut: 18 January 1936.
Born: Wolverhampton, 18 July 1905. Died: 1980.
5ft 9½ins. 11st 3lbs.
Career: Wolverhampton Schools. Army football (Royal Horse Artillery). Wolverhampton Wanderers late-1928. Everton July 1935. LIVERPOOL January 1936. Bristol Rovers March 1936 to 1938.
Representative honours: British Army.
Club honours: Wolverhampton Wanderers, Division Two champions 1932.
Two of Bill Hartill's Liverpool appearances were at outside-right but he had built a great reputation with Wolves as one of the country's leading centre-forwards, netting 164 goals in 221 League games for them. He was dubbed 'Hartillery' at Molineux, a play on his surname, former regiment and shooting skills. After retiring from soccer he was a Wolverhampton licensee.

HARTLEY, Abraham **1897-98**
Forward. 7 apps; 1 goal.
League debut: 25 December 1897.
Born: Dumbarton, 8 February 1872. Died: 9 October 1909.
5ft 7½ins. 12st.
Career: Artizan Thistle (Dumbarton). Dumbarton FC. Everton 1892. LIVERPOOL December 1897. Southampton May 1898. Woolwich Arsenal cs 1898 to 1899.
Club honours: Everton, FA Cup runners-up 1897; Southampton, Southern League champions 1899.
Abe Hartley, the son of a tailor and one of three brothers who assisted Dumbarton, graduated from Artizan Thistle, the junior club which also produced George Livingston. He was generally regarded as a useful centre-forward, although at Anfield he also played inside- and outside-left. He scored 28 goals in 61 League and Cup matches for Everton. Hartley eventually settled in Southampton and died suddenly at Southampton Docks aged only 37.

HATELEY, Anthony **1967-68**
Centre-forward. 42 apps; 17 goals.

League debut: 19 August 1967.
Born: Derby, 13 June 1941.
6ft 1½ins. 12st 7lbs.
Career: Normanton Sports. Notts County groundstaff, professional June 1958. Aston Villa July 1963 (£22,000). Chelsea October 1966 (£100,000, Chelsea record). LIVERPOOL June 1967 (£96,000). Coventry City September 1968 (£80,000). Birmingham City August 1969 (£60,000). Notts County October 1970 (£20,000). Oldham Athletic July 1972 (£5,000). Bromsgrove Rovers 1974. Prescot (Cheshire League) August 1975. Keyworth United December 1978.
Club honours: Chelsea, FA Cup runners-up 1967; Notts County, Division Four champions 1971.
Tony Hateley was a much-travelled striker who commanded some notable transfer fees. He was especially noted for his powerful heading, a talent inherited by his son, Mark, the England international. Tony Hateley's career spanned 434 League matches (five as a substitute) and 211 goals.

HEIGHWAY, Stephen Derek **1970-81**
Forward. 312 (17) apps; 50 goals.
League debut: 3 October 1970 (sub).
Born: Dublin, 25 November 1947.
5ft 10½ins. 11st 7lbs.
Career: Manchester City amateur. Warwick University. Skelmersdale United. LIVERPOOL amateur early 1970, professional May 1970. Minnesota Kicks, USA, 1981.
International honours: Republic of Ireland.
Club honours: Liverpool, European Cup winners 1977, 1978 (sub). UEFA Cup winners 1973, 1976. Division One champions 1973, 1976, 1977, 1979. FA Cup winners 1974, runners-up 1971, 1977. Football League Cup runners-up 1978.
A major figure in the Reds' many triumphs of the 1970s, Steve Heighway was a fast, high-stepping attacker whose athletic style was described as 'running with the ball rather than after it and possessing the balance to ride ill-timed and late tackles'. His parents were English and the family moved back to England when Heighway was ten. He represented both Cheshire and

England Grammar Schools and later the English Universities. He is a BA (Econs) graduate from Warwick University.

HENDERSON, Alastair **1931-33**
Right-half. 5 apps.
League debut: 10 October 1931.
Born: Shettleston, Glasgow.
Career: Yoker Athletic. LIVERPOOL July 1931. Clapton Orient July 1933 to 1935.
Alastair Henderson could also play at left-half and did so in his final League appearance for Liverpool. He played 19 Third Division South matches during his two seasons with Clapton Orient.

HENDERSON, David **1893-94**
Centre-forward. 21 apps; 10 goals.
League debut: 23 September 1893.
Born: Stirling district, 1868.
Career: King's Park (Stirling). LIVERPOOL September 1893, returned to Scotland November 1894, later assisted Partick Thistle.
Club honours: Liverpool, Division Two champions 1894.
David Henderson replaced James Henderson (no relation) and proved a valuable asset in Liverpool's successful quest for promotion in their first League season. When George Dewhurst deputized for him against Crewe Alexandra in March 1894, a reporter wrote that the England international did not perform as well as the former King's Park man.

HENDERSON, James **1893-94**
Centre-forward. 3 apps.
League debut: 2 September 1893.
Born: Scotland.
Career: Annbank 1891. LIVERPOOL cs 1893 to 1894.
Annbank was a crack Scottish senior club in the 1890s, winning the prized Ayrshire Cup in 1892 and 1893. James Henderson, however, found life difficult in the Second Division with newly elevated Liverpool. He lost his place to David Henderson, who was signed from King's Park in September 1893.

HEWITT, Charles **1907-08**
Inside-right. 16 apps; 6 goals.
League debut: 2 September 1907.
Born: Greatham nr Hartlepool, Co Durham, 1882. Died: 31 December 1966.
5ft 6ins. 11st 4lbs.
Career: Junior football. Middlesbrough *c.*1904. Tottenham Hotspur May 1906. LIVERPOOL cs 1907. West Bromwich Albion April 1908. Spennymoor United 1910. Crystal Palace later in 1910 to 1915. Later joined Hartlepools United to 1922.
Charlie Hewitt arrived at Anfield as an experienced forward, having been a regular at Middlesbrough and Tottenham, also having played outside-right for the former. Hewitt appeared in Liverpool's first six League fixtures of 1907-08 but thereafter his appearances were spasmodic. His career picked up again with West Brom and Palace and as a veteran of around 40, he played six League games during Hartlepools' initial League season, 1921-2.

HEWITT, Joseph **1904-10**
Centre-forward/inside-left. 153 apps; 67 goals.
League debut: 30 January 1904.
Born: Chester, 3 May 1881. Died: November 1971.
5ft 9ins. 11st 8lbs.
Career: Chester works team. Sunderland September 1901. LIVERPOOL January 1904. Bolton Wanderers August 1910. LIVERPOOL coaching staff in 1911-12.
Club honour: Liverpool, Division One champions 1906.
Joe Hewitt signed as an inside-forward but served Liverpool mainly at centre-forward. In the 1905-06 Championship season he made 37 appearances and scored 23 goals, following a season when he had mostly figured on the injured list. Hewitt was associated with the Reds for 60 years, as player and coach and then in other jobs, the last as press-box attendant.

HEYDON, John **1948-53**
Right-/centre-half. 63 apps.
League debut: 7 October 1950.
Born: Birkenhead, 19 October 1928.
5ft 11½ins. 11st 3lbs.
Career: Junior football. Everton amateur. LIVERPOOL professional December 1948. Millwall May 1953 (around £3,000). Tranmere Rovers June 1956 to 1961.
Although most of John Heydon's career was spent at right-half, 23 of his League games for the Reds were at centre-half, for he was particularly good in the air. With Millwall and Tranmere he added another 148 League games to his tally.

HICKSON, David **1959-61**
Centre-forward. 60 apps; 37 goals.
League debut: 7 November 1959.
Born: Ellesmere Port, Cheshire, 30 October 1929.
5ft 10½ins. 12st 10lbs.
Career: Ellesmere Port FC. Everton amateur 1947, professional May 1949. Aston Villa September 1955 (£17,500). Huddersfield Town November 1955 (£16,000). Everton July 1957 (£6,500). LIVERPOOL November 1959 (£10,500). Cambridge City July 1961. Bury January 1962 (£1,000 paid to Liverpool). Tranmere Rovers July 1962 (originally on two months' trial). Ballymena United player-manager 1964. Ellesmere Port Town early 1965, player-manager March 1965. Northwich Victoria. Winsford United September 1967. Also assisted Fleetwood and in 1973 started a second spell as Ellesmere Port Town manager.
Dave Hickson, a colourful, dashing centre-forward who excelled in the air, was often in the headlines, sometimes because of his brushes with authority. Yet off the field he was quiet and unassuming, even shy. After leaving football he became a bookmaker in the Liverpool area.

HIGNETT, Alan J. **1962-66**
Full-back. 1 app.
League debut: 26 April 1965.

Born: Liverpool, 1 November 1946.
5ft 6ins. 10st 9lbs.
Career: Liverpool Schools. LIVERPOOL apprentice cs 1962, professional November 1963. Chester August 1966 (three months' trial).
International honours: England Schoolboys.
Alan Hignett made his only League appearance for Liverpool at Molineux in the last game of 1964-5. He played six times in Division Four for Chester before leaving the League scene.

HIGNETT, A. 1907-08
Right-half. 1 app.
League debut: 12 October 1907.
Born: Liverpool, mid-1880s.
5ft 6ins. 10st 4lbs.
Career: Merseyside junior football. LIVERPOOL *c.*1906 to *c.*1908.
Hignett's League appearance was against Sunderland at Anfield, when Liverpool won by a first-half goal scored by Harold Fitzpatrick.

HOARE, Joseph Henry 1903-04
Right-/left-back. 7 apps.
League debut: 24 October 1903.
Born: Southampton, 1881. Died: 24 March 1947.
Career: Junior football. Southampton 1902. LIVERPOOL cs 1903. Southampton cs 1904. Bitterne Guild 1905. Salisbury City 1908. Bitterne Guild 1909-10.
Joe Hoare was a sound defender but he did not get much of a look-in at The Dell, being in competition with ex-Liverpudlain Tom Robertson and England players, Benson and Molyneux. At Liverpool he was in the shadows of Billy Dunlop and Alf West. Although a carpenter by trade, he later became a tobacconist in Southampton.

HOBSON, Alfred 1936-38
Goalkeeper. 26 apps.
League debut: 29 August 1936.
Born: Co Durham, 9 September 1913.
Career: Shildon Colliery. LIVERPOOL April 1936. Chester October 1938 (wartime guest for Liverpool, Southport and Burnley) South Liverpool 1946-7.

Alf Hobson quickly became a regular for Liverpool with 25 League games in his first full season. He played in 172 wartime games for the Reds but when peacetime soccer resumed he drifted into non-League football.

HODGSON, David James 1982-84
Forward. 21 (7) apps; 4 goals.
League debut: 28 August 1982.
Born: Gateshead, 6 August 1960.
5ft 10ins. 11st 12lbs.
Career: Redleugh Boys Club (Gateshead). Middlesbrough August 1978. LIVERPOOL August 1982 (£450,000). Sunderland August 1984 (£125,000). Norwich City July 1986. Jerez (Spain) July 1987. Sheffield Wednesday July 1988.
International honours: England Under-21.
Club honours: Liverpool, Division One champions 1983.
Dave Hodgson followed the trail of Graeme Souness and Craig Johnston from Middlesbrough but did not have anything like the same impact at Anfield, despite glowing reports during his Ayresome Park days.

HODGSON, Gordon **1925-36**
Inside-right. 359 apps; 232 goals.
League debut: 27 February 1926.
Born: Johannesburg, South Africa, 16 April 1904. Died: 14 June 1951.
6ft 0¼ins. 13st 5lbs.
Career: Transvaal FC, South Africa. LIVERPOOL December 1925. Aston Villa January 1936 (£3,000). Leeds United March 1937 (wartime guest for Hartlepools United), retired during the war. Leeds coaching staff. Port Vale manager October 1946 to his death.
International honours: England. South Africa. Football League.
Burly Gordon Hodgson, a boilermaker, went to England with a South African touring party which also provided the Reds with Riley and James Gray. Hodgson, who was born of English parents, played his first few games for the Reds at centre-forward. He appeared in first-class cricket for Lancashire between 1928 and 1933, for Forfarshire from 1934 to 1936 and also excelled at baseball.

HOLDEN, Ralph **1911-14**
Half-back. 2 apps.
League debut: 8 January 1913.
Born: Blundellsands nr Liverpool.
Career: St Helens Recreation. LIVERPOOL in 1911-12. Tranmere Rovers cs 1914.
Ralph Holden caught the eye in Lancashire Combination football. He had a testing introduction to League soccer when he played at left-half in a 4-1 defeat by Manchester City at Hyde Road. His other First Division appearance was at centre-half in a goalless draw against West Brom at Anfield.

HOLMES, John **1895-98**
Left-half. 42 apps.
League debut: 14 September 1895.
Born: Preston, Lancs.
Career: Junior football. Preston North End *c.*1890. LIVERPOOL cs 1895. Burton Swifts cs 1898. New Brighton Tower cs 1899 to cs 1901 when the club folded.
Club honours: Liverpool, Division Two champions 1896.
John Holmes was signed after the 1894-5 relegation season and helped Liverpool return immediately to Division One. He was 'two-footed', a fact demonstrated by his switching to right-half entirely in his Burton Swifts and New Brighton Tower years. He was the brother of Bob Holmes, of Preston 'Invincibles' and England fame.

HOOD, William John **1937-38**
Right-back. 3 apps.
League debut: 20 November 1937.
Born: Belfast, 3 November 1914.
Career: Cliftonville. LIVERPOOL March 1937. Derry City 1938, where he ended his senior career.
International honours: Northern Ireland Amateurs.
Bill Hood played in successive League fixtures during November and December 1937, as deputy for Tom Cooper. Just before joining Liverpool he played in Northern Ireland's famous 5-1 win over England in an amateur international.

HOOPER, Michael D. **1985-**
Goalkeeper. 30 apps.
League debut: 23 August 1986.
Born: Bristol, 10 February 1964.
6ft 1in. 13st.
Career: Junior football. Bristol City 1983-4 season. Wrexham, loan, February 1985, permanently July 1985 (£4,000). LIVERPOOL October 1985.

Mick Hooper proved a reliable deputy to Bruce Grobbelaar. He played only once for his home-town club before his form in a run of 34 League outings for Wrexham brought him to Liverpool's attention.

HOPKIN, Frederick **1921-31**
Outside-left. 335 apps; 9 goals.
League debut: 27 August 1921.
Born: Dewsbury, Yorks, 23 September 1895. Died: March 1970.
5ft 7¾ins. 12st 5lbs.
Career: Darlington. Manchester United cs 1919. LIVERPOOL cs 1921 (£2,800). Darlington August 1931-2.
Club honours: Liverpool, Division One champions 1922, 1923.

Unfortunately, Fred Hopkin is remembered as much for his lack of goals as for his teamwork and ability to centre the ball accurately. It is also part of Reds' folklore that one of Hopkin's rare goals coincided with a fire in the Kemlyn Road stand. The League fined Manchester United £350 for paying him more than the regulation maximum wage and promising an illegal percentage on his transfer fee. Hopkin, the last survivor of the 1922 and 1923 Championship sides, played in an England trial in 1923.

HOUGHTON, Raymond J. **1987-**
Midfield. 64 (2) apps; 12 goals.
League debut: 24 October 1987.
Born: Glasgow, 9 January 1962.
5ft 7ins. 10st 10lbs.
Career: Junior football. West Ham United, professional July 1979. Fulham July 1982. Oxford United September 1985 (£125,000). LIVERPOOL October 1987 (£825,000).
International honours: Republic of Ireland.
Club honours: Oxford United, Football League Cup winners 1986; Liverpool, Division One champions 1988. FA Cup winners 1989, runners-up 1988.

Ray Houghton fitted in admirably at Anfield with his old Oxford colleague, John Aldridge. His career blossomed at Fulham after a single substitute appearance for West Ham. Houghton, the son of an Irishman, was one of the great successes of the Eire team that did so well in the 1988 European Championships.

HOWE, Fred **1935-38**
Centre-/inside-forward. 89 apps; 36 goals.
League debut: 6 April 1935.
Born: Bredbury, Cheshire, 24 September 1912.
5ft 9½ins. 11st 12lbs.
Career: Wilmslow. Stockport County amateur May 1931, professional September 1931. Hyde United 1933. LIVERPOOL March 1935. Manchester City June 1938. Grimsby Town October 1938 (wartime guest Stockport County and Watford). Oldham Athletic July 1946 to cs 1947.
Fred Howe was recommended to Liverpool by 'Tosh' Johnson. He played mainly at centre-forward, although he was an outside-left with Hyde United. At Grimsby, he proved a useful successor to the renowned Pat Glover before war intervened. Howe was a plumber by trade.

HOWELL, Raby **1898-1901**
Right-half. 59 apps.
League debut: 16 April 1898.
Born: Wincobank, Sheffield, 12 October 1869. Died: 1937.
5ft 5¼ins. 9st 8lbs.
Career: Ecclesfield. Rotherham Swifts 1889. Sheffield United cs 1890 (over £200). LIVERPOOL April 1898 (£200). Preston

North End June 1901, retired through injury late-1903.
International honours: England.
Club honours: Sheffield United, Division One champions 1898.
Raby Howell was famous as the first full-blooded gypsy to be capped by England. Despite his size, Howell played at centre-half before Sheffield United moved him to wing-half. He possessed tremendous stamina but his career was ended by a broken leg sustained in September 1903.

HUGHES, Abel **1894**
Right-back. 1 app.
League debut: 3 February 1894.
Born: Wrexham, 1869. Died: 14 June 1946.
Career: Wrexham 1892. Rhosllanerchrngog 1894. LIVERPOOL. Wrexham 1896 to 1897.
International honours: Wales.
Club honours: Wrexham, Welsh Cup winners 1893.
Abel Hughes' single appearance for Liverpool came while he was a Rhos player. He was a skilful though vigorous player, 'spoiled by his roughness', according to one writer. He played right-back for his Liverpool appearance against Northwich Victoria but won his caps at left-back and left-half.

HUGHES, Emlyn Walter OBE 1967-79
Midfield. 474 apps; 35 goals.
League debut: 4 March 1967.
Born: Barrow-in-Furness, 28 August 1947.
5ft 10½ins. 11st 13lbs.
Career: North Lancashire Schools. Roose FC (Blackpool). Blackpool September 1964. LIVERPOOL February 1967 (£65,000). Wolverhampton Wanderers August 1979 (£90,000). Rotherham United player-manager July 1981. Hull City March 1983. Mansfield Town August 1983. Swansea City September-October 1983.
International honours: England. England Under-23. Football League.
Club honours: Liverpool, European Cup winners 1977, 1978. UEFA Cup winners 1973, 1976. Division One champions 1973, 1976, 1977, 1979. FA Cup winners 1974, runners-up 1971, 1977. Football League Cup runners-up 1978; Wolverhampton Wanderers, Football League Cup winners 1980.
Emlyn Hughes had an infectious enthusiasm that earned him the nickname 'Crazy Horse'. He captained club and country, scored some spectacular goals from midfield and could also play at full-back and centre-half. His father was a Rugby League international, his brother and an uncle were RL professionals and an aunt played hockey for England. Emlyn Hughes, who won 62 full England caps, later became a TV personality.

HUGHES, James 1904-09
Wing-half. 14 apps.
League debut: 1 September 1904.
Born: Bootle.
5ft 9ins. 11st 4lbs.
Career: Merseyside junior football. LIVERPOOL *c.*1904. Crystal Palace cs 1909. Chatham cs 1920.
Representative honours: Southern League.
Jim Hughes' career took off when he joined Palace and became one of the best wing-halves in the south. He made 200 peacetime Southern League appearances and scored 15 goals for the Glaziers. He managed 17 games and one goal in 1919-20 when in the veteran stage.

HUGHES, John ('Geezer') 1903-06
Left-half. 31 apps; 2 goals.
League debut: 19 September 1903.
Born: Flint, 1877.
Career: New Brighton Tower in 1898-9. Aberdare. LIVERPOOL cs 1903. Plymouth Argyle cs 1906, soon retiring through a knee injury. Harrowby FC trainer 1908 to late-1920s.
International honours: Wales.
All John Hughes' appearances were in season, 1903-04, his first at Anfield. Similarly his three caps were all won in 1904-05. His Liverpool career overlapped with that of James Hughes and constitutes an occupational hazard for soccer historians.

HUGHES, Lawrence **1943-60**
Centre-half. 303 apps; 1 goal.
League debut: 31 August 1946.
Born: Waterloo, Liverpool, 2 March 1924.
6ft. 12st 4lbs.
Career: Merseyside schools and junior football. Tranmere Rovers amateur 1942. LIVERPOOL professional February 1943, retired May 1960.
International honours: England. England 'B'.
Club honours: Liverpool, Division One champions 1947. FA Cup runners-up 1950.
Laurie Hughes had all the qualities necessary for a top-class centre-half and he maintained a high level of performance throughout his career. He was out of action for the bulk of 1948-9 and 1952-3, the versatile Bill Jones taking over.

HUNT, Roger **1958-69**
Inside-right. 401 (3) apps; 245 goals.
League debut: 9 September 1959.
Born: Golborne, Lancs, 20 July 1938.
5ft 9ins. 11st 10lbs.
Career: Lancashire schools football. Croft Youth Club. Stockton Heath. LIVERPOOL amateur 1958, professional

July 1959. Bolton Wanderers December 1969 (£31,000), retired cs 1972.
International honours: England. Football League.
Club honours: Liverpool, European Cup-winners' Cup runners-up 1966. Division One champions 1964, 1966. Division Two champions 1962. FA Cup winners 1965.
Roger Hunt scored more League goals for Liverpool than any other player, both in a single season and in aggregate, with 41 and 245 respectively, and his 285 goals also puts him top of the list of overall Reds' goalscorers. Hunt, a natural opportunist striker, was a member of the England team which won the World Cup in 1966. He represented the British Army when on National Service, when he also played for Devizes Town. Since retiring from soccer he has worked in the family haulage business.

HUNTER, John ('Sailor') **1899-1902**
Centre-/inside-forward. 37 apps; 10 goals.
League debut: 2 September 1899.
Born: Johnstone, Renfrews, 6 April 1878.
Died: 12 January 1966.
5ft 6ins. 10st 7lbs.
Career: Westmarch XI (Paisley).

Abercorn. LIVERPOOL 1899. Heart of Midlothian May 1902 (£300 including another player). Woolwich Arsenal cs 1904. Portsmouth cs 1905. Dundee May 1907. Clyde 1910. Motherwell manager May 1911, secretary-manager February 1913, relinquished managership May 1946, remaining secretary until 1959.
International honours: Scotland.
Club honours: Heart of Midlothian, Scottish Cup runners-up 1903; Dundee, Scottish Cup winners 1910.
John Hunter was a strong, incisive forward who paraded a distinctive rolling gait that earned him the 'Sailor' nickname. His playing career was notable but nevertheless dwarfed by his achievements as a manager. His long managerial career encompassed Motherwell's great period of the 1930s, when their marvellous side was built and motivated by Hunter.

HUNTER, T. **1899-1902**
Centre-half. 5 apps.
League debut: 25 November 1899.
Career: LIVERPOOL late-1899 to 1902.
Hunter was a reserve who stood in for the immaculate Alex Raisbeck on a few occasions, although his League debut was at outside-right. He apparently did not let the side down, his five League outings including three wins and a draw.

HUNTER, William **1908-09**
Inside-right. 1 app.
League debut: 20 March 1909.
Born: *c.*1887.
5ft 9ins. 11st 7lbs.
Career: Junior football. LIVERPOOL 1908. Sunderland May 1909. Lincoln City cs 1910 to 1911.
Hunter's League appearance for Liverpool was in a 2-0 defeat at Deepdale. He made no senior appearances for Sunderland but played in ten Second Division games for Lincoln in 1910-11.

IRELAND, Robert Johnstone **1929-31**
Right-half. 1 app.
League debut: 26 December 1930.
Born: Darvel, Ayrshire, 22 July 1900. Died: 12 July 1962.
5ft 9½ins. 12st.
Career: Junior football. Rangers February 1923. LIVERPOOL November 1929. St Johnstone 1931 to 1934.
Bob Ireland's natural position was centre-half and he spent almost seven years as a reserve with Rangers, in the shadows of Arthur Dixon and Davie Meiklejohn, appearing in only 18 Scottish League games in that time. He had been at Liverpool only three months when 'Tiny' Bradshaw arrived. Ireland eventually sampled more regular first-team football with newly-promoted St Johnstone.

IRVINE, Alan J. **1986-87**
Forward. 0 (2) apps.
League debut: 20 December 1986.
Born: Broxburn, West Lothian, 29 November 1962.
6ft 2ins. 11st 6lbs.
Career: Hibernian. Falkirk 1983. LIVERPOOL November 1986 (£75,000). Dundee United August 1987 (£100,000).
Alan Irvine did not play in the Scottish League for Hibs but made 118 appearances for Falkirk. The fee paid by Liverpool would have been increased by a further £25,000 if he had played in a specified number of first-team games, but Irvine managed only substitute appearances at Charlton and against Southampton at Anfield.

IRWIN, Colin Thomas **1974-81**
Defender. 26 (3) apps; 3 goals.
League debut: 25 August 1979.
Born: Liverpool, 9 February 1957.
6ft. 12st 6lbs.
Career: Merseyside junior football. LIVERPOOL, professional December 1974. Swansea City August 1981 (£350,000), retired 1984.
Colin Irwin was a valuable player to have in reserve and would have been a regular first-teamer with almost any other club. He captained Swansea, who were then in Division One, before injury forced his retirement at the age of 27.

JACKSON, Brian H. **1951-58**
Outside-right. 124 apps. 12 goals.
League debut: 10 November 1951.
Born: Walton-on-Thames, Surrey, 1 April 1933.
5ft 7¼ins. 10st 6lbs.
Career: Weybridge Schools. Chase of Chertsey (Arsenal amateur). Leyton Orient professional October 1950. LIVERPOOL November 1951 (£6,500 plus Donald Woan). Port Vale June 1958 (£3,000). Peterborough United July 1962 (£2,000). Lincoln City May 1964. Burton Albion early 1965.
International honours: England Schoolboys.
Club honours: Port Vale, Division Four champions 1959.
Brian Jackson was described by a critic

as one of the outstanding discoveries of 1950-51, 'a speedy, brilliantly clever outside-right'. Jackson made his League debut as a 17-year-old and was only 18 when he moved to Liverpool. His time at Anfield coincided with an unsuccessful period and he would almost certainly have prospered in happier times. At Peterborough he appeared at right-half.

JACKSON, Revd. James ('Parson') **1925-33**
Right-back/centre-half. 212 apps. 2 goals.
League debut: 14 November 1925.
Born: Newcastle-upon-Tyne, 4 December 1900.
5ft 10¾ins. 11st 10lbs.

Career: Queen's Park. Motherwell May 1919. Aberdeen cs 1923. LIVERPOOL May 1925, retired 1933.
Representative honours: Scottish League. Football League.
Jimmy Jackson was studying for the ministry while playing professional soccer, his move to the Reds enabling him to attend Liverpool University. He later went up to Cambridge and was ordained as a Presbyterian minister in 1933, serving in Liverpool and Bournemouth. He was a popular footballer and it was recorded that 'Jackson is all grit and determination' and 'has a way of combining business-like methods with brains'. He was a versatile player, able to take almost any position. His father was a well-known pre-1914 player, his brother, Archie, played for Tranmere before World War Two and his cousin, another Archie Jackson, played Test cricket for Australia.

JAMES, Norman Leslie **1929-33**
Centre-half. 8 apps.
League debut: 28 February 1931.
Born: Liverpool, 25 March 1908. Died: October 1985.
5ft 11ins. 11st.
Career: Bootle St James'. Braby's Athletic (Liverpool). LIVERPOOL April 1929. Bradford City May 1933. Queen's Park Rangers October 1936 to 1939.
Norman James was a stand-in for 'Tiny' Bradshaw. He showed promise but could not oust Bradshaw from the team. A reserve at Bradford City, he had better luck at QPR, for whom he made 67 League appearances.

JENKINSON, William **1919-21**
Right-/left-back. 13 apps.
League debut: 30 August 1919.
Born: Golborne, Lancs, 2 March 1892. Died: 3 April 1967.
5ft 9½ins. 11st 6lbs.
Career: Golborne United. LIVERPOOL cs 1919. Wigan Borough June 1921. Wallasey United cs 1923.
Bill Jenkinson first played for Liverpool in wartime football, making 59 appearances at left-back from 1916-17 to 1918-19 inclusive. He lost his place in the first post-war season, when Longworth and Lucas held the full-back positions. He made only ten appearances for Wigan, all in his first season (which was also Wigan's first in the League). Jenkinson played cricket for Bootle CC.

JOHNSON, David Edward **1976-82**
Forward. 128 (20) apps; 55 goals.
League debut: 21 August 1976.
Born: Liverpool, 23 October 1951.
5ft 10ins. 12st 4lbs.
Career: Liverpool Schools. Everton apprentice May 1967, professional April 1969. Ipswich Town October 1972 (in exchange for another player). LIVERPOOL August 1976 (£200,000, Liverpool record). Everton August 1982 (£100,000) (Barnsley, loan, February 1984). Manchester City March 1984. Tulsa Roughnecks, USA, briefly. Preston North End during 1984-5.
International honours: England. England Under-23.
Club honours: Liverpool, European Cup winners 1981. Division One champions 1977, 1979, 1980. FA Cup runners-up 1977.
David Johnson was at his best in tight situations. Sharp near goal, he had some delightful touches. He scored on his debut for Everton in four competitions — Central League, Football League, FA Cup and European Cup — netted their fastest goal and scored in his first Merseyside derby.

JOHNSON, Richard Kemp **1920-25**
Centre-forward: 78 apps; 28 goals.
League debut: 5 April 1920.
Born: Gateshead, 1895. Died: January 1933.
5ft 7ins. 10st 8lbs.
Career: Felling Colliery (wartime guest for Sunderland 1918-19). LIVERPOOL January 1920. Stoke February 1925. New Brighton September 1929. Connah's Quay August 1931.
Club honours: Liverpool, Division One champions 1923; Stoke, Division Three North champions 1927.
Dick Johnson's Anfield career was marred by knee trouble and he missed the entire 1921-2 Championship-winning season before returning to win a medal the following campaign. A lively player, he could open up a game with sweeping passes and had speed, control and was good in the air. He sometimes played at inside-forward.

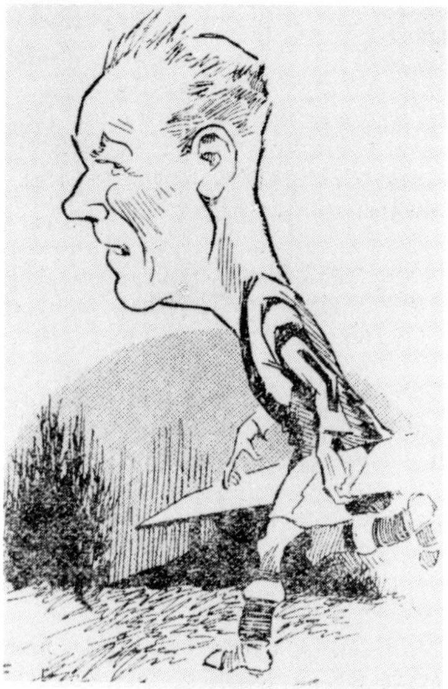

JOHNSON, Thomas Clark Fisher ('Tosh') **1934-36**
Centre-forward/inside-left. 37 apps; 8 goals.
League debut: 3 March 1934.
Born: Dalton-in-Furness, Lancs, 19 August 1901. Died: 29 January 1973.

5ft 9ins. 12st 5lbs.
Career: Dalton Athletic. Dalton Casuals. Manchester City February 1919. Everton March 1930 (£6,000). LIVERPOOL March 1934. Darwen August 1936.
International honours: England. Football League.
Club honours: Manchester City, Division Two champions 1928. FA Cup runners-up 1926; Everton, Division One champions 1932. Division Two champions 1931. FA Cup winners 1933.
Originally a Manchester City amateur, Tosh Johnson was a prominent player for most of the inter-war period. He probably reached his peak in 1928-9, when he scored 38 goals in 39 League games. He is still holder of City's seasonal and aggregate League goal total records. Johnson formerly worked as an apprentice shipyard riveter.

JOHNSTON, Craig Peter **1981-88**
Midfield. 168 (22) apps; 30 goals.
League debut: 29 August 1981 (sub).
Born: Johannesburg, 8 December 1960.
5ft 8ins. 10st 13lbs.
Career: Lake McQuarrie FC (Australia). Sydney City. Middlesbrough apprentice, professional February 1978. LIVERPOOL April 1981 (£575,000).
International honours: England Under-21.
Club honours: Liverpool, European Cup winners 1984, runners-up 1985 (sub). Division One champions 1982, 1983, 1984, 1986, 1988. FA Cup winners 1986, runners-

up 1988 (sub). Football League Cup winners 1983, 1984, runners-up 1987.
Craig Johnston was born in South Africa of English and Welsh parentage and graduated from Australian football to this country. He paid his own way from Australia to break into League football. A ball-winning midfielder who likes to move forward for a crack at goal, Johnston is a '90-minute' player, mounting an attack one minute and back helping his defence the next. In May 1988, he created a minor sensation by announcing his retirement from professional football at the age of 27 and returning to Australia.

JONES, Alan P. 1957-63
Right-back. 5 apps.
League debut: 19 December 1959.
Born: Flint, 6 January 1940.
5ft 10ins. 10st 7lbs.
Career: Flint Schools. LIVERPOOL professional April 1957. Brentford August 1963 (about £6,000) to 1970.
International honours: Wales Schoolboys. Wales Youth.
Alan Jones won Welsh schoolboy honours at centre-half but converted to full-back while on Liverpool's groundstaff. First-team chances were hard to come by at Anfield but when he moved to newly-promoted Brentford, he had a prolonged taste of League football. In seven years at Griffin Park, Jones made 249 League appearances (five as substitute).

JONES, Harold 1952-54
Inside-left. 1 app.
League debut: 5 September 1953.
Born: Liverpool, 22 May 1933.
5ft 10ins. 12st 2lbs.
Career: Merseyside schools and junior football. LIVERPOOL January 1952. Rhyl June 1954.
Harry Jones made his only League appearance in a 4-0 defeat at Newcastle during the 1953-4 relegation season. He was given a free transfer at the end of that season.

JONES, John H. 1924-25
Goalkeeper. 4 apps.
League debut: 8 November 1924.
Born: Holyhead.
Career: Holyhead FC. Liverpool amateur season 1924-5. Llandudno FC.
International honours: Wales Amateur
John Jones won his Welsh amateur cap against England in March 1924, at a time when Holyhead fielded a strong side. They finished third in the Welsh National League (Northern Section) that season. His First Division debut was against Preston at Anfield and the last against Spurs, also at home. Liverpool won two and lost two of his four appearances.

JONES, J(ohn) Mervyn 1951-53
Inside-/outside-left. 4 apps.
League debut: 1 March 1952.
Born: Bangor, Caernarfons, 30 April 1931.
5ft 4ins. 10st 3lbs.
Career: Bangor City. LIVERPOOL November 1951. Scunthorpe United July 1953. Crewe Alexandra June 1959 (£3,000). Chester August 1961. Lincoln City October 1963. Gainsborough Trinity cs 1964.
Club honours: Scunthorpe Utd, Division Three North champions 1958.
Mervyn Jones was a sprightly little forward who normally played on the left wing. He enjoyed six good years with Scunthorpe, playing in 240 League games and scoring 29 goals. His inside partner was usually another ex-Liverpudlian, Jack Haigh. Altogether Jones totalled 392 League appearances and 53 goals.

JONES, Joseph Patrick **1975-78**
Left-back. 72 apps; 3 goals.
League debut: 16 August 1975.
Born: Llandudno, 4 March 1955.
5ft 10ins. 11st 1lb.
Career: Junior football. Wrexham January 1973. LIVERPOOL July 1975 (£110,000). Wrexham September 1978 (£20,000). Chelsea October 1982 (£34,500). Huddersfield Town August 1985.
International honours: Wales. Wales Under-23.
Club honours: Wrexham, Welsh Cup winners 1975; Liverpool, European Cup winners 1977. Division One champions 1976, 1977. FA Cup runners-up 1977; Chelsea, Division Two champions 1984.
Joey Jones was a regular in the Wales team, winning 72 full caps. Although primarily a full-back, Jones can also play at centre-half. Rightly regarded as a bargain buy for Chelsea, his worth was well known to their then manager, John Neal, from his time in charge of Wrexham.

JONES, Ronald **1938-39**
Outside-/inside-right. 5 apps; 1 goal.
League debut: 26 March 1938.
Born: Mold, Flintshire.
5ft 7ins. 10st 5lbs.
Career: Junior football. Wrexham 1935-6 season. LIVERPOOL March 1938 (war-time guest for Wrexham).
Ronnie Jones soon won a first-team place at outside-right for Wrexham, making 78 Third Division North appearances and scoring 21 goals for them before joining the Reds. He did not reappear in League football after the war.

JONES, William Henry **1938-54**
Utility player. 257 apps; 17 goals.
League debut: 31 August 1946.
Born: Whaley Bridge, Derbys, 13 May 1921.
5ft 11ins. 13st 1lb.

Career: Hayfield St Matthew's (Derbyshire). LIVERPOOL September 1938 (wartime guest for York City, Leeds United and Reading). Ellesmere Port Town player-manager May 1954. Liverpool scout in 1960s and 1970s.
International honours: England. England 'B'. Football League.
Club honours: Liverpool, Division One champions 1947. FA Cup runners-up 1950.
Bill Jones was perhaps the most versatile player in Liverpool's history. His England appearances were at centre-half and he also played at full-back and in the forward line for the Reds. In the 1946-7 Championship side he played in six different positions. Jones won the Military Medal during the Allies' crossing of the Rhine in World War Two.

JOWITT, C. H. **1896-97**
Goalkeeper. 1 app.
League debut: 3 April 1897.
Jowitt's senior outing for the Reds was in the penultimate League game of 1896-7, a 2-2 draw with Sheffield Wednesday at Anfield, in the era when Harry Storer ruled supreme in Liverpool's goal. (The player may be Charles Herbert B.Jowett, born Liverpool in 1896, but this has not been proven).

KANE, Stanley **1935-36**
Goalkeeper. 6 apps.
League debut: 20 March 1935.
Born: Workington, 17 April 1912. Died: 13 February 1976.
5ft 11ins. 11st 10lbs.
Career: Junior football. Birmingham 1934. LIVERPOOL early 1935 to 1937.
Stan Kane did not make a senior appearance for Birmingham. During his time at St Andrew's the Blues had the current England goalkeeper, Harry Hibbs, and could also call on Frank Clack. Kane was soon deputizing for Arthur Riley at Anfield, however, making three appearances before the season ended. He also played in three League games in 1935-6, when Alf Hobson arrived to share the goalkeeper's job.

KAYE, George Harold **1941-47**
Right-half. 1 app.
League debut: 5 April 1947.
Born: Liverpool, 19 April 1919.
5ft 11ins. 12st 4lbs.
Career: Merseyside junior football. LIVERPOOL 1940-41 (wartime guest for Bradford City). Swindon Town May 1947 to 1953.
George Kaye made nearly 160 wartime appearances for Liverpool but he had to compete with the classy Phil Taylor when peacetime football returned. Kaye asked for a transfer and went on to make 169 League appearances for Swindon, despite some bad injuries, the first of which was a broken ankle.

KEECH, William **1895-97**
Right-/centre-half. 6 apps.
League debut: 26 October 1895.
Born: Irthlingborough, Northants, 1872.
5ft 9ins. 12st 7lbs.
Career: Wellingborough. Barnsley September 1894. LIVERPOOL cs 1895. Blackpool cs 1897. Leicester Fosse during 1897-8. Loughborough early 1899. Queen's Park Rangers late 1899. Brentford cs 1902 to 1903.
Bill Keech could play anywhere in the half-back line. At Loughborough he was used exclusively as a centre-forward, scoring five goals in 13 Second Division matches for the Leicestershire club. Keech was a member of QPR's first professional side and his younger brother, Ben, also played for Rangers.

KEEGAN, J(oseph) Kevin OBE **1971-77**
Forward. 230 apps; 68 goals.
League debut: 14 August 1971.
Born: Armthorpe near Doncaster, 14 February 1951.
5ft 8ins. 10st 10lbs.
Career: Schools football. Lonsdale Hotel FC (Doncaster Sunday League). Scunthorpe United apprentice December 1967, professional December 1968. LIVERPOOL May 1971 (£33,000). SV Hamburg June 1977 (£500,000). Southampton July 1980 (£400,000). Newcastle United August 1982 (£100,000), retired May 1984.
International honours: England. England Under-23.
Club honours: Liverpool, European Cup winners 1977. UEFA Cup winners 1973, 1976. Division One champions 1973, 1976, 1977. FA Cup winners 1974, runners-up 1977; SV Hamburg, European Cup runners-up 1980. Bundesliga champions 1979.
Kevin Keegan was a leading star of the 1970s and a good example of the 'self-made' player, who rose to international fame as much through dedication as skill. Keegan was sharp and creative, making and scoring goals throughout his career. He captained England, was Player of the Year in Europe (1978 and 1979), England (1976 and 1982) and West Germany (1978). Keegan's last great triumph was to help Newcastle United back to Division One in 1984.

KEETLEY, Joseph Frederick **1923-25**
Forward. 9 apps; 3 goals.
League debut: 22 December 1923.
Born: Derby, 28 June 1897. Died: 30 March 1958.
5ft 9ins. 11st.
Career: Victoria Ironworks (Derby). Bolton Wanderers during 1920-21. Accrington Stanley June 1923. LIVERPOOL November 1923. Wolverhampton Wanderers May 1925. Wrexham, then Doncaster Rovers during 1925-6. Horwich RMI.
Joe Keetley was a recognized inside-left but he also appeared at inside-right, outside-right and left-half for Liverpool. He was one of five brothers who played League football, four of whom, including Joe, played for Doncaster in the 1920s. Joe, Tom and Harold were in Doncaster's forward line on 20 February 1926 but Frank did not sign for the Belle Vue club until after Joe had left. The youngest member of the quintet was Charlie, who played for Leeds United.

KEMP, Dirk J. **1936-44**
Goalkeeper. 30 apps.
League debut: 27 March 1937.
Born: Cape Town, South Africa, 15 October, year unknown.
Career: South African football. LIVERPOOL December 1936 (wartime guest for York City, Brighton & Hove Albion and Southport).
Dirk Kemp was one several South Africans to join Liverpool between the wars and he followed in the footsteps of another Springbok, Arthur Riley. Kemp soon got a chance in League football, playing in a 2-0 win over Manchester United at Anfield, three months after arriving in England.

KENNEDY, Alan Phillip **1978-85**
Left-back. 247 (2) apps; 15 goals.
League debut: 19 August 1978.
Born: Sunderland, 31 August 1954.
5ft 9ins. 10st 7lbs.

Career: Junior football. Newcastle United apprentice July 1971, professional September 1972. LIVERPOOL August 1978 (£330,000). Sunderland September 1985 (£100,000). Hartlepool United cs 1987. Beerschot (Belgium) November 1987. Wigan Athletic December 1987 (originally on trial).
International honours: England. England 'B'. England Under-23.
Club honours: Newcastle United, FA Cup runners-up 1974. Football League Cup runners-up 1976; Liverpool, European Cup winners 1981, 1984, runners-up 1985. Division One champions 1979, 1980, 1982, 1983, 1984. Football League Cup winners 1981, 1982, 1983, 1984.
Alan Kennedy was a brave, hard-tackling defender with an attacking instinct which brought him some vital and sometimes memorable goals. He was first selected for England nine years before his international debut, initially missing out through injury. His elder brother, Keith, played for Bury from 1972 to 1982.

KENNEDY, Raymond 1974-82
Inside-forward/midfield. 272 (3) apps; 51 goals.
League debut: 31 August 1974.
Born: Seaton Delaval, Northumberland, 28 July 1951.
5ft 11ins. 13st 4lbs.
Career: South Northumberland Schools (Port Vale trial). New Hartley Juniors (Seaton Delaval). Arsenal apprentice May 1968, professional November 1968. LIVERPOOL July 1974 (£180,000). Swansea City January 1982 (£160,000) to October 1983. Hartlepool United November 1983 to 1985. Sunderland part-time coach February 1987, first-team coach April 1987.
International honours: England. England Under-23.
Club honours: Arsenal, Division One champions 1971. FA Cup winners 1971, runners-up 1972 (sub); Liverpool, European Cup winners 1977, 1978, 1981. UEFA Cup winners 1976. Division One champions 1976, 1977, 1979, 1980, 1982. FA Cup runners-up 1977. Football League Cup winners 1981, runners-up 1978; Swansea City, Welsh Cup winners 1982, 1983.
Ray Kennedy always liked to attack and scored some important goals for Arsenal and Liverpool. In his Arsenal days he was used as an attacker and was top scorer in his first season with the London club. Early in his Anfield career, however, Bill Shankly converted him to a midfield role. One of his most important goals was in the second leg of the 1980-81 European Cup semi-final, when he gave Liverpool the lead against Bayern Munich after a goalless draw at Anfield. Kennedy, who won 17 England caps, later became a licensee in the North-East.

KERR, Neil **1894-95**
Outside-right. 12 apps; 3 goals.
League debut: 13 September 1894.
Born: Bowling, Dunbartonshire, 13 April 1871. Died: December 1901.
Career: Cowlairs; Rangers May 1890. LIVERPOOL June 1894 to 1895. Falkirk.
Club honours: Rangers, Scottish League champions (joint) 1891.
Neil Kerr took full advantage of the goalscoring chances created by his colleagues, especially his Rangers days, when he was surrounded by many great players. He was ever-present in 1890-91, the very first season of the Scottish League. Normally an inside-right or centre-forward, at Anfield — apart from his first game — he was employed at outside-right.

KETTLE, Brian **1973-80**
Left-back. 3 apps.
League debut: 2 December 1975.
Born: Prescot, Lancs, 22 April 1956.
5ft 8ins. 10st 7lbs.
Career: Junior football. LIVERPOOL apprentice, professional May 1973. Wigan Athletic September 1980 (£25,000), contract cancelled October 1981.
International honours: England Youth.
Although Brian Kettle made only four senior appearances for Liverpool (one of them in European competition), he was a member of the Reds' strong reserve team for some years. At Wigan he managed only 14 Fourth Division games.

KEWLEY, Kevin **1972-78**
Forward. 0 (1) apps.
League debut: 2 January 1978.
Born: Liverpool, 2 March 1955.
5ft 8ins. 10st 7lbs.
Career: Junior football. LIVERPOOL, apprentice, professional March 1972, contract cancelled February 1978.
Kevin Kewley enters this book with the minimum qualification — a single substitute appearance in a peacetime competitive match. He played against Middlesbrough at Anfield but left Liverpool the following month.

KINGHORN, William John Darroch **1938-45**
Outside-left. 19 apps; 4 goals.
League debut: 27 August 1938.
Born: Strathblane, Stirlings, 27 February 1912.

Career: Junior football. Queen's Park mid-1930s. LIVERPOOL professional April 1938 (wartime guest for Leicester City, Brighton & Hove Albion, Manchester City, Newcastle United, Leeds United, Blackburn Rovers and Burnley).
International honours: Scotland Amateur.
Bill Kinghorn had four amateur caps and top-flight experience in the Scottish League (12 goals in 51 games) when he joined Liverpool. He played his last game for the Reds on 12 May 1945.

KIPPAX, F(rederick) Peter **1948-50**
Outside-left. 1 app.
League debut: 12 March 1949.
Born: Burnley, 17 July 1922.
Career: Schoolboy football. Burnley during 1939-40 (wartime guest for Charlton Athletic, Grimsby Town, Manchester United, West Ham United,

Fulham, Liverpool, Heart of Midlothian and Hibernian). LIVERPOOL amateur during 1948-9 season. Preston North End late 1950. Yorkshire Amateurs from 1948.
International honours: Great Britain (1948 Olympic Games). England Amateurs. Football League.
Club honours: Burnley, FA Cup runners-up 1947.
Peter Kippax was a leading amateur player in the 1940s. He graduated through Burnley's junior ranks, becoming an outside-left in an emergency. Kippax enjoyed a fine season in 1946-7, when Burnley won promotion and reached the FA Cup Final. That season he also played for the Football League. However, he was relegated to the Reserves the following season and his solitary appearance for Liverpool was his last in the Football League.

KYLE, Peter **1899-1900**
Inside-right. 4 apps.
League debut: 2 September 1899.
Born: Scotland.
Career: Clyde. LIVERPOOL cs 1899. Leicester Fosse cs 1900. Kettering cs 1901.
Peter Kyle started in Liverpool's first team, his appearances coming during the first five games of 1899-1900. Kyle's only other senior appearance was in the FA Cup first-round replay on 1 February 1900. He missed only four League games during his Fosse season. Kyle could also play at inside-left and centre-forward.

LACEY, William **1912-24**
Half-back/forward. 229 apps; 18 goals.
League debut: 2 March 1912.
Born: Wexford, 24 September 1889. Died: 30 May 1969.
5ft 9¾ins. 12st 4lbs.
Career: Shelbourne. Everton 1908. LIVERPOOL February 1912 (together with Tom Gracie for H.J.Uren). New Brighton cs 1924. Shelbourne cs 1925.
International honours: Ireland. Republic of Ireland. League of Ireland.
Club honours: Liverpool, Division One champions 1922, 1923. FA Cup runners-up 1914.
Billy Lacey was a great soccer character, as someone wrote, 'a rounded, lovable personality whose jutting chin was the delight of cartoonists'. His career spanned well over 20 years and he made his last international appearance when he was in his 41st year. Lacey was outstandingly versatile and could play in any outfield position, although his best was probably on the wing.

LAMBERT, Raymond **1936-57**
Right-/left-back. 309 apps; 2 goals.
League debut: 14 September 1946.
Born: Bagillt, Flintshire, 18 July 1922.
5ft 9½ins. 12st 3lbs.
Career: Flint Schools. LIVERPOOL amateur January 1936, professional July 1939 (wartime guest for New Brighton and Reading), retired cs 1956.
International honours: Wales. Wales Wartime. Wales Schoolboys.
Club honours: Liverpool, Division One champions 1947. FA Cup runners-up 1950.
Ray Lambert was only 13 years 189 days old when he joined Liverpool, then the youngest-ever player to be signed by a League club. As a schoolboy he played at centre-half but matured into a classy, unflappable full-back. Lambert later ran a newsagent's business at Queensferry in his native Flintshire. His son, Wayne, was on Manchester City's books for a spell.

LANE, Frank **1971-75**
Goalkeeper. 1 app.
League debut: 2 September 1972.
Born: Wallasey, 20 July 1948.
6ft 1in. 12st 10lbs.
Career: Stanley Arms FC (Wallasey). Tranmere Rovers August 1968. LIVERPOOL September 1971 (£15,000). Notts County July 1975. Kettering Town 1977.
At Tranmere, Frank Lane earned a reputation as a sound goalkeeper, making 76 League appearances before joining Liverpool as Ray Clemence's deputy. His chances at Anfield were few, thanks to Clemence's brilliance and freedom from injury. At Second Division Notts County, Lane managed only two senior games as understudy to the consistent Eric McManus. Latterly, he worked as a self-employed kitchen and bathroom fitter in the Nottingham area.

LATHOM, George, Capt. **1902-09**
Half-back. 18 apps.
League debut: 8 April 1905.
Born: Newtown, Montgomeryshire, 1 January 1881. Died: 9 July 1939.
5ft 8ins. 12st 6lbs.
Career: Newtown FC. LIVERPOOL amateur cs 1902, professional 1903. Southport Central cs 1909. Cardiff City player-coach 1911, later trainer to 1932. Chester trainer 1932 to 1934. Cardiff City trainer 1934 to 1937.
International honours: Wales.
Club honours: Cardiff City, Welsh Cup winners 1912.
George Lathom was at home in any of the half-back positions but it was as a trainer that he emerged as a major soccer personality, highly popular and having a major part in Cardiff's progress to two Wembley FA Cup Finals besides looking after successful Welsh national sides. He served in the Boer War and held a commission in the Royal Welch Fusiliers in World War One, when he was awarded the MC. The Newtown FC ground, Lathom Park, is named after him. He made one League appearance for Cardiff during an emergency in 1921-2.

LAWLER, Christopher **1959-75**
Right-back. 406 apps; 41 goals.
League debut: 20 March 1963.
Born: Liverpool, 20 October 1943.
6ft. 12st 10lbs.
Career: Liverpool Schools. LIVERPOOL FC amateur May 1959, professional October 1960. Portsmouth October 1975. Stockport County August 1977. Bangor City cs 1978. Coached in Norway. October

1981 Wigan Athletic assistant manager. Liverpool's coaching staff.

International honours: England. England Under-23. England Youth. England Schoolboys.

Club honours: Liverpool, European Cup-winners' Cup runners-up 1966. UEFA Cup winners 1973. Division One champions 1966, 1973. FA Cup winners 1965, runners up 1971.

Chris Lawler was a cultured, composed full-back who was dubbed 'The Silent Knight' by the Anfield faithful. Lawler could also give an effective performance at centre-half but he was perhaps most noted for his goals which came, not from penalties or free-kicks but as a result of his great attacking flair. In 546 senior games for the Reds he scored 61 goals, probably a record for a defender.

LAWRENCE, Thomas **1957-71**

Goalkeeper. 306 apps.
League debut: 27 October 1962.
Born: Dailly, Ayrshire, 14 May 1940.
5ft 11ins. 13st 12lbs.
Career: Warrington. LIVERPOOL FC amateur, professional September 1957. Tranmere Rovers September 1971 (originally on trial). Chorley August 1974 (trial).

International honours: Scotland. Scotland Under-23.

Club honours: Liverpool, European Cup-winners' Cup runners-up 1966. Division One champions 1964, 1966. FA Cup winners 1965.

Agile and quick, despite his bulk, Tommy Lawrence was affectionately known to the Kop as 'Flying Pig'. He had to wait some time for a regular first-team place but went on to become a vital member of the team which effectively launched the Reds on their great modern era.

LAWRENSON, Mark Thomas 1981-88
Left-back/central defender. 233 (7) apps; 11 goals.
League debut: 29 August 1981.
Born: Preston, Lancs, 2 June 1957.
6ft. 11st 7lbs.
Career: Preston Schools. Preston North End on 'S' forms aged 14, professional August 1974. Brighton & Hove Albion July 1977 (£100,000). LIVERPOOL August 1981 (£900,000, then Liverpool record), retired through injury March 1988. Oxford United manager April 1988-October 1988.
International honours: Republic of Ireland.
Club honours: Liverpool, European Cup winners 1984, runners-up 1985. Division One champions 1982, 1983, 1984, 1986. FA Cup winners 1986. Football League Cup winners 1982, 1983, 1984.
Mark Lawrenson was reckoned to be the finest defender in British soccer in the mid-1980s. Elegant, unruffled and with an excellent turn of speed, Lawrenson tackled with perfect timing. An Achilles tendon injury sustained in 1987 caused a premature retirement and he immediately took the Oxford job. The son of a former Preston and Southport player, Lawrenson qualified for the Republic of Ireland through his mother and made 37 appearances for them.

LAWSON, Hector Stewart Ramsay 1924-26
Outside-left. 12 apps.
League debut: 19 January 1924.
Born: Shettleston, Glasgow, 21 May 1896.
5ft 7½ins. 11st.
Career: Shettleston FC. Rangers August 1916. LIVERPOOL January 1924. Aberdeen cs 1926. Brighton & Hove Albion June 1928. Newport County August 1929. Shamrock Rovers August 1931.
Hector Lawson spent his last four years at Ibrox understudying the great Alan Morton and, altogether, made only ten peacetime Scottish League appearances. At Anfield, Fred Hopkin was difficult to oust but Lawson enjoyed greater sucess at Aberdeen (24 appearances) and Newport (56). Lawson also appeared at outside-right and left-half.

LEAVEY, Herbert James 1910-11
Outside-right/centre-forward. 5 apps.
League debut: 24 December 1910.
Born: Guildford, 1886.
5ft 9½ins. 11st 2lbs.
Career: Woodland Villa (Plymouth). Plymouth Argyle cs 1907. Derby County early 1909. Plymouth Argyle May 1909.

LIVERPOOL cs 1910. Barnsley September 1911. Bradford May 1913. Llanelli player-manager cs 1919. Portsmouth March 1921. Boscombe United's player-coach later 1921.

Bert Leavey was a versatile forward who made most of his Liverpool appearances at outside-left. He was a key member of the Barnsley team in 1911-12 but had the misfortune to break his leg in an FA Cup Cup quarter-final second replay and was sidelined for the rest of that season as Barnsley went on to win the Cup. His appointment at Boscombe came a couple of years prior to the club's entry into the Football League as Bournemouth & Boscombe Athletic.

LEE, Samuel **1975-86**

Midfield. 190 (7) apps; 13 goals.
League debut: 8 April 1978 (sub).
Born: Liverpool, 7 February 1959.
5ft 7ins. 10st llb.

Career: Merseyside schools football. LIVERPOOL apprentice 1975, professional April 1976. Queen's Park Rangers August 1986 (£200,000). Osasuna (Spain) July 1987 (£200,000).

International honours: England. England Under-21. England Youth.

Club honours: Liverpool, European Cup winners 1981, 1984. Division One champions 1982, 1983, 1984. Football League Cup winners 1981, 1982, 1983, 1984.

Sammy Lee was an enthusiastic little player, constructive, full of running and a fierce ball-winner. Between 1980 and 1984 he had a magnificent spell at Anfield, during which time he won his major honours, but then lost his form during 1984-5 and eventually drifted out of League football.

LEISHMAN, Thomas **1959-63**

Left-half. 107 apps; 6 goals.
League debut: 28 December 1959.
Born: Stenhousemiur, Stirlings, 3 September 1937.
6ft. 11st 6lbs.

Career: Camelon Juniors. St Mirren cs 1953. LIVERPOOL November 1959 (£9,000). Hibernian January 1963 (£10,000). Linfield player-manager July 1965-February 1968.

Club honours: St Mirren, Scottish Cup winners 1959; Liverpool, Division Two champions 1962; Linfield, Irish Cup runners-up 1966.

Tommy Leishman, easily recognized by his crew-cut hair-style, was a part-timer with St Mirren and full-time training at Anfield improved his game immensely. Leishman, who was fast and possessed a biting tackle, played his part in the 1961-2 promotion season but First Division soccer highlighted his shortcomings and he returned to Scotland.

LESTER, Henry **1911-13**
Outside-left. 2 apps.
League debut: 8 April 1912.
Born: Liverpool area.
5ft 8½ins. 11st 7lbs.
Career: Merseyside junior football. LIVERPOOL during 1911-12 season to 1913.
Harry Lester was a 'local outside-left of ability', according to the *Liverpool Express Guide* for 1912. With versatile Billy Lacey on the books, however, Lester soon became surplus to requirements.

LEWIS, Henry **1916-23**
Inside-forward. 59 apps; 10 goals.
League debut: 30 August 1919.
Born: Birkenhead, 19 December 1896.
Died: 11 July 1976.
5ft 6½ins. 11st 3lbs.
Career: The Comets FC (Liverpool). LIVERPOOL September 1916. Hull City late-1923 to 1925. Mold 1927.
Club honours: Liverpool, Division One champions 1922.
Harry Lewis played at centre-forward for a dozen games during Liverpool's League Championship season of 1921-2. In wartime soccer, Lewis made 99 appearances and scored 56 goals, playing exclusively at inside-left. He drifted out of League soccer after leaving the Reds, re-emerging in the Welsh League.

LEWIS, Kevin **1960-63**
Outside-right/outside-left. 71 apps; 39 goals.
League debut: 20 August 1960.
Born: Ellesmere Port, Cheshire, 19 September 1940.
5ft 11ins. 10st.
Career: Sheffield United Juniors. Sheffield United amateur 1955, professional October 1957. LIVERPOOL June 1960 (£13,000, then a Liverpool record). Huddersfield Town August 1963 (£18,000). Port Elizabeth, South Africa, July 1965.
International honours: England Youth.
Club honours: Liverpool, Division Two champions 1962.
Kevin Lewis, although a tall, lightweight winger, sometimes led the Reds' attack. Quick, clever and packing a hard shot, Lewis netted 75 goals in 180 League games during his career.

LIDDELL, William Beveridge **1938-61**
Forward. 495 apps; 216 goals.

League debut: 31 August 1946.
Born: Dunfermline, 10 January 1922.
5ft 10ins. 12st 11lbs.
Career: Lochgelly Violet. LIVERPOOL amateur July 1938, professional April 1939 (wartime guest for Chelsea, Cambridge Town, Dunfermline Athletic, Linfield and Toronto Scottish, Canada), retired May 1961.
International honours: Scotland. Scotland Wartime. Great Britain (twice played against Rest of Europe).
Club honours: Liverpool, Division One champions 1947. FA Cup runners-up 1950.
Billy Liddell was one of the great names of post-war British soccer. Although best remembered as an outside-left, Liddell was superbly 'two-footed' and also played on the other wing, as well as leading the Reds' attack with great distinction. With Liverpool he established a new club appearance record (since surpassed) and stands in the top six of the Reds' overall leading goalscorers. During the war he served as a navigator in the RAF. An accountant by profession, Liddell later became an assistant bursar at Liverpool University and a Justice of the Peace.

LINDSAY, Alec **1969-77**
Left-back. 168 (2) apps; 12 goals.
League debut: 18 October 1969 (sub).
Born: Bury, Lancs, 27 February 1948.
5ft 9½ins. 11st.
Career: Junior football. Bury FC apprentice, professional March 1965. LIVERPOOL March 1969 (£67,000). Stoke City, loan, August 1977, permanently September 1977 (£20,000). Oakland (USA) March 1978. Came out of retirement late-1982 to assist Newton FC (North-West Counties League).
International honours: England. England Youth.
Club honours: Liverpool, UEFA Cup winners 1973. Division One champions 1973. FA Cup winners 1974, runners-up 1971.
Alec Lindsay played wing-half and inside-forward for Bury, moving to left-back at Liverpool. Extremely fast, he was a great success as a modern 'overlapping' full-back. A robust performer, he possessed a

strong left foot. Outside the game Lindsay has worked as a scrap metal merchant, a licensee and has run a fish and chip shop.

LINDSAY, John **1928-30**
Half-back/forward. 14 apps; 2 goals.
League debut: 1 December 1928.
Born: Fifeshire.
5ft 9ins. 11st 7lbs.
Career: Rhyl Athletic. LIVERPOOL April 1928. Swansea Town January 1930 to 1931.
John Lindsay was one of those handy footballers who could play almost anywhere. In his 14 League matches for the Reds, he played in six different positions, two in the half-back line and four in attack. For Swansea he played in 16 Second Division games, scoring three goals.

LIPSHAM, John Reginald 1906-07
Outside-left. 3 apps.
League debut: 25 December 1906.
Born: Chester, 1881. Died: 13 December 1959.
Career: Junior football. Chester. LIVERPOOL cs 1906 to 1907. Chester.
Club honours: Chester, Welsh Cup winners 1908, runners-up 1910.
Jack Lipsham was the younger brother of England international, H.B.Lipsham, who was also an outside-left. Between his Chester spells, Jack had a season at Anfield, understudying Cox. Chester were then a strong non-League side, never finishing below third in their competition in the six seasons from 1905-6 to 1910-11 inclusive. Lipsham gained a rare distinction for a non-League player, being awarded a benefit by Chester in 1912-13, when it was said that 'he has accomplished some excellent work for the club.'

LIVERMORE, Douglas Ernest 1965-70
Midfield. 13 (3) apps;
League debut: 20 April 1968 (sub).
Born: Liverpool, 27 December 1947.
5ft 8ins. 10st 7lbs.
Career: Junior football (Bolton Wanderers amateur). LIVERPOOL November 1965. Norwich City November 1970 (£22,000). (AFC Bournemouth, loan, March 1975). Cardiff City August 1975 (£15,000). Chester October 1977 to 1979. Coaching with Cardiff City, Norwich City and Swansea City. Tottenham Hotspur reserve-team manager.
Club honours: Norwich City, Division Two champions 1972. Football League Cup runners-up 1973; Cardiff City, Welsh Cup winners 1976, runners-up 1977.
Doug Livermore made his mark after leaving Anfield, particularly at Norwich where his shrewd tactical knowledge contributed much to the Canaries' promotion to Division One. Livermore has been a successful coach, not least as part-time assistant manager to the Welsh national side. In 1987 he became caretaker manager of Spurs, between the demise of David Pleat and the appointment of Terry Venables.

LIVINGSTON, George Turner 1902-03
Inside-right. 31 apps; 4 goals.
League debut: 6 September 1902.
Born: Dumbarton, 5 May 1876. Died: 15 January 1950.
5ft 9ins. 11st 10lbs.
Career: Sinclair Swifts (three seasons). Artizan Thistle (Dumbarton). Parkhead FC (Glasgow). Dumbarton FC *c.*1895. Heart of Midlothian cs 1896. Sunderland May 1900 (£175). Celtic May 1901. LIVERPOOL May 1902. Manchester City May 1903. Rangers January 1907. Manchester United during 1908-9, retired during World War One. Dumbarton manager January 1919. Rangers trainer 1920 to season 1926-7. Bradford City trainer 1928-35.
International honours: Scotland. Scottish League.
Club honours: Celtic, Scottish Cup runners-up 1902; Manchester City, FA Cup winners 1904.
George Livingston was an expert at shielding the ball and was difficult to dispossess, as well as being a constructive player who set up many attacks. Off the field he was a jovial character who did much for dressing-room harmony. Besides his long soccer career, he ran a plumbing and gas-fitting business.

LLOYD, Laurence Valentine 1969-74
Centre-half. 150 apps; 4 goals.
League debut: 27 September 1969.
Born: Bristol, 6 October 1948.
6ft 2ins. 12st 4lbs.

Career: Bristol schoolboy and junior football. Bristol Rovers amateur, professional July 1967. LIVERPOOL April 1969 (£50,000). Coventry City August 1974 (£225,000). Nottingham Forest November 1976 (£60,000, after a month's loan). Wigan Athletic player-manager March 1981 to 1983. Notts County team manager July 1983-October 1984.
International honours: England. England Under-23. England Youth.
Club honours: Liverpool, UEFA Cup winners 1973. Division One champions 1973. FA Cup runners-up 1971; Nottingham Forest, European Cup winners 1979, 1980. Division One champions 1978. Football League Cup winners 1978, 1979.
Larry Lloyd was the typical 'sheet-anchor' pivot, a dominant figure whose physical presence alone did much to inspire confidence in his fellow defenders. His spells with Liverpool and Forest coincided with some vintage years for both clubs.

LOCK, Frank William **1953-55**
Right-/left-back. 41 apps.
League debut: 26 December 1953
Born: Whitechapel, London, 12 March 1922. Died: April 1985.
5ft 8¾ins. 12st 6lbs.
Career: Finchley. Army football. Charlton Athletic December 1945. LIVERPOOL December 1953 (£7,500). Watford June 1955. Cambridge United July 1957. Clacton Town July 1959, retired 1960.
Frank Lock was a classy defender, 'two-footed' and with fine anticipation. He was 31 when he went to Anfield with his Charlton colleague, John Evans, for a combined fee of £20,000. Lock was a member of the FA touring party to Australia in 1951, playing once against the national side. Latterly a representative of a Clacton soft-drinks firm.

LONGWORTH, Ephraim **1910-28**
Right-/left-back. 342 apps.
League debut: 19 September 1910.
Born: Halliwell, Bolton, 2 October 1887.
Died: 7 January 1968.
5ft 8½ins. 11st 6lbs.
Career: Bolton schools. Bolton St Luke's Boys (three seasons). Chorley Road Congregationals (two seasons). Bolton St Luke's (Lancashire Combination). Halliwell Rovers. Hyde, professional. Bolton Wanderers cs 1907. Leyton late-1908. LIVERPOOL May 1910, retired cs 1928, subsequently serving on the coaching staff.
International honours: England. England Victory. Football League.
Club honours: Liverpool, Division One champions 1922, 1923. FA Cup runners-up 1914.
Eph Longworth was a full-back of immense talent whose fine positional play enabled him to remain in the first-class game until he was 40. He could use either foot equally well and always looked to place clearances to advantage. He captained both the Reds and his country — the first Liverpool player to skipper England.

LOW, Norman Harvey **1933-36**
Centre-half. 13 apps.
League debut: 5 September 1934.
Born: Aberdeen, 23 March 1914.
6ft. 12st.
Career: Newcastle Schools. Rosehill FC (Newcastle). (Newcastle United amateur). LIVERPOOL October 1933. Newport County November 1936 (wartime guest for Bristol City, Everton, Liverpool and Swindon Town). Norwich City October 1946 to 1950. Norwich City manager May 1950-April 1955. Workington manager January 1956. Port Vale manager February 1957-October 1962. Liverpool chief scout 1965 to 1967, when he emigrated to North America.
Club honours: Newport County, Division Three South champions 1939.
Norman Low's father was Scottish international, Wilf Low, and an uncle, Harry Low, was left-half in Sunderland's great team which reached the 1913 FA Cup Final. Norman Low dominated in the air and was a most difficult opponent. He made a total of 265 peacetime League appearances for Newport and Norwich.

LOWE, Henry Charles **1911-20**
Centre-/wing-half. 122 apps; 2 goals.
League debut: 4 September 1911.
Born: Whitwell, Derbys, 20 March 1886. Died: 25 October 1958.
5ft 10ins. 12st 7lbs.
Career: Whitwell FC. Gainsborough Trinity cs 1907. LIVERPOOL April 1911 (wartime guest for Nottingham Forest). Nottingham Forest March 1920 to 1921.
Harry Lowe was a wonderfully consistent footballer, able to play anywhere in the half-back line. Lowe skippered the Reds but had to miss the 1914 FA Cup Final through injury. In 1920, a Nottingham football annual wrote of his 'admirable powers of imparting steadiness and solidarity to his wing, both in attack and defence, feeding and supporting his forwards well'. Lowe, however, failed to make a first-team appearance for Forest in the ensuing season.

LOWRY, Thomas **1963-66**
Full-back. 1 app.
League debut: 26 April 1965.
Born: Liverpool, 26 August 1945.
5ft 8½ins. 9st 8lbs.
Career: Junior football. LIVERPOOL apprentice, professional April 1963. Crewe Alexandra June 1966, retired 1977.
Tom Lowry's progress at Liverpool was blocked by the presence of Byrne, Lawler and Moran, but he gave Crewe splendid service, setting a club appearances record (which still stands) of 435 (1) League games.

LUCAS, Thomas **1916-33**
Right-/left-back. 341 apps; 3 goals.
League debut: 13 September 1919.
Born: St Helens, Lancs, 20 September 1895. Died: 11 December 1953.
5ft 6½ins. 11st 4lbs.
Career: Sherdley Villa. Sutton Commercial. Heywood United. Peasley Cross. Eccles Borough (Manchester United trial). LIVERPOOL cs 1916. Clapton Orient July 1933, retired cs 1934. Ashford manager.
International honours: England. Football League.
Club honours: Liverpool, Division One champions 1922.
Tommy Lucas shared the full-back positions with Longworth and McKinlay for a decade or so, otherwise his total of appearances would have been even higher. He made 21 Southern Section appearances

for Orient when in his 39th year and was in charge of their nursery club, Ashford, for a short while. For 18 years until his death, he was a licensee at Stoke Mandeville, Bucks.

LUMSDEN, J. 1897-98
Outside-left. 6 apps; 2 goals.
League debut: 27 November 1897.
Career: Burton Wanderers. LIVERPOOL cs 1897. Glossop cs 1898 to 1900.
Lumsden signed for the Reds after an excellent season with Burton Wanderers in which he missed only one Second Division match and scored five goals. At Liverpool he deputized for Harry Bradshaw. For Glossop he was ever-present in the 1898-9 side that won promotion to Division One, scoring 15 goals and sometimes playing at inside-left.

McAVOY, Douglas Haig 1947-49
Inside-left. 2 apps.
League debut: 3 January 1948.
Born: Kilmarnock, 29 November 1918.
5ft 7ins. 10st.
Career: Cumnock Juniors. Kilmarnock c.1936-7. LIVERPOOL December 1947 (£7,000). Queen of the South September 1949 to 1950.
Club honours: Kilmarnock, Scottish Cup runners-up 1938.
Doug McAvoy was a typical Scottish ball-player who made his reputation in the years leading up to the war. By the time peacetime football was suspended, he had made 63 appearances in the Scottish First Division and scored 14 goals. At Anfield his senior appearances were limited to one in 1947-8 and one in 1948-9.

McBAIN, Neil 1928
Right-back/left-half. 12 apps.
League debut: 10 March 1928.
Born: Campbeltown, Argyll, 15 November 1895. Died: 13 May 1974.
5ft 8ins. 12st 3lbs.
Career: Campbeltown Academicals. Ayr United cs 1914 (wartime guest for Portsmouth and Southampton). Manchester United November 1921 (£4,600). Everton January 1923 (£4,200). St Johnstone July 1926 (£1,000). LIVERPOOL March 1928. Watford player-manager November 1928 to 1931, manager to August 1937. Ayr United manager 1937-8. Luton Town manager June 1938-June 1939. New Brighton secretary-manager June 1946. Leyton Orient assistant manager February 1948, manager April 1948 to 1949. Subsequently Ayr United manager 1955-6 and 1962-3. Watford manager August 1956-February 1959. In between he scouted for Watford, Mansfield Town, Everton and Chelsea and coached Estudiantes de la Plata FC, Argentina.
International honours: Scotland.
Neil McBain was a centre or wing-half — 'there was no more stylish half-back', wrote one commentator — yet ten of his 12 appearances for Liverpool were at right-back. McBain's greatest claim to fame, however, was as the oldest player to have appeared in a Football League game, when he turned out in goal for New Brighton during an injury crisis. He was 51 years and four months old, also creating a record playing span which exceeded 32 years.

McBRIDE, James **1892-95**
Left-half. 30 apps; 3 goals.
League debut: 2 September 1893.
Born: Renton, Dunbartonshire, 30 December 1873.
5ft 4ins. 10st.
Career: Renton Wanderers. Renton FC *c.*1891. LIVERPOOL cs 1892 to 1895.
Club honours: Liverpool, Division Two champions 1894.
Jim McBride came to prominence at an early age and was the reserve for the Scottish League in the inaugural fixture against the Football League at Bolton in April 1892, when he was only 18. During the 1890-91 season, McBride was caught up in the litigation surrounding Renton, who had been expelled by the SFA for professionalism. McBride was certainly a paid player when he joined Liverpool.

McCALLUM, D. **1901-03**
Right-back. 2 apps.
League debut: 11 October 1902.
Born: Scotland.
Career: Junior football. Queen's Park. LIVERPOOL cs 1901 to 1903.
McCallum was described in the *Athletic News* of 15 August 1902 as 'a sturdy full-back'. He spent 1901-02 in the Reserves but was retained for 1902-03, when he deputized twice for John Glover. (Note: the player is possibly Donald McCallum, who joined Sunderland from Morton in May 1904, moving to Middlesbrough the following December and Kilmarnock cs 1906.)

McCANN, W. **1894-95**
Goalkeeper. 15 apps.
League debut: 1 September 1894.
Born: Scotland (probably in Renfrewshire).
Career: Junior football. Abercorn early 1890s. LIVERPOOL cs 1894, released March 1895.
McCann played in the opening 13 League fixtures of 1894-5 but thereafter appeared in only two more League games, plus an FA Cup-tie in January 1895. Unfortunately for McCann, his season at Anfield coincided with relegation and he was on the receiving end of some emphatic defeats, including 5-0 reverses at West Bromwich Albion, Aston Villa and Sheffield Wednesday. The month following his release by Liverpool he was reported to be living in Paisley.

McCARTHY **1893-94**
Right-back. 1 app.
League debut: 6 January 1894.
A player named McCarthy was shown as occupying the right-back position in the above fixture. However, two versions of Liverpool's team that day were published and it is doubtful if such a player existed. The late Morley Farror, who compiled original seasonal totals, working from the archives of the British Museum Newspaper Library at Colindale, included no player named McCarthy for season 1893-4.

McCARTNEY, John **1892-98**
Right-half. 128 apps; 5 goals.
League debut: 1 September 1893.
Born: Newmilns, Ayrshire.
Career: Newmilns FC. St Mirren. LIVERPOOL October 1892. New Brighton Tower cs 1898-1900.
Club honours: Liverpool, Division Two champions 1894, 1896.
John McCartney was a stalwart of the Reds' early days and the regular right-half for their first five League seasons. He tackled hard and distributed the ball accurately. Apparently, he joined the

Anfield club during a lace strike, so he may have been employed in Paisley's then important cotton industry.

McCONNELL, John Morrison 1909-12
Left-half. 50 apps; 1 goal.
League debut: 18 December 1909.
Born: Cambusnethan, Lanarks, 9 December 1890.
5ft 8ins. 10st 8lbs.
Career: Junior football. Motherwell c.1907. Airdrieonians May 1908. LIVERPOOL April 1909 (£80). Aberdeen cs 1912 to 1913.
John McConnell was playing in Motherwell's first team before his 17th birthday. With Airdrieonians, the following season, he appeared at right-half in 22 Scottish League and two Scottish Cup matches. In August 1909, the *Athletic News* said that he 'can play with equal facility on either wing'.

McCOWIE, Andrew 1896-99
Inside-forward. 33 apps; 11 goals.
League debut: 3 April 1897.
Born: Scotland.
Career: LIVERPOOL during 1896-7. Woolwich Arsenal cs 1899. Middlesbrough October 1900 to 1901.
Andy McCowie was a canny inside-forward who could also play in the other attacking positions. He found stiff competition at Anfield, however, with international players John Walker, Becton and Hugh Morgan on the staff. McCowie had a useful season with Woolwich Arsenal in 1899-1900, scoring ten goals in 26 Second Division games.

McDERMOTT, Terence 1974-82
Midfield. 221 (11) apps; 54 goals.
League debut: 16 November 1974.
Born: Kirkby, Liverpool, 8 December 1951.
5ft 9ins. 12st 13lbs.
Career: Liverpool schools football. Bury apprentice, professional October 1969. Newcastle United February 1973 (£22,000). LIVERPOOL November 1974 (£170,000). Newcastle United September 1982 (£100,000) to September 1984. Cork City January 1985. Apoel FC (Cyprus).

International honours: England. England 'B'. England Under-23.
Club honours: Newcastle United, FA Cup runners-up 1974; Liverpool, European Cup winners 1977, 1978, 1981. Division One champions 1977, 1979, 1980, 1982. FA Cup runners-up 1977. Football League Cup winners 1981, 1982, runners-up 1978.
Terry McDermott was a hard-running player who scored some spectacular goals, often the result of strong surges from deep positions, a ploy for which he became well-known. He did not consolidate his place in the Reds' line-up until 1977-8, thereafter winning a rich collection of medals. In 1980 he became the first man to win the PFA and Football Writers' Association 'Player of the Year' awards in the same season. He played only five games for Cork before going to Cyprus.

McDEVITT, William **1923-25**

Centre-half. 4 apps.
League debut: 17 November 1923.
Born: Belfast, 5 January 1898. Died: 10 January 1966.
5ft 11½ins. 11st 10lbs.
Career: Junior football. Swansea Town 1920-21. Belfast United 1922. LIVERPOOL cs 1923. Exeter City May 1925, player-manager April 1929-31, manager 1931 to September 1935.

Billy McDevitt, a deputy to Walter Wadsworth, had a notable run with Exeter after leaving the Reds. He moved to inside-right and, although on the slow side and no great goalscorer, he became the 'brains' of the team with his vision and subtle promptings. His managership took in Exeter's famous FA Cup run of 1930-31, when they reached the quarter-finals.

McDONALD, John **1909-12**

Outside-left. 76 apps; 4 goals.
League debut: 4 September 1909.
Born: Kirkcaldy, 1886.
5ft 8ins. 11st 7lbs.
Career: Wemyss Harp. Vale of Wemyss. Raith Rovers *c.*1902. Rangers January 1907 (£100 and proceeds from a match). LIVERPOOL May 1909. Newcastle United May 1912 (£650). Raith Rovers (briefly) 1919-20.
Club honours: Rangers, Scottish Cup runners-up 1909.

John McDonald was an early Raith Rovers star. He was a versatile performer and although the bulk of his Liverpool appearances were on the left wing, he played in each of the other forward positions during his last season. A member of the Raith team that won the 1907 Qualifying Cup, his appearance for Rangers in the 1909 Scottish Cup Final replay was the occasion of the notorious 'Hampden Riot'.

MacDONALD, Kevin D. **1984-**

Midfield. 29 (11) apps; 1 goal.
League debut: 29 December 1984.
Born: Inverness, 22 December 1960.
6ft 1in. 12st 1lb.
Career: Inverness Caledonian. Leicester City May 1980 (£26,000, a Highland League record). LIVERPOOL November 1984 (£400,000). (Leicester City, loan, December 1987).
Club honours: Liverpool, FA Cup winners 1986.

Kevin MacDonald created a good impression with Inverness Caley, progressing through their youth team to semi-professional status and reaching the first team in 1979. He helped Leicester City regain their First Division place and played around 150 games for them before moving to Liverpool. In September 1987 he had the misfortune to break his leg.

McDOUGALL, James **1928-38**
Left-half/inside-left. 339 apps; 12 goals.
League debut: 25 August 1928.
Born: Port Glasgow, 23 January 1904.
Died: July 1984.
5ft 11ins. 11st 6lbs.
Career: Port Glasgow Athletic. Partick Thistle *c.*1925. LIVERPOOL April 1928. South Liverpool player-youth coach cs 1938, retired 1939.
International honours: Scotland.
Jimmy McDougall started with the Reds at inside-left, a position he occupied at Firhill. He switched to left-half in the second half of his first season at Anfield and remained there for almost a decade. Together with Busby and 'Tiny' Bradshaw formed an all-Scottish international half-back line around 1936-7. He was a cultured and sportsmanlike player and a younger brother of John McDougall (Airdrieonians & Scotland). Jimmy had a successful chandlery business in Liverpool.

McDOUGALL, R. **1913-15**
Outside-right. 7 apps; 1 goal.
League debut: 24 January 1914.
Born: Glasgow.
5ft 7½ins. 11st 4lbs.
Career: Junior football. LIVERPOOL during 1913-14. Falkirk 1919. Ayr United cs 1921-2.
McDougall was a promising young winger who, like so many of his generation, saw his career interrupted by war. However, when peace was restored, he enjoyed three good seasons of top-flight Scottish League football, making 73 appearances for Falkirk (11 goals) and 35 for Ayr United (three goals).

McFARLANE, John **1928-30**
Inside-right/centre-forward. 2 apps.
League debut: 9 February 1929.
Born: Shettleston, Glasgow.
5ft 7ins. 11st 2lbs.
Career: Junior football. Aberdeen mid-1920s. LIVERPOOL November 1928. Halifax Town July 1930. Northampton Town cs 1932. Kidderminster Harriers 1934. Darlington cs 1935 to 1938.
Throughout his career John McFarlane was mostly a reserve and in more than a decade he managed only 93 games and 16 goals in the Scottish and Football Leagues. His best spell, by far, was with Halifax, for whom he made 63 appearances and scored 14 goals.

McGUIGAN, Andrew 1900-02
Inside-left. 31 apps; 14 goals.
League debut: 6 October 1900.
Born: Newton Stewart, Dumfries, 24 February 1878.
5ft 9ins. 11st 5lbs.
Career: Newton Stewart FC. Hibernian May 1898. LIVERPOOL May 1900. Middlesbrough 1902. Accrington Stanley. Exeter City cs 1908 to cs 1910. Also Burslem Port Vale and Bristol City. Liverpool in the 1920s.
Club honours: Liverpool, Division One champions 1901.
Andy McGuigan was the first player to score five goals in a League game for Liverpool (against Stoke on 4 January 1902). Earlier he had been described as 'the finest Hibs player since Groves' — Willie Groves being a famous Scottish international of the 1880s. McGuigan later did much voluntary work on behalf of Merseyside pensioners.

McINNES, James Sloan 1938-46
Left-half. 48 apps; 2 goals.
League debut: 19 March 1938.
Born: Ayr. Died: 5 May 1965 aged 53.
5ft 8¾ins. 11st 7lbs.
Career: Third Lanark mid-1930s LIVERPOOL March 1938 (£5,500). (Wartime guest for Brighton & Hove Albion, Newcastle United, York City, Leeds United, Luton Town, Millwall, Queen's Park Rangers, Fulham and Manchester United). Retired August 1946 and joined Liverpool's administrative staff. Assistant secretary, then secretary from August 1955 until his death.
Club honours: Third Lanark, Scottish Cup runners-up 1936.
Jimmy McInnes was a talented wing-half with over 100 Scottish League First Division appearances to his credit before signing for Liverpool for a substantial fee. He was well established when war arrived. McInnes gained a BSc at Edinburgh University.

McKENNA, John 1906-07
Outside-right. 1 app.
League debut: 26 January 1907.
Born: almost certainly Liverpool area.
Career: Merseyside schools football. Old Xaverians (Liverpool). LIVERPOOL 1906-07.
John McKenna's appearance came as stand-in for the consistent Arthur Goddard against Birmingham at Anfield. The Reds won 2-0, with goals in each half from Jack Parkinson and Willie McPherson.

McKINLAY, Donald 1910-29
Left-back/left-half. 393 apps; 33 goals.
League debut: 20 April 1910.
Born: Newton Mearns, near Glasgow, 25

July 1891. Died: 16 September 1959.
5ft 9ins. 11st 9lbs.
Career: Newton Swifts. Newton Villa. LIVERPOOL January 1910. Prescot Cables July 1929.
International honours: Scotland.
Club honours: Liverpool, Division One champions 1922, 1923. FA Cup runners-up 1914.
A celebrated name in Liverpool's history, Don McKinlay captained the side for some years and skippered them to consecutive Championships. Extraordinarily versatile, he began at left-half and played at right-half and centre-half as well as all five forward positions before settling at left-back after the war.

McKINNEY, Peter **1920-23**
Centre-/inside-forward. 3 apps; 1 goal.
League debut: 9 October 1920.
Born: Consett, Co Durham, 16 December 1897. Died: 23 December 1979.
5ft 9½ins. 10st 10lbs.
Career: Consett FC. LIVERPOOL cs 1920 to 1923. New York Giants mid-1920s, retiring *c.*1928.
Peter McKinney's Football League outings were all in 1920-21, at centre-forward and both inside-forward positions. He scored on his debut and could also play at wing-half. Emigrating to the United States in the mid-1920s, he remained there and died in New York.

McLAUGHLIN, John T. **1967-76**
Midfield. 38 (2) apps; 2 goals.
League debut: 18 April 1970.
Born: Liverpool, 25 February 1952.
5ft 8ins. 10st 3lbs.
Career: Kirkby Schools (Liverpool). LIVERPOOL apprentice 1967, professional February 1969 (Portsmouth, loan, October 1975) to April 1976.
John McLaughlin's best season was the 1970-71 campaign, when he made 33 League appearances. He played five Second Division games during his month on loan with Pompey.

McLEAN, Duncan **1892-95**
Left-back. 53 apps; 5 goals.
League debut: 2 September 1893.
Born: Dumbarton, 12 September 1869.
5ft 10½ins. 13st 7lbs.
Career: Renton Union. Renton FC *c.*1888. Everton 1890. LIVERPOOL 1892. Edinburgh St Bernard's October 1895.
International honours: Scotland.
Club honours: Liverpool, Division Two champions 1894.
Duncan McLean partnered Andy Hannah in Liverpool's early years. Both men were generously built and must have have presented an intimidating sight to opponents. McLean skippered St Bernard's and won his two Scotland caps while with that club.

McLEAN, James **1903-04**
Right-back. 4 apps.
League debut: 19 September 1903.
Born: Scotland.
Career: Vale of Leven. LIVERPOOL cs 1903-04.
'He comes South with the highest possible credentials,' the *Liverpool Football Echo* said of Jimmy McLean in August 1903. Alf West arrived from Notts County during the following November, however, and thereafter McLean's opportunities were curtailed.

McLEAN, John **1894-97**
Left-half. 27 apps.
League debut: 10 November 1894.
Born: Port Glasgow, 22 May 1870.
5ft 6ins. 12st 7lbs.
Career: Greenock Volunteers when 18. LIVERPOOL professional 1894. Grimsby Town June 1897. Bristol City May 1898 (£40). Bristol Rovers cs 1902. Millwall Athletic April 1904. Queen's Park Rangers May 1906 to 1908.
Club honours: Queen's Park Rangers, Southern League champions 1908.
John McLean distinguished himself with his first club, twice representing Renfrewshire and winning a Scottish junior international cap. In his early Grimsby days he was summed up as 'a splendid footballer, a hard worker, and a fearless tackler'. He could also play at centre-half and ended his senior career in that position, in QPR's 1908 championship side.

McLEOD, Thomas **1945-51**
Inside-left. 7 apps.
League debut: 4 April 1947.
Born: Musselburgh, Midlothian, 26 December 1920.
5ft 9ins. 10st 5lbs.
Career: Army football (BAOR). LIVERPOOL 1945. Chesterfield July 1951. Wisbech Town cs 1952.
Tommy McLeod came to Liverpool's notice when he was playing Services soccer in Germany towards the end of World War Two and he joined them after being demobbed. Although no heavyweight, he possessed a surprisingly powerful shot. In his season at Saltergate he appeared in 25 Third Division North matches. McLeod also played successfully in the half-back line.

McMAHON, Stephen **1985-**
Midfield. 128 (1) apps; 23 goals.
League debut: 14 September 1985.

Born: Liverpool, 20 August 1961.
5ft 7ins. 10st 9lbs.
Career: Liverpool schools football. Everton on 'S' forms (aged 14), apprentice December 1977, professional August 1979. Aston Villa May 1983 (£350,000). LIVERPOOL September 1985 (£350,000).
International honours: England. England Under-21.
Club honours: Liverpool, Division One champions 1986, 1988. FA Cup winners 1989, runners-up 1988, Football League Cup runners-up 1987.
Steve McMahon was an Everton regular by the time he was 19. He declined to renew his contract in 1983 and spent a couple of years with Villa before returning to his native city. With the Reds he benefited enormously in the company of exceptional players and earned his first England caps early in 1988. McMahon is particularly noted for his stern tackling.

McMULLAN, David 1925-28
Right-half. 31 apps.
League debut: 17 October 1925.
Born: Belfast.
5ft 7¾ins. 11st.
Career: Belfast Distillery, early 1920s. LIVERPOOL October 1925. New York Giants, USA, July 1928. Belfast Celtic 1928-9. Exeter City May 1929, retired 1930.
International honours: Northern Ireland. Irish League.
Club honours: Belfast Distillery, Irish Cup winners 1925.
David McMullan was certainly a useful player to have around. Although he made most of his Liverpool appearances at right-half, he was versatile enough to also appear at left-half and in four different forward positions for the Reds. Indeed, he won his Irish Cup medal at outside-left and played there and at left-half for Exeter. For good measure he went between the posts for the last home game of 1929-30, when both Exeter goalkeepers were injured.

McNAB, John S. 1919-28
Right-half. 200 apps; 6 goals.
League debut: 1 January 1920.
Born: Cleland, Lanarks, 17 April 1894.
Died: 2 January 1949.
6ft 1in. 11st 7lbs.
Career: Army football. Bellshill Athletic. LIVERPOOL November 1919. Queen's Park Rangers June 1928 to 1930.
International honours: Scotland.
Club honours: Liverpool, Division One champions 1922, 1923.
Jock McNab grabbed his chance in the big-time when Jack Bamber was sidelined. A strong-tackling wing-half, McNab reached his peak in the early 1920s, winning consecutive League Championship medals with the Reds. After retiring from the game he became a publican in Bootle.

McNAMARA, Anthony 1957-58
Outside-right. 10 apps; 3 goals.
League debut: 21 December 1957.
Born: Liverpool, 3 October 1929.
5ft 11¾ins. 12st 4lbs.
Career: Merseyside schools and amateur football. Everton May 1950. LIVERPOOL December 1957 (£4,000). Crewe Alexandra July 1958. Bury September 1958. Runcorn cs 1959.
The principle part of Tony McNamara's career was the seven and a half years he spent at Everton, when he played 113 senior games and scored 22 goals. He was heavily built for a winger, yet was described as an elegant footballer.

McNAUGHTON, Harold **1920-21**
Goalkeeper. 1 app.
League debut: 23 October 1920.
Born: Edinburgh.
5ft 10ins. 12st.
Career: Edinburgh St Bernard's. LIVERPOOL cs 1920 to 1921.
Harry McNaughton earned a fine reputation with St Bernard's but after signing for Liverpool he found the great Elisha Scott impossible to displace. McNaughton's sole appearance for the Reds came when Scott was on international duty, yet he did have the satisfaction of making his debut in a Merseyside derby. A local reporter commented that 'McNaughton, at the outset, struck one as being a rather cool customer and quite undisturbed by the size of the giant crowd'. The Reds beat Everton 1-0 before 50,000 spectators.

McNULTY, Thomas **1954-58**
Full-back. 36 apps.
League debut: 24 February 1954.
Born: Salford, 30 December 1929.
5ft 7ins. 11st 7lbs.
Career: Salford Boys Club. Manchester United June 1947. LIVERPOOL February 1954 (£7,000) to 1958. Hyde United.
Club honours: Manchester United, Division One champions 1952.
Tom McNulty made 57 First Division appearances for Manchester United before joining Liverpool. He played on both flanks before the Molyneux-Moran partnership developed and he found himself out of the reckoning.

McOWEN, William Arthur **1892-94**
Goalkeeper. 23 apps.
League debut: 2 September 1893.
Born: Blackburn, 1871. Died 27 December 1950.
Career: Blackburn Rovers 1886. Darwen 1890. LIVERPOOL cs 1892 to late-1894. Blackpool.
Club honour: Liverpool, Division Two champions 1894.
Billy McOwen was the lone Englishman among Liverpool's early recruitment of nine 'Macs'. He was a brilliant goalkeeper who conceded only 16 goals when the Reds won the Second Division title in 1893-4 without losing a game. He made his senior debut for Blackburn when he was only 15 and left Ewood Park after being dropped within sight of an FA Cup Final appearance. After leaving Liverpool he resumed his profession as a dentist. When he signed for Blackpool he was reinstated as an amateur.

McPHERSON, Archibald **1929-34**
Inside-left. 130 apps; 18 goals.
League debut: 23 November 1929.
Born: Alva, Clackmannanshire, 10 February 1910. Died: 1969.
5ft 8½ins. 10st 13lbs.
Career: Bathgate. Rangers March 1928. LIVERPOOL November 1929. Sheffield United December 1934. Falkirk cs 1937-8. Alloa Athletic manager after World War Two.
Club honours: Sheffield United, FA Cup runners-up 1936.
Archie McPherson was a teenager with half-a-dozen Scottish League appearances for Rangers to his name when he joined Liverpool. He soon won approval. In 1930, one commentator wrote that he was 'an accurate purveyor . . .is also a fine manipulator and excellent controller of the ball.' Those qualities were still his hallmark after he converted to left-half, the position he played in the 1936 FA Cup Final.

McPHERSON, William **1906-08**
Inside-left. 48 apps; 16 goals.
League debut: 6 October 1906.
Born: Beith, Ayrshire.
5ft 8½ins. 11st 6lbs.
Career: Beith FC. St Mirren late-1904. LIVERPOOL cs 1906. Rangers cs 1908. Heart of Midlothian 1911-13.
Club honours: Rangers, Scottish Cup runners-up 1909.
Billy McPherson enjoyed two useful years with Liverpool before coming to prominence in Rangers' Scottish Cup run of 1908-09. He scored the goals in three successive 1-0 wins up to and including the semi-final. 'He was not a great manipulator,' records the first Rangers' historian, 'but had always his wits about him.' Some time later McPherson was the subject of a £250 offer from Motherwell, a not inconsiderable amount for the Lanarkshire club in those days. He was the nephew of the Rangers and Scotland star, John ('Kitey') McPherson.

McQUE, Joseph **1892-98**
Centre-half. 108 apps; 10 goals.
League debut: 2 September 1893.
Born: Scotland.
Career: Celtic. LIVERPOOL cs 1892 to 1898. Also assisted Third Lanark.
Club honours: Liverpool, Division Two champions 1894, 1896.
Joe McQue had the thankless task of understudying the great James Kelly at Celtic. Nevertheless, deputizing for such a fine player had its benefits and McQue no doubt picked up plenty of tips that helped him in his later career. Indeed, he gave Liverpool many years' valuable service. A dominating player, he attacked and defended in the usual centre-half style of his day and was a regular member of the 1892-3 (Lancashire League) side. He played in Liverpool's first-ever match and their first game in the Football League.

McQUEEN, Hugh **1892-95**
Outside-left. 40 apps; 13 goals.
League debut: 2 September 1893.
Born: Harthill, Lanarks, 1 October 1867.
Died: 8 April 1944.
5ft 8ins. 12st 2lbs.
Career: Leith Athletic 1890. LIVERPOOL October 1892. Derby County July 1895. Queen's Park Rangers May 1901. Gainsborough Trinity July 1902. Fulham cs 1903, trainer 1904. Norwich City trainer.
Club honours: Liverpool, Division Two champions 1894; Derby County, FA Cup runners-up 1898.
Hugh McQueen's place in the Reds' history is inevitably overshadowed by his older brother, Matt, who dominated the club's first 30 years. Nevertheless, Hugh McQueen was a force in his own right, a winger who made and scored goals. He once had a narrow escape after jumping off the diving board into Southport baths. He had to be hauled out and later admitted that he could not swim. The magazine *Football Chat* voted him the best player on the losing side in the 1898 Cup Final. Up to World War Two, he ran a confectioners' and tobacconists' shop in Norwich.

McQUEEN, Matthew **1892-99**
Utility player. 79 apps; 1 goal.
League debut: 2 Sepember 1893.
Born: Harthill, Lanarks, 18 May 1863. Died: 29 September 1944.
Career: Leith Athletic. Heart of Midlothian 1887. Leith Athletic 1889. LIVERPOOL professional October 1892 to 1899. Later qualified as a referee and, towards the end of the World War One, was appointed a Liverpool director. Liverpool manager February 1923-February 1928.
International honours: Scotland.
Club honours: Liverpool, Division Two champions 1894, 1896.
Matt McQueen was one of the most remarkable figures of pre-World War One football. He was exceptionally versatile and could keep goal as effectively as he could play in outfield positions. Indeed, he was the Reds' goalkeeper in over half the matches of the 1895-6 championship campaign. He appeared in almost all the outfield berths at some time and, after refereeing in the League, he continued to make his mark, this time as Liverpool's manager. In December 1923, he lost a leg after a road accident whilst travelling back from a scouting mission in Sheffield.

McRORIE, Daniel **1930-33**
Outside-right. 33 apps; 6 goals.
League debut: 29 November 1930.
Born: Glasgow, 25 June 1906. Died: 26 July 1963.
5ft 8½ins. 11st.
Career: Queen's Park Strollers. Airdrieonians 1925-6. Stenhousemuir *c.*1927. Morton 1928. LIVERPOOL November 1930. Rochdale October 1933. Morton December 1933. Runcorn cs 1934.
International honours: Scotland. Scottish League.
Danny McRorie was signed exactly four weeks after winning his Scottish cap. He had won a reputation with Morton as a dangerous and penetrative winger and was a star of the Greenock club's 1928-9 promotion side. He went on to score 24 goals in 40 Scottish League First Division games. At Liverpool, however, he was usually reserve to Harold Barton and drifted from the first-class scene when only 28

McVEAN, Malcolm **1892-97**
Outside-/inside-right. 94 apps; 24 goals.
League debut: 2 September 1893.
Born: Jamestown, Dunbartonshire, 7 March 1871. Died: 6 June 1907.
Career: Junior football. Third Lanark. LIVERPOOL cs 1892. Burnley March 1897. Dundee cs 1897. Bedminster cs 1898 to 1899.
Club honours: Liverpool, Division Two champions 1894, 1896.
Malcolm McVean appeared in all five forward positions for Liverpool. He was a speedy player whose pace was described as 'blistering' and he scored the Reds' first-ever League goal. Before becoming a full-time professional he began an apprenticeship (apparently uncompleted) as a boiler-maker in a shipyard. After leaving football he returned to the shipyards as a labourer.

MALONEY, Joseph J. **1951-54**
Wing-half/inside-forward. 12 apps.
League debut: 4 March 1953.
Born: Liverpool, 26 January 1954
5ft 8½ins. 11st 7lbs.
Career: Schools and junior football.

LIVERPOOL January 1951. Shrewsbury Town July 1954. Port Vale July 1961. Crewe Alexandra August 1961. Winsford United cs 1963.
Joe Maloney was another versatile footballer, who also played at centre-half and full-back during his career. He made his senior debut at 19 before moving to Shrewsbury with Russell Crossley. In a seven-year career at Gay Meadow he made 237 League appearances, averaging 34 games per season.

MARSH, Michael A. **1987-**
Forward. (1) app.
League debut: 1 March 1989 (sub).
Born: Kirkby, Liverpool, 21 July 1969.
5ft 11ins. 11st 2lb.
Career: Kirkby Town. LIVERPOOL 1987-8.
Mike Marsh had a first taste (some 34 minutes) of the big time when he replaced the injured Jan Molby in a home fixture against Charlton Athletic. He won the approval of a local reporter, being complimented on some nice touches and generally making a promising impression. 'He could be a player with a real future' the writer concluded. Marsh joined Kirkby Town when only 15.

MARSHALL **1901-02**
Goalkeeper. 1 app.
League debut: 11 January 1902.
Marshall was recruited after the 1901-02 season had begun. He stood in for Bill Perkins — Perkin's only absence that term — in a Merseyside derby at Goodison. It was an unhappy day for the new goalkeeper, however, as Everton won 4-0.

MARSHALL, Robert G. **1897-99**
Outside-right. 20 apps; 2 goals.
League debut: 4 September 1897.
Born: 1876.
Career: Leith Athletic. LIVERPOOL cs 1897. Portsmouth cs 1899. Brighton & Hove Albion cs 1904.
Club honours: Portsmouth, Southern League champions 1902.
Bobby Marshall was a clever player, originally first choice at Anfield before being ousted, first by Fred Geary, then Jack Cox. His football career was most notable for his five years at Portsmouth, during which he played in 258 first-team games and scored 40 goals. His teammates in Pompey's 1902 championship side included ex-Liverpudlians Tom Wilkie and Tom Cleghorn.

MATTHEWS, R(obert) William **1919-22**
Centre-forward. 9 apps; 4 goals.
League debut: 3 April 1920.
Born: Plasbennion, nr Wrexham, 14 April 1897. Died: 18 December 1987.
6ft 1½ins. 12st 8lbs.
Career: Welsh junior football. LIVERPOOL 1918-19. Bristol City March 1922. Wrexham November 1923. Northwich Victoria cs 1925. Barrow late 1925. Bradford January 1926. Stockport County May 1930. New Brighton October 1930. Chester January 1932. Oswestry Town cs 1932. Witton Albion September 1932. Sandbach Ramblers November 1932. Colwyn Bay later in 1932-3. Rossendale United August 1933. Blackpool scout in 1960s.
International honours: Wales. Wales Victory.
Club honours: Bristol City, Division Three South champions 1923; Wrexham, Welsh Cup winners 1924; Bradford, Division Three North champions 1928.
Although Bill Matthews played mostly at centre-forward in Liverpool's first team, he was a centre-half for the bulk of his career. He enjoyed the rare experience of winning championship medals in both Third Division sections.

MELIA, James **1953-64**
Inside-left. 269 apps; 76 goals.
League debut: 17 December 1955.
Born: Liverpool, 1 November 1937.
5ft 8½ins. 10st 12lbs.
Career: Liverpool Schools. LIVERPOOL groundstaff 1953, professional November 1954. Wolverhampton Wanderers March 1964 (£55,000). Southampton December 1964 (£30,000). Aldershot player-coach November 1968 (£9,000), player-manager April 1969-January 1972. Crewe Alexandra player-manager May 1972-December 1974. Southport manager July-September 1975. Coach in Middle East. California Lasers (USA) scout. Brighton & Hove Albion scout, manager March-October 1983. Worked in Portugal before becoming Stockport manager July-November 1986.
International honours: England. England Schoolboy. England Youth. Football League.
Club honours: Liverpool, Division One champions 1964. Division Two champions 1962.
Jimmy Melia, the fifth of 11 children, was a hard-working inside-forward who moved to wing-half later in his career. His brief spell as Brighton manager took in the club's appearance in a Wembley FA Cup Final.

METCALF, Arthur **1912-19**
Inside-forward. 52 apps; 23 goals.
League debut: 28 September 1912.
Born: Sunderland, 8 April 1889.
5ft 7ins. 11st.
Career: Herrington Swifts. North Shields Athletic. Newcastle United April 1909 (£100). LIVERPOOL May 1912 (£150). Stockport County cs 1919. Swindon Town cs 1920. Accrington Stanley cs 1922. Aberdare Athletic cs 1923. Norwich City July 1925-6.
Club honours: Liverpool, FA Cup runners-up 1914.
Arthur Metcalf occupied all five forward positions for Liverpool and also appeared at right-half. He was forceful and an opportunist, as his scoring record shows. With Accrington he netted 21 goals in 32 Third Division matches and his final peacetime League record was 76 goals in 235 appearances. His brother was on the books of Sunderland and Huddersfield Town before World War One.

MICHAEL, William **1896-97**
Inside-forward. 19 apps; 4 goals.
League debut: 5 September 1896.
Born: Wishaw, Lanarks, 1874. Died: July 1938.
Career: Wishaw Thistle. Heart of Midlothian May 1893. LIVERPOOL cs 1896. Heart of Midlothian again cs 1897. Bristol City May 1900 to 1901.

Representative honours: Scottish League.
Club honours: Hearts, Scottish League champions 1895, Scottish Cup winners 1896.
Bill Michael was noted for his extreme robustness ('. . .could charge into a bull elephant and come off best,' said one report). He became known as the 'India-rubber man'. He had a keen eye for goals and is thought to be the first player to score for Hearts in ten consecutive matches (1893-4). His season with Bristol City was likewise productive with 15 goals in 20 matches. He was president of his old junior club, Wishaw Thistle, in the 1920s.

MILLAR, William 1928-30
Inside-right/centre-forward. 3 apps; 2 goals.
League debut: 25 August 1928.
Born: Ballymena, Co Antrim, 22 March (year not known).
5ft 8¾ins. 11st 10lbs.
Career: Lochgelly United. Linfield. LIVERPOOL cs 1928. Barrow January 1930. Newport County June 1933. Carlisle United July 1934-5.
International honours: Northern Ireland.
Billy Millar is still the only player to have won a full international cap whilst on Barrow's books. In 1931-2, he also set their scoring record with 30 goals in 30 League games, a figure passed by Jimmy Shankly two years later. Millar had originally played wing-half for Lochgelly United, later finding his best position as a centre-forward. In 1931, a Barrow journalist wrote that Millar 'last season solved the centre-forward problem, showing speed, ability to keep the front line together, and quickness in grasping scoring chances.'

MILLER, John 1918-21
Outside-/inside-right. 8 apps.
League debut: 18 October 1919.
Born: Dalziel, Motherwell, 12 March 1897.
5ft 9½ins. 10st 11lbs.
Career: Larkhall Thistle. Hamilton Academical *c.*1914. LIVERPOOL 1918. Aberdeen June 1921 (for Aberdeen's then record fee). Partick Thistle December 1924. Aberdeen cs 1926. Clyde February 1927 (£350) (briefly).
John Miller was a member of a famous Lanarkshire footballing family that included his brother, Tom (below). The family contributed a quartet of players to Hamilton Accies and later produced John Govan (Hibs & Scotland), a nephew of both John and Tom Miller. Although John Miller's peacetime Liverpool appearances were on the right wing, he subsequently made a name as Aberdeen's goalscoring centre, with aggregate Scottish League figures of 109 matches and 54 goals.

MILLER, Thomas 1912-20
Centre-forward/inside-left. 127 apps; 52 goals.
League debut: 17 February 1912.
Born: Motherwell, 29 June 1890. Died: 3 September 1958.
5ft 9ins. 11st 4lbs.
Career: Larkhall Hearts. Gleniven. Lanark United. Third Lanark. Hamilton Academical. LIVERPOOL February 1912 (£400). Manchester United September 1920. Heart of Midlothian cs 1921 (£550, the deal including Arthur Lochhead valued at £2,300). Torquay United in 1922-3. Hamilton Academical 1923 (£100). Raith Rovers December 1926-7.
International honours: Scotland.
Club honours: Liverpool, FA Cup runners-up 1914.
Tom Miller was the most distinguished member of a family that supplied four players to Hamilton Academical, including brother John (above). Tom showed lots of pace and formidable shooting power.

MILNE, Gordon **1960-67**
Right-half. 234 (2) apps; 18 goals.
League debut: 31 August 1960.
Born: Preston, Lancs, 29 March 1937.
5ft 7½ins. 11st 3lbs.
Career: Preston Amateurs. Morecambe. Preston North End January 1956. LIVERPOOL August 1960 (£16,000). Blackpool May 1967 (£30,000). Wigan Athletic player-manager January 1970 (England Youth-team manager from 1971). Coventry City manager June 1972, executive-manager May 1981. Leicester City manager August 1982, general manager June 1986. Besiktas FC (Turkey) manager 1987.
International honours: England. Football League.
Club honours: Liverpool, European Cup-winners' Cup runners-up 1966. Division One champions 1964, 1966. Division Two champions 1962.
A tireless, stocky, skilful wing-half, Gordon Milne showed a flair for management in his spell in charge of Wigan and was much sought after in consequence. This early reputation was consolidated at Coventry and Leicester. He is the son of Jimmy Milne, a renowned Preston half-back between the wars.

MINSHULL, Raymond **1946-51**
Goalkeeper. 28 apps.
League debut: 19 October 1946.
Born: Bolton, 15 July 1920.
5ft 10½ins. 11st 10lbs.
Career: Southport schools and junior football (Southport FC amateur cs 1939). Army football. High Park FC (Southport). LIVERPOOL September 1946. Southport June 1951. Bradford December 1957 (£500). Wigan Rovers player-manager cs 1959. Retired cs 1960. Southport assistant trainer for two years. Later coached in Gibraltar and Austria before serving as Everton's youth development officer.
Ray Minshull moved with his family to Southport at the age of 13. One of Cyril Sidlow's capable deputies, he subsequently earned a reputation as one of Division Three's best goalkeepers, twice representing the Northern Section against the Southern. He was most unlucky with injuries yet his confidence and clean handling were not impaired.

MITCHELL, Frank W. **1920-23**
Goalkeeper. 18 apps.
League debut: 9 February 1921.
Born: Elgin, Morayshire, 25 May (year not known)
5ft 9ins. 12st.
Career: Junior football. Motherwell. Everton cs 1913. LIVERPOOL cs 1920. Tranmere Rovers June 1923 to 1925.
At Motherwell, Frank Mitchell had to vie with the Scottish League representative player, Colin Hampton; at Goodison he was in contention with Tommy Fern at his peak, although he did manage 24 peacetime and many wartime senior appearances. Competition was, of course, hot at Anfield too, Elisha Scott being around. Mitchell, an efficient 'keeper, played 55 Northern Section games for Tranmere.

MOLBY, Jan **1984-**
Midfield. 105 (10) apps; 24 goals.
League debut: 25 August 1984.
Born: Kolding, Denmark, 4 July 1963.
6ft 1in. 14st 7lbs.
Career: Danish football. Ajax (Amsterdam). LIVERPOOL August 1984 (£200,000).

International honours: Denmark.
Club honours: Liverpool, Division One champions 1986. FA Cup winners 1986, runners-up 1988 (sub). Football League Cup runners-up 1987.
Jan Molby is a tremendously strong player with excellent ball control. He was a key performer in the Reds' Double triumph of 1986 but was sidelined through injury in 1988 and in October that year received a three-month prison sentence for a motoring offence.

MOLYNEUX, John Alan 1955-62
Right-back. 229 apps; 2 goals.
League debut: 3 September 1955.
Born: Warrington, 3 February 1931.
5ft 11ins. 12st 13lbs.
Career: Orford Youth Club. Chester

amateur 1947, professional February 1949. LIVERPOOL June 1955 (£4,500). Chester August 1962 (£2,000). New Brighton cs 1965.
International honours: England Youth.
Club honours: Chester, Welsh Cup runners-up 1953, 1955.
John Molyneux was an extremely popular figure at Anfield; a first-team regular in the seasons when the Reds came tantalizingly near to promotion but never achieved First Division football. He was blessed with an excellent physique and proved a steadying influence on the defence. His brother, Geoff, was also on Chester's books in the 1960s.

MOLYNEUX, William S. 1961-67
Goalkeeper. 1 app.
League debut: 26 April 1965.
Born: Liverpool, 10 January 1944.
5ft 9ins. 11st.
Career: Earle FC (Liverpool Combination). LIVERPOOL amateur 1961, professional November 1963. Oldham Athletic June 1967 to 1969.
Bill Molyneux was one of several reserve goalkeepers in the shadow of Tommy Lawrence. His only League appearance was in a 3-1 win at Wolves in the last game of 1964-5. He made eight Third Division appearances for Oldham.

MONEY, Richard **1980-82**
Defender. 12 (2) apps.
League debut: 13 September 1980 (sub).
Born: Lowestoft, 13 October 1955.
5ft 11½ins. 11st 5lbs.
Career: Lowestoft Town. Scunthorpe United July 1973. Fulham November 1977 (£40,000). LIVERPOOL May 1980 (£50,000) (Derby County, loan, January-March 1982). Luton Town April 1982 (£100,000, after being on loan from 25 March). Portsmouth August 1983 (£55,000). Scunthorpe United October 1985.
Club honours: Luton Town, Division Two champions 1982.
A Scunthorpe product, Richard Money followed such names as Clemence and Keegan to Anfield but never made anywhere near the same impact. He eventually returned to the Iron after useful spells with other clubs.

MORAN, Ronald **1952-69**
Left-back. 343 apps; 14 goals.
League debut: 22 November 1952.
Born: Crosby, Liverpool, 28 February 1934.
5ft 9½ins. 13st 2lbs.
Career: Crosby Schools. LIVERPOOL amateur, professional January 1952. Retired during 1968-9 season and joined the club's training staff.
Representative honours: Football League.
Club honours: Liverpool, Division One champions 1964. Division Two champions 1962.
Ronnie Moran has proved a great Anfield

loyalist of many years standing. As a player, despite being on the heavy side, he was rarely beaten for speed and was a penalty expert. In later seasons he was plagued by injuries. For many years now Moran has been an invaluable member of the famed 'boot-room' brigade. In his first season as reserve-team trainer (1972-3) the Reds won the Central League championship.

MORGAN, Hugh **1898-1900**
Inside-left. 59 apps; 15 goals.
League debut: 2 April 1898.
Born: Longriggend, Lanarks, 20 September 1869.
5ft 6ins. 10st.
Career: Junior football. St Mirren. LIVERPOOL March 1898. Blackburn Rovers June 1900 to 1903.
International honours: Scotland. Scottish League.
Signed shortly after his Scotland debut, Hugh Morgan gained another cap while on Liverpool's staff. An excellent dribbler, he was brave and hard-working and had an eye for goal. He did well at Blackburn, where he and the inside-right, fellow Scottish international Peter Somers, were described as players who 'made' the centre-forward.

MORRIS, Frederick William **1958-60**
Outside-right. 47 apps; 14 goals.
League debut: 3 September 1958.

Born: Pant, near Oswestry, 15 June 1929.
5ft 10ins. 12st 2lbs.
Career: Oswestry Town. Walsall May 1950 (£500). Mansfield Town March 1957 (£1,500). LIVERPOOL March 1958 (£7,000). Crewe Alexandra June 1960 (£4,000). Gillingham January 1961 (£1,500). Chester July 1961. Altrincham cs 1962.
Fred Morris had spent eight seasons in the lower divisions before Liverpool signed him when he was nearly 29. Seven of these seasons were at Walsall and he made 210 Football League appearances (43 goals) for the Saddlers, although military service limited his availability early on. He was speedy and progressive and had 'a tearaway style' according to a Mansfield reporter, who said he was a player who 'pleased the crowd with his dashing work.'

MORRIS, Richard **1902-05**
Inside-left. 38 apps; 5 goals.
League debut: 19 April 1902.
Born: Newtown, Montgomeryshire, 1879.
Career: Druids (Ruabon). Newtown FC. LIVERPOOL April 1902. Leeds City July 1905. Grimsby Town June 1906. Plymouth Argyle cs 1907-09. Huddersfield Town.
International honours: Wales.
An established international before joining Liverpool, Dick Morris also represented Wales at inside-right and outside-left and played for the Reds in those positions, too. In April 1903 he also played a couple of games at left-back. His spell with Huddersfield was brief and came before they entered the Football League.

MORRISON, Thomas **1927-35**
Right-half. 240 apps; 4 goals.
League debut: 11 February 1928.
Born: Coylton, Ayrshire.
5ft 9ins. 11st.
Career: Troon Athletic. St Mirren 1923-4. LIVERPOOL November 1927 (£4,000). Sunderland November 1935 to cs 1936; in season 1936-7 he assisted a Cambridgeshire junior side under the pseudonym of 'Anderson'. Ayr United cs 1937. Drumcondra FC coach August 1939.
International honours: Scotland.
Club honours: St Mirren, Scottish Cup winners 1926; Sunderland, Division One champions, 1936.
Tom Morrison was a highly constructive player and a crisp tackler who maintained a consistent level of excellence over a dozen years. He actually left Anfield at the end of season 1934-5. His League championship medal with Sunderland was won at right-back.

MORRISSEY, John J. 1957-62
Outside-right/outside-left. 36 apps; 6 goals.
League debut: 23 September 1957.
Born: Liverpool, 18 April 1940.
5ft 7ins. 10st 4lbs.
Career: Liverpool Schools. LIVERPOOL professional April 1957. Everton August 1962 (£10,000). Oldham Athletic May 1972. Retired through injury January 1973.
International honours: England Schoolboy. Football League.
Club honours: Everton, Division One champions 1963, 1970. FA Cup runners-up 1968.
Outside-left was Johnny Morrissey's main position but Alan A'Court was very much the first choice at Anfield and Morrissey eventually moved to Goodison. It was a good move for the player who won Championship and Cup medals in a decade of service with the Blues. He was a tenacious player whose powerful shooting delighted the crowd.

MUIR, Alexander J. 1947-49
Outside-right. 4 apps.
League debut: 21 February 1948.
Born: Inverkeithing, Fife, 10 December 1923.
5ft 6ins. 9st 10lbs.
Career: Lochgelly Violet. LIVERPOOL July 1947. South Liverpool 1949.
A diminutive winger recruited from good class Scottish junior football, Alex Muir was one of four players to occupy the right-wing position in 1947-8. He was twice partnered by Jack Balmer and twice by Kevin Baron. This was the extent of his senior career.

MURDOCH, W(illiam) Robert 1954-59
Inside-right. 17 apps; 5 goals.
League debut: 26 December 1957.
Born: Garston, Liverpool, 25 January 1936.
5ft 9ins. 10st 7lbs.
Career: South Liverpool when 16½ (Bolton Wanderers amateur). LIVERPOOL amateur 1954-5, professional May 1957. Barrow September 1959. Stockport County July 1960 (£3,000). Carlisle United January 1962 (in exchange for another player). Southport July 1962. Wigan Athletic July 1963. South Liverpool July 1965, later player-manager then manager until the mid-1970s. In 1976-7 was coaching in America at Ohio State University.
Bobby Murdoch was a promising player whose 15-appearance run in late 1957-8 was not continued the next season when Jimmy Harrower monopolized the number-eight shirt. Murdoch, a skilful inside man, later rendered good service to a number of smaller clubs in the North-West. He career figures were 160 League matches and 51 goals.

MURRAY, David B. 1904-05
Right-/left-back. 15 apps.
League debut: 1 September 1904.
Born: Glasgow, 1882.
5ft 9ins. 12st 4lbs.
Career: Rangers. Everton 1903. LIVERPOOL May 1904. Hull City late 1905. Leeds City December 1905. Mexborough Town 1909. Also Burslem Port Vale.
Club honours: Liverpool, Division Two champions 1905.
David Murray was a former Rangers reserve who had two League outings for Everton prior to his arrival at Anfield. He

started off as first-choice right-back, playing in 12 of the first 17 fixtures — enough to qualify for a Championship medal — before Alf West took over. He had a good run with Leeds City (85 League and Cup games, seven goals.)

MURRAY, William Thomas 1927-30
Centre-half/centre-forward. 4 apps; 1 goal.
League debut: 28 April 1928.
Born: Alexandria, Dunbartonshire, 9 November 1904. Died: 1940.
5ft 10¾ins. 12st.
Career: Junior football. Clydebank. New Brighton October 1926. Clydebank 1927. LIVERPOOL November 1927. Barrow January 1930. Bristol Rovers December 1933. Folkestone 1936.
Two matches as centre-forward (1927-8) and a couple at centre-half (1929-30) summed up Bill Murray's League career at Anfield, but he was essentially a wing-half. He captained Barrow and won high praise there. One writer said of him '. . . a clever player and a hard worker in both attack and defence,' and '. . .one of the best left-half-backs in the Northern Section'.

NEAL, Philip George 1974-85
Right-back. 453 (2) apps; 41 goals.
League debut: 16 November 1974.
Born: Irchester, Northants, 20 February 1951.
5ft 11ins. 12st 2lbs.
Career: Irchester FC. Northampton Town apprentice July 1967, professional December 1968. LIVERPOOL October 1974 (£66,000). Bolton Wanderers player-manager December 1985.
International honours: England (50 apps).
Club honours: Liverpool, European Cup winners 1977, 1978, 1981, 1984, runners-up 1985. UEFA Cup winners 1976. Division One champions 1976, 1977, 1979, 1980, 1982, 1983, 1984. FA Cup runners-up 1977. Football League Cup winners 1981, 1982, 1983, 1984, runners-up 1978.
Phil Neal was a fine defender, who possessed great skill and was remarkably consistent. He had excellent positional sense and loved to overlap down the flank. Neal missed only one League match in ten

seasons (1975-6 to 1984-5). His high goals tally (for a full-back) was mostly due to his expertise as a penalty-taker.

NEIL, Robert Scott Gibson 1896-97
Centre-half. 23 apps; 2 goals.
League debut: 17 October 1896.
Born: Govan, Glasgow, 24 September 1875. Died: 7 March 1913.
5ft 4ins. 10st 8lbs.
Career: Glasgow Ashfield. Hibernian June 1894. LIVERPOOL May 1896. Rangers April 1897. Retired cs 1904.
International honours: Scotland. Scottish League.
Club honours: Hibernian, Scottish Cup runners-up 1896; Rangers, Scottish League champions 1899, 1900, 1901, 1902. Scottish Cup winners 1898, runners-up 1899.
In the days before World War One, when there were plenty of centre-halves who were on the small side, Bobby Neil was smaller than most. That did not prevent him from being a most effective pivot. An early Rangers' historian recorded that 'there was nothing florid about Neil's style. He was always cool and thoughtful, and his methods were essentially constructive.' Later he was a Glasgow restauranteur.

NICHOLL, James 1914-15
Inside-/outside-left. 52 apps; 12 goals.
League debut: 24 January 1914.
Born: Port Glasgow.
5ft 8ins. 11st 8lbs.
Career: Junior football. Middlesbrough c.1910. LIVERPOOL during 1913-14 season to 1915.
Club honours: Liverpool, FA Cup runners-up 1914.
Jimmy Nicholl was mostly used at outside-left, although his first appearances in a Liverpool shirt were at inside-left. During his comparatively brief period at Anfield he also played at centre-forward in two League games. A bright, incisive forward, he had 50 First Division outings for Middlesbrough, scoring 13 goals.

NICHOLSON, John P. 1957-61
Centre-half. 1 app.
League debut: 10 October 1959.
Born: Liverpool, 2 September 1936. Died: 3 September 1966.
6ft. 12st.
Career: Merseyside junior football. LIVERPOOL January 1957. Port Vale August 1961. Doncaster Rovers September 1965 (£5-6,000) to his death.
Club honours: Doncaster Rovers, Division Four champions 1966.
John Nicholson, possessed the traditional centre-half's physique, was an understudy to Dick White. He found greater opportunities in the lower divisions and was an ever-present for four seasons in Port Vale's League side. Nicholson was also a regular in Doncaster's 1965-6 championship line-up. He lost his life in a car crash, the day after his 30th birthday.

NICOL, Stephen 1981-
Defender/midfield. 175 (9) apps; 25 goals.
League debut: 31 August 1982.
Born Irvine, Ayrshire, 11 December 1961.
5ft 10ins. 12st.
Career: Ayr United Boys Club. Ayr United 1979. LIVERPOOL October 1981 (£300,000).
International honours: Scotland. Scotland Under-21.
Club honours: Liverpool, European Cup winners 1984 (sub), runners-up 1985. Division One champions 1984, 1986, 1988. FA Cup winners 1986, 1989, runners-up 1988.
Steve Nicol has proved a reliable and versatile footballer, whose attacking instincts have produced some memorable goals. Nicol enjoyed a fair amount of Scottish League experience as a teenager (70 matches for Ayr) before being nurtured in the Reds Central League side ready for League soccer. His 14 appearances for Scotland Under-21 set a record. He was voted Footballer of the Year in 1989.

NIEUWENHUYS, Berry ('Nivvy') 1933-47
Outside-right. 239 apps; 74 goals.
League debut: 23 September 1933.
Born: Boskburg, Transvaal, 5 November 1911. Died: June 1984.

5ft 11ins. 11st 7lbs.
Career: Boksburg FC. Germiston Calies (South Africa). LIVERPOOL September 1933 (wartime guest for West Ham United and Arsenal). Retired cs 1947.
International honours: Great Britain (twice played against England).
Club honours: Liverpool, Division One champions 1947.
Berry Nieuwenhuys headed the 1930s wave of South African recruits to Anfield. He was a dynamic personality, loping down the wing, deceptively fast and often finishing with a thunderous shot. He served in the wartime RAF, returning to South Africa in 1949 where, being a considerable golfer, he was assistant professional to the famous Bobby Locke. Nieuwenhuys had originally worked as an engineer after leaving school. The nickname 'Nivvy' derives from the pronunciation of his surname, which is 'Nivvenhuys'.

OGRIZOVIC, Steven **1977-82**
Goalkeeper. 4 apps.
League debut: 8 March 1978.
Born: Mansfield, 12 September 1957.
6ft 3ins. 14st 7lbs.
Career: Youth club football. Chesterfield July 1977. LIVERPOOL November 1977 (£70,000). Shrewsbury Town August 1982 (in part exchange for Bob Wardle). Coventry City June 1984 (£72,500).
Club honours: Coventry City, FA Cup winners 1987.
Steve Ogrizovic was the giant custodian

brought to Anfield after only four months (and 16 Third Division games) as a full-time professional with Chesterfield. At Liverpool he understudied Ray Clemence for nearly five years, getting few opportunities before being exchanged for another goalkeeper, who, incidentally, had to retire the following year. Ogrizovic did not miss a League match for Shrewsbury before achieving regular First Division football at Coventry. In the top-flight he has proved a consistent performer who commands his goal area.

OGSTON, John Kessack **1965-68**
Goalkeeper. 1 app.
League debut: 7 April 1967.
Born: Aberdeen, 15 January 1939.
6ft 2ins. 14st 7lbs.
Career: Aberdeen schools. Banks o' Dee. Aberdeen FC 1957. LIVERPOOL September 1965 (£10,000). Doncaster Rovers, loan, August 1968 for season 1968-9, permanently July 1969 (£2,500) to 1971.
International honours: Scotland Under-23.
Club honours: Doncaster Rovers, Division Four champions 1969.
Not surprisingly, considering his bulk, John Ogston was nicknamed 'Tubby' at Aberdeen where he played a lot of first-team soccer. With Liverpool, however, he had to contend with Tommy Lawrence in his prime. At Doncaster he again enjoyed regular League football with 70 appearances. He represented The Army when on National Service.

ORR, Ronald **1908-12**
Inside-left. 108 apps; 35 goals.
League debut: 4 April 1908.
Born: Bartonholm, Irvine, Ayrshire, 6 August 1880.
5ft 5ins. 11st 6lbs.
Career: Kilwinning Eglinton 1896. Glossop North End. St Mirren May 1898. Newcastle United May 1901. LIVERPOOL April 1908 (£350). Raith Rovers January 1912. South Shields March 1913.
International honours: Scotland.
Club honours: Newcastle United, Division One champions, 1905, 1907. FA Cup runners-up 1906.
'The "Wee Orr", as his admirers love to call him,' wrote a commentator in 1910, 'is a man of few words, but great deeds — a credit to the game, his club and his country.' This came at the end of a long paragraph that began 'Ronald Orr, Liverpool's sub-captain. A great little forward and as plucky as he is clever.' He was an outstanding success on Tyneside and proved equally successful during his four years at Anfield.

OXLEY, Cyril **1925-28**
Outside-right. 31 apps; 6 goals.
League debut: 31 October 1925.
Born: Worksop, Notts, 2 May 1904. Died: 20 December 1984.
5ft 7¾ins. 11st.
Career: Whitwell Colliery (Derbyshire). Chesterfield January 1924. LIVERPOOL October 1925 (around £2,000). Southend United September 1928. Kettering Town 1929. Morecambe cs 1930. Southend United August 1931-2.
As a youngster Cyril Oxley played in 30 Third Division North matches in three seasons with Chesterfield. In 1925 a critic wrote that he was 'a good outside-left from Whitwell, capable of using either foot with advantage.' For Liverpool he immediately took over the right-wing spot from Archie Rawlings but was himself displaced by Dick Edmed in 1926-7. His brother, Bernard, played in the League between 1927 and 1938, including a spell with Chesterfield.

PAGNAM, Frederick **1914-19**
Inside-right/centre-forward. 37 apps; 28 goals.
League debut: 10 October 1914.
Born: Poulton-le-Fylde, Lancs, 4 September 1891. Died: 7 March 1962.
5ft 9ins. 12st.
Career: Poulton Grammar School. Lytham. Blackpool Wednesday. Huddersfield Town 1910. Southport Central cs 1912. Blackpool February 1913. LIVERPOOL cs 1914. Arsenal October 1919 (£1,500) Cardiff City March 1921 (£3,000). Watford December 1921 (£1,000, Watford's first four-figure fee), manager

1926 to 1929. Later Turkey's national coach and for some eight years, a coach in Holland.
From the time he joined Liverpool, Fred Pagnam was noted as a prolific goalscorer. His early days were spent at outside-right and, after moving to inside-forward, he developed into a brave, lively centre-forward who packed considerable shooting power. This was most evident in the last peacetime season. In the two seasons following (1915-16 and 1916-17) he netted 42 goals in 48 games. The son of a Blackpool bank manager, Pagnam was also engaged in the licensed trade after giving up playing.

PAISLEY, Robert OBE **1939-54**
Left-half. 253 apps; 10 goals.
League debut: 7 September 1946.
Born: Hetton-le-Hole, County Durham, 23 January 1919.
5ft 7ins. 11st 4lbs.
Career: Bishop Auckland. LIVERPOOL professional May 1939 (wartime guest for Bristol City). Retired July 1954. Liverpool assistant trainer, trainer, assistant manager, manager July 1974-June 1983, director.
Club honours: Bishop Auckland, FA Amateur Cup winners 1939; Liverpool, Division One champions 1947.
A gritty, tenacious little wing-half, Bob Paisley scored a vital goal in the 1950 FA Cup semi-final against Everton. It set the Reds on the road to a famous victory but when the Cup Final team to meet Arsenal was named, Paisley was left out. His later managerial career dwarfed his playing accomplishments and he ranks as the most successful manager in Football League history; in nine years he led Liverpool to the European Cup three times, the Championship six times, the League Cup in three consecutive seasons and the UEFA Cup. The FA Cup still eluded him as a manager, as it had when he was a player. He was voted 'Manager of the Year' a record six times and awarded the OBE in 1977. As a Liverpool director, he became an adviser to the club.

PARKINSON, John **1902-14**
Centre-/inside-forward. 203 apps; 123 goals.
League debut: 3 October 1903.
Born: Bootle, September 1883. Died: 13 September 1942.
5ft 9ins. 12st.
Career: Hertford Albion and Valkyrie FC (Merseyside junior football). LIVERPOOL amateur season 1901-02, professional 1903. Bury cs 1914. Retired during World War One.
International honours: England. Football League.
Club honours: Liverpool, Division Two champions 1905.
An early Liverpool star, Jack Parkinson spent some time on the injured list during the 1900s, one consequence of which was that he missed a Championship medal in 1906. He was fast and had a fine scoring record. Parkinson ran a couple of Liverpool newsagents' shops after leaving football.

PARR, Stephen V. **1948-55**
Right-/left-back. 20 apps.
League debut: 18 August 1951.
Born: Bamber Bridge, Preston, 22 December 1926.
5ft 8¾ins. 12st 5lbs.
Career: Farrington Villa (Preston). LIVERPOOL May 1948. Exeter City May 1955. Rochdale December 1956. Retired 1958.
Steve Parr made most of his Reds' appearances at left-back (16 in 1951-2) and the remainder (in 1952-3) on the right flank. He played several games at centre-half for Exeter City but suffered from injury and, altogether, played only 24 Third Division games for Exeter and Rochdale before retiring.

PARRY, Edward **1921-26**
Right-/left-back. 13 apps.
League debut: 9 April 1921.
Born: Colwyn Bay, 8 December 1892. Died: 1976.
Career: Colwyn Bay FC. LIVERPOOL professional February 1921. Walsall cs 1926. Colwyn Bay July 1927.
International honours: Wales. Wales Amateur.
Ted Parry was a talented full-back whose chances at Anfield were nevertheless limited by the presence of international stars Lucas, Longworth and McKinlay. He came into the professional game late — in his 29th year — and he earned the last of his full caps when in his 34th. He played 27 Division Three North matches during his season with Walsall.

PARRY, Maurice Pryce **1900-09**
Right-half. 207 apps; 3 goals.
League debut: 13 October 1900.
Born: Trefonen near Oswestry, 1878. Died: 24 March 1935.
5ft 11½ins. 13st.
Career: Newtown. Long Eaton Rangers. Leicester Fosse cs 1898. Loughborough February 1899. Brighton United cs 1899. LIVERPOOL March 1900. Partick Thistle May 1909. Rotherham County manager 1921-3. Subsequently coach in Barcelona, Frankfurt, Cologne and with Liverpool FC.

International honours: Wales.
Club honours: Liverpool, Division One champions 1906. Division Two champions 1905.
Maurice Parry was a prominent Liverpool and Wales half-back of the 1900s. His son, Frank, was an outside-right with Everton in the early 1920s and later assisted Grimsby, Accrington Stanley and Nelson. Brother of Tom Parry (Oswestry and Wales).

PATERSON, George L. **1937-46**
Outside-left. 2 apps.
League debut: 27 December 1938.
Born: Aberdeen, 19 December 1916.
5ft 8½ins. 11st 11lbs.
Career: Hall, Russell's FC (Aberdeen). LIVERPOOL May 1937 (wartime guest for Brighton & Hove Albion, York City, Leeds United, Queen's Park Rangers, Reading and Burnley). Swindon Town October 1946 to 1950. Later worked on Liverpool's coaching staff in Bill Shankly's time.
George Paterson, who also played inside-left, was a Scottish junior international, who arrived at Anfield together with a teammate named Penrose from his

Aberdeen junior club. He qualified as an FA coach before leaving Swindon's playing staff, during which period he also worked as an assistant warden at a Swindon youth club.

PAYNE, James B. 1942-56

Outside-right. 224 apps; 37 goals.
League debut: 11 September 1948.
Born: Bootle, 10 March 1926.
5ft 7¼ins. 10st.
Career: Bootle Schools. Bootle ATC. LIVERPOOL amateur 1942, professional November 1944. Everton April 1956 (about £5,000), Retired during 1956-7 season.
International honours: England 'B'.
Club honours: Liverpool, FA Cup runners-up 1950.

Jimmy Payne possessed excellent ball-control and a deceptive body swerve that saw him dubbed 'The Merseyside Matthews'. As a contemporary of Stan Matthews and Tom Finney, however, he did not collect a full cap. He switched to inside-left for a spell during the 1951-2 campaign and this, together with injuries, was thought to have taken the edge off his game. He retired early and became owner of newsagent and confectionery shops in the Liverpool area.

PEAKE, Ernest 1908-14

Centre-half/left-half. 51 apps; 5 goals.
League debut: 20 February 1909.
Born: Aberystwyth, 1888. Died: November 1931.
5ft 9ins. 11st 7lbs.
Career: Aberystwyth FC 1904. LIVERPOOL professional cs 1908. Third Lanark 1914. Blyth Spartans 1919-20. Aberaman manager 1920 to February 1922. Caerphilly manager June 1922.
International honours: Wales. Wales Amateur.

Ernie Peake was 'energetic yet skilful' according to the *Athletic News* in August 1908. He also played at left-back, right-half and centre-forward in the Reds' League side. He had a brother who also won a Welsh Amateur cap, in the same match as Ernie, against England at Stockport on 22 February 1908.

PEARSON, Albert Victor 1919-21

Outside-left. 44 apps; 4 goals.
League debut: 30 August 1919.
Born: Tynemouth, 6 September 1892.
Died: 24 January 1975.
5ft 8½ins. 10st 10lbs.
Career: Hebburn Argyle. Sheffield United cs 1912. Port Vale *c.*1914. LIVERPOOL March 1919. Port Vale cs 1921. Llanelli cs 1922. Rochdale cs 1923. Stockport County during season 1925-6. Ashton National June 1929.

Bert Pearson was a 'traditional' winger, although no great goalscorer and he found the net only 23 times in 187 matches between the wars. His best spell was the two and a half seasons he spent with Rochdale, during which he netted 12 goals in 53 outings.

PENMAN, James **1919-21**
Right-back. 1 app.
League debut: 6 November 1920.
Born: Kelty, Fife, 26 May 1896. Died: 11 October 1976.
Career: Glasgow Ashfield. LIVERPOOL 1919-21.
Jim Penman was a reserve full-back. His League appearance was in a home game defeat by Bradford (Park Avenue). His other senior run-out for the Reds was in the last fixture of wartime competition, on 26 April 1919. He was the father of Willie Penman, for many years a Raith Rovers forward, who appeared in the 1949 Scottish League Cup Final. Jim played for Ashfield in the 1914 Scottish Junior Cup Final.

PEPLOW, Stephen Thomas **1965-70**
Inside-right. 2 apps.
League debut: 15 November 1969.
Born: Liverpool, 8 January 1949.
5ft 8ins. 10st 10lbs.
Career: Liverpool Schools. LIVERPOOL apprentice, professional January 1966. Swindon Town May 1970 (loan in season 1970-71). Nottingham Forest July 1973 (Mansfield Town, month's loan, December 1973). Tranmere Rovers January 1974 (£6,000) to 1981.
Steve Peplow had made less than 50 League appearances until settling at Tranmere. Back in his native Merseyside, he made 232 appearances plus 16 substitutions, scoring 44 goals. He did a good job in a midfield/forward role and, when he left Tranmere, he was one of Prenton Park's longest-serving players.

PERKINS, William Harry **1899-1903**
Goalkeeper. 107 apps.
League debut: 3 April 1899.
Born: Wellingborough, Northants, 1875.
5ft 11ins. 12st.
Career: Kettering. Luton Town cs 1898. LIVERPOOL March 1899. Northampton Town cs 1903 to 1906.
Club honours: Liverpool, Division One champions 1901.
Bill Perkins was a sound goalkeeper who was ever-present in the 1900-01 Championship team and he missed only one League match in the next season. He was just as consistent after leaving Anfield. In his three years with Northampton, Perkins played in 100 out of a possible 102 Southern League matches.

PERRY, Frederick N. **1954-57**
Right-back. 1 app.
League debut: 31 December 1955.
Born: Cheltenham, 30 October 1933.
5ft 11ins. 11st 5lbs.
Career: Worthing FC. LIVERPOOL July 1954. Sittingbourne January 1957.
Fred Perry, who could also play at half-back, signed from the same junior club as Alan Arnell. He did not, however, establish himself as a League player as did Arnell, returning to minor soccer after two and a half years. His only senior appearance was against Blackburn Rovers at Anfield, a game which Rovers won 2-1.

PETERS, Keith **1936-40**
Left-back. 1 app.
League debut: 2 January 1939.
Born: Port Sunlight, Cheshire, 19 July 1915.
Career: Junior football. LIVERPOOL amateur *c.*1936, professional 1936-7 season (wartime guest for Brighton & Hove Albion). Retired before peacetime football resumed.
One of Jim Harley's several deputies in the late 1930s — others included Dabbs and the emerging Barney Ramsden — Keith Peter's solitary League outing was against Middlesbrough at Ayresome Park, when Liverpool were defeated 3-0.

PITHER, George **1926-28**
Outside-left. 12 apps; 1 goal.
League debut: 1 January 1927.
Born: Kew, Surrey, 24 June 1899. Died: 3 June 1966.
5ft 8½ins. 11st 7lbs.
Career: Junior football. Brentford August 1921. Millwall Athletic cs 1922. Bristol Rovers June 1924. Torquay United 1925. Merthyr Town cs 1926. LIVERPOOL late 1926. Crewe Alexandra May 1928. New Brighton June 1929. Tunbridge Wells Rangers August 1931. Margate September 1932.

Apart from his time at Liverpool, all George Pither's career was spent with Third Division and non-League clubs. He scored freely for Torquay, then in the Southern League, before going to Anfield as Fred Hopkin's deputy. He enjoyed better days in the Third Division North with Crewe (38 matches, 11 goals) and New Brighton (69 matches, nine goals). With the latter club he formed a useful left wing partnering an old Millwall colleague, Alf Oakes.

PLATT, Peter **1902-04**
Goalkeeper. 44 apps.
League debut: 11 October 1902.
Born: Oldham, 1883. Died: 11 January 1922.
Career: Oswaldtwistle Rovers. Blackburn Rovers. LIVERPOOL cs 1902-04. Nuneaton FC.
Peter Platt was still a teenager when he made his only League appearance for Blackburn and he spent his time at Ewood Park in good-class soccer with Blackburn Reserves in the Lancashire League and Oswaldtwistle (Lancashire Combination). Although still quite young, he became a first choice, making 22 Football League appearances in each of his seasons. He later settled in Nuneaton, entering the licensed trade. At the time of his demise he was the landlord of 'The White Swan' in that town.

POLK, Stanley **1940-48**
Inside-left. 13 apps.
League debut: 12 February 1947.
Born: Liverpool, 28 October 1921.
Career: South Liverpool. LIVERPOOL 1940. Port Vale July 1948. Worcester City August 1952.
'Brainy type possessing ability to think a move or so ahead' and 'a clever dribbler and ball manipulator who needed speeding up,' were two contemporary verdicts on Stan Polk. He made a lot of appearances for Liverpool during the first five wartime seasons. For Port Vale he made 159 League appearances and scored 14 goals, latterly turning out at wing-half.

PRATT, David **1923-27**
Centre-/left-half. 77 apps; 1 goal.
League debut: 17 February 1923.
Born: Lochore, Fife, 5 March 1896.
5ft 10¾ins. 11st 10lbs.
Career: Hill o' Beath FC (Fife). Celtic June 1919. Bradford City November 1921. LIVERPOOL January 1923. Bury November 1927. Yeovil & Petters United player-manager June 1929. Notts County manager April 1935. Heart of Midlothian manager June 1935 to February 1937. Bangor City manager July-October 1937. Port Vale manager December 1944 to July 1945.
Dave Pratt was a highly efficient half-back with some 200 appearances in top class Scottish and Football League soccer to his name. As Hearts manager he made some improbable sounding captures, such as Fred Warren, the Welsh international, and Walsh of Oldham Athletic.

PRICE, John G. 1954-57
Left-back. 1 app.
League debut: 19 November 1955.
Born: Aberystwyth, 22 November 1936.
5ft 10ins. 11st 12lbs.
Career: Fordhouse Youth Club, Wolverhampton. LIVERPOOL October 1954. Aston Villa March 1957. Walsall July 1957. Shrewsbury Town July 1958 to 1959.
John Price was signed from his Wolverhampton youth club, together with a left-half named Graham Wood, who did not make the Reds' senior team. Price did not play in the League for Villa or Walsall, but made nine appearances for Shrewsbury, which brought his Football League total to double figures.

PRIDAY, Robert H. 1945-49
Outside-right/outside-left. 33 apps; 6 goals.
League debut: 4 September 1946.
Born: Cape Town, South Africa, 29 March 1925.
5ft 9ins. 11st 2lbs.
Career: South African football. LIVERPOOL 1945. Blackburn Rovers March 1949. Clitheroe cs 1951. Northwich Victoria *c*.1952. Accrington Stanley December 1952. Rochdale (trial) August 1953.
A red-haired winger, Bob Priday played in the final wartime season, his debut coming on 22 December 1945. He finished the season with 11 appearances (four goals), all at outside-left. He was quick and incisive and proved a useful deputy for Billy Liddell, in addition to playing on the right wing in 18 games during the 1947-8 season. He scored 11 goals in 44 Football League games for Blackburn.

PURSELL, Robert Russell 1911-20
Left-back. 99 apps.
League debut: 30 September 1911.
Born: Campbeltown, Argyll, 18 March 1889. Died: 24 May 1974.
5ft 11ins. 12st.
Career: Aberdeen University. Queen's Park. LIVERPOOL professional September 1911. Port Vale cs 1920. Retired through injury 1922.
Club honours: Liverpool, FA Cup runners-up 1914.

Cool under pressure, fast and brainy, Bob Pursell was coveted by several clubs when he was an amateur. Liverpool moved quickly and suffered a £250 fine for signing him without first approaching Queen's Park. At Port Vale he partnered his elder brother, Scottish international Peter Pursell. He also partnered Peter in a Hanley tobacconists' business for 43 years until their retirement in 1965. The pair married two sisters and Peter's son, Bob junior, later played full-back for Port Vale.

RACE, Henry 1927-30
Inside-left. 43 apps; 18 goals.
League debut: 15 February 1928.

Born: Evenwood, County Durham, 7 January 1906.
5ft 8ins. 10st 13lbs.
Career: Raby United (County Durham). LIVERPOOL late 1927. Manchester City July 1930 (£3,000). Nottingham Forest June 1933. Shrewsbury Town cs 1937.
Club honours: Shrewsbury Town, Welsh Cup winners 1938.
Harry Race played some of his Liverpool games at centre-forward, the position in which he made his League debut. He was a reserve with Manchester City but a popular figure in Nottingham, as the local annual reported: 'He was the hardest worker and most consistent member of the attack and, on sticky grounds, the brains and driving force of the line.' Another verdict was '. . .the forward line always languished without him. Harry is a schemer who makes openings for others.'

RAISBECK, Alexander Galloway **1898-1909**
Centre-half. 312 apps; 19 goals.
League debut: 3 September 1898.
Born: Wallacestone near Polmont, Stirlings, 26 December 1878. Died: 12 March 1949.
5ft 9¾ins. 12st 9lbs.
Career: Blantyre Boys' Brigade. Larkhall Thistle. Royal Albert. Hibernian 1896. Stoke March 1898. LIVERPOOL May 1898 (£350). Partick Thistle cs 1909 (£500). Hamilton Academical April 1914, director 1917, manager for a year. Bristol City secretary-manager December 1921-June 1929. Halifax Town secretary-manager July 1930. Chester secretary-manager May 1936-April 1938. Liverpool scout. Bath City manager.
International honours: Scotland. Scottish League.
Club honours: Liverpool, Division One champions 1901, 1906. Division Two champions 1905.
Alex Raisbeck was a personality renowned throughout the football world for half a century. One of the greatest centre-halves of the era, he was a commanding captain. His brother, William, also a half-back, was well-known with Derby County and other clubs at the turn of the century.

RAMSDEN, Bernard **1935-48**
Left-back. 60 apps.
League debut: 28 August 1937.
Born: Sheffield, 8 November 1917.
5ft 9½ins. 11st 2lbs.
Career: Hampton Sports (Sheffield). Sheffield Victoria. LIVERPOOL March 1935 (wartime guest for Brighton & Hove Albion, Leeds United and York City). Sunderland March 1948. Hartlepools United January 1950. Retired cs 1950 and emigrated to the United States.
Barney Ramsden linked up with Jim Harley to form an effective full-back partnership. It carried over to the post-war seasons, although its wartime activity was confined to season 1939-40. He made only 13 senior appearances while at Roker Park. He settled in California.

RAWLINGS, Archibald 1924-26

Outside-right. 663 apps; 8 goals.
League debut: 15 March 1924.
Born: Leicester, 2 October 1891. Died: 11 June 1952.
5ft 11½ins. 11st 10lbs.
Career: Wombwell. Shirebrook. Northampton Town early in 1908. Barnsley 1911. Rochdale cs 1914. Dundee 1919. Preston North End June 1920 (£1,500) LIVERPOOL March 1924. Walsall June 1926. Bradford February 1927. Southport July 1928. Dick Kerr's FC (Preston) December 1928. Burton Town cs 1931. Preston North End assistant trainer.
International honours: England.
Club honours: Preston North End, FA Cup runners-up 1922.

Archie Rawlings, who spent well over two decades as a professional player, was exceptionally tall and weighty for a winger. This physique combined with pace and hard shooting to make him a dangerous opponent. His son, Syd, also an outside-right, served several League clubs in the 1930s, including Millwall with whom he won a Division Three South championship medal in 1938.

RAYBOULD, Samuel F. 1900-07

Centre-forward. 211 apps; 119 goals.
League debut: 13 January 1900.
Born: Chesterfield, 1875.
5ft 10ins. 13st.

Career: Ilkeston Town. Chesterfield Town. Derby County 1894-5. Derbyshire junior football. New Brighton Tower 1899. LIVERPOOL January 1900. Sunderland May 1907. Woolwich Arsenal May 1908-cs 1909.
Representative honours: Football League.
Club honours: Liverpool, Division One champions 1901, 1906. Division Two champions 1905.

Sam Raybould established a League record with his 31 goals in season 1902-03, a figure which stood as a Liverpool club record for 29 years. He played a fair number of games at inside-left around the mid-1900s, moving over to accommodate Joe Hewitt. His three inter-League medals were all won while at Anfield, all against the Scottish League.

REID, Thomas Joseph 1926-29

Centre-forward. 51 apps; 31 goals.
League debut: 1 May 1926.
Born: Motherwell, 15 August 1905. Died: 1972.
5ft 9½ins. 11st 3lbs.
Career: Blantyre Victoria. Clydebank cs 1925. LIVERPOOL April 1926 (£1,000). Manchester United January 1929. Oldham Athletic (loan) March 1933, permanently June 1933 (£400). Barrow September 1935 to 1936. Rhyl Athletic.

Tommy Reid was described as 'a robust, dashing Scot. No artist but a scorer in any grade of football.' He continued that form with Manchester United (63 goals in 96 League outings), at a time when United suffered from an otherwise indifferent attack. His final total of Football League and Scottish League appearances was 276 matches (165 goals).

RILEY, Arthur Jack **1925-40**

Goalkeeper. 322 apps.
League debut: 24 October 1925.
Born: Boksburg, Transvaal, 26 December 1903.
6ft 1in. 12st 8lbs.
Career: Boksburg FC. LIVERPOOL August 1925. Returned to South Africa 1940.
International honours: South African Amateur.
Arthur Riley and Gordon Hodgson were the pick of the South African FAs 1924 touring side. Riley signed for the Reds four months ahead of Hodgson and eventually took over from the long-serving Elisha Scott. Ideally built for a goalkeeper, he was a classy performer and generally reliable, although he suffered some loss of form in the 1930s. He was an engineer by trade.

ROBERTS, John Edgar ('Nipper') **1933-34**

Centre-forward. 1 app.
League debut: 4 September 1933.
Born: Blundellsands, Liverpool, 15 March 1910. Died: 1 June 1985.
5ft 9ins. 11st 8lbs.
Career: Marine (Crosby). Orrell. Blundellsands FC. Southport on amateur forms September 1931. LIVERPOOL professional May 1933. Wigan Athletic June 1934. Port Vale December 1935 (in exchange for another player) to 1940.
International honours: England Amateur.
One of Merseyside's best inter-war amateurs, John Roberts scored a goal in the first minute of his Amateur international appearance. He was reserve to Sam English and Tommy Johnson in his Anfield season. Sixty-six goals in 55 matches for non-League Wigan paved his return to the Football League soccer. By the outbreak of war he had made 95 League appearances for Port Vale and scored 56 goals. He served with the Irish Guards during the war and afterwards pursued his trade as a lithographer in South Africa and Rhodesia. He died in Cape Town. As a young man he captained England at baseball.

ROBERTS, Sydney **1929-37**
Inside-left. 57 apps; 10 goals.
League debut: 23 April 1932.
Born: Bootle, 1911.
5ft 9½ins. 10st 4lbs.
Career: Bootle JOC. LIVERPOOL 1929. Shrewsbury Town August 1937. Chester January 1938. Northfleet August 1939.
Syd Roberts spent three years working his way through the 'A' and Central League sides to first-team recognition. He formed an effective left wing with Alf Hanson, who also graduated from Bootle JOC. Shrewsbury were a non-League side when Roberts joined them but he returned to the League with Chester, scoring five goals in 29 Northern Section appearances for them.

ROBERTSON, John Thomas **1900-02**
Right-back. 42 apps; 1 goal.
League debut: 1 September 1900.
Born: Newton Mearns, Renfrews. *c.*1877.
Career: Newton Thistle. Edinburgh St Bernard's. Stoke cs 1894. Hibernian 1896. Stoke again cs 1897. LIVERPOOL cs 1900. Southampton May 1902. Brighton & Hove Albion cs 1904-06, captaining the Reserves in season 1905-06.
Club honours: Hibernian, Scottish Cup runners-up 1896; Liverpool, Division One champions 1901; Southampton, Southern League champions 1903, 1904.
In 1905, a Sussex newspaper reported that Jack Robertson was 'a brave and daring player whose best years were spent at Stoke'. It was a strange statement, considering all the honours he had won with other clubs. Liverpool had no wish to lose him and that was justified when he won consecutive Southern League championship medals with Southampton. He became a Hove licensee in the mid-1900s.

ROBERTSON, Thomas **1898-1902**
Outside-left. 126 apps; 34 goals.
League debut: 11 April 1898.
Born: probably in Lanarkshire.
Career: East Benhar Heatherbell. Motherwell. Fauldhouse. Heart of Midlothian August 1896. LIVERPOOL March 1898 (£350 including John Walker). Heart of Midlothian May 1902 (£300 including 'Sailor' Hunter). Dundee October 1902.
International honours: Scotland.
Club honours: Hearts, Scottish League champions 1897; Liverpool, Division One champions 1901.
Tom Robertson could play on either flank. He laid on plenty of goals as well as scoring well himself. While with Liverpool he was said to be earning £4 per week, a good income at the turn of the century.

ROBINSON, Michael John **1983-84**
Forward. 26 (4) apps; 6 goals.
League debut: 27 August 1983.

Born: Leicester, 12 July 1958.
6ft. 12st 7lbs.
Career: Blackpool Schools (Coventry City on 'S' forms). Waterloo Wanderers (Blackpool Sunday League). Dolphinstone FC. Preston North End apprentice July 1974, professional July 1976. Manchester City June 1979 (£756,000). Brighton & Hove Albion July 1980 (£400,000). LIVERPOOL August 1983 (£200,000). Queen's Park Rangers December 1984 (£100,000). Osasuna FC (Spain) 1987.
International honours: Republic of Ireland.
Club honours: Brighton & Hove Albion, FA Cup runners-up 1983; Liverpool, European Cup winners 1984. Division One champions 1984; Queen's Park Rangers, Football League Cup runners-up 1986.
Michael Robinson attracted a lot of transfer money in his time. An aggressive, roving player, he scored 37 League goals in 113 matches (two as substitute) for Brighton, his best club spell. He qualified for the Republiuc of Ireland, for whom he won 23 caps, through parentage.

ROBINSON, Robert Smith **1904-12**
Right-half/inside-right. 254 apps; 64 goals.
League debut: 13 February 1904.

Born: Sunderland, October 1879.
5ft 9ins. 12st 5lbs.
Career: Sunderland Royal Rovers. Sunderland FC November 1902. LIVERPOOL February 1904. Tranmere Rovers 1912.
Club honours: Liverpool, Division One champions 1906. Division Two champions 1905.
'Robbie' Robinson was an inspired signing from Sunderland, for whom he scored seven goals in 25 senior games. He gave Liverpool eight years' sterling service. He began at inside-forward and switched to wing-half at Anfield around 1909, as replacement for Maurice Parry.

ROGERS, Fred **1933-40**
Right-/centre-half. 70 apps.
League debut: 27 October 1934.
Born: Frodsham, Cheshire, 17 April 1910.
Died: 1 April 1967
Career: Helsby Athletic. LIVERPOOL March 1933 to 1940.
Fred Rogers was known to the Kop as 'The Bullet', a nickname that derived from his close-cropped hairstyle. He was a strong half-back who was well-suited to the 'policeman' role at centre-half. He did not resume in the first-class game when peace returned, by then being in his mid-30s.

ROGERS, Thomas **1907-12**
Left-back. 38 apps.
League debut: 27 April 1906.
Born: Prescot, Lancs, 1885.
Career: Rossendale United. LIVERPOOL April 1907 to 1912.
Tom Rogers quickly graduated after signing from Lancashire Combination football, playing in the last League match of the 1906-07 season. The following term he deputized for Percy Saul on a dozen occasions but, in his five years at Anfield, was never an automatic selection. A solid reserve, he could also play at right-back.

ROSS, Ian **1965-72**
Utility player. 42 (6) apps; 2 goals.
League debut: 14 January 1967 (sub).
Born: Glasgow, 26 November 1947.
5ft 8ins. 10st 8lbs.
Career: Schools and junior football. LIVERPOOL August 1965. Aston Villa February 1972 (£60,000), (Notts County, loan, October 1976; Northampton Town, loan, November 1976; Peterborough United, loan, December 1976-March 1977). Peterborough United permanently, player-coach cs 1977. Wolverhampton Wanderers August 1979. Hereford United, non-contract player during 1982-3.
Club honours: Aston Villa, Division Three champions 1972. Football League Cup winners 1975.

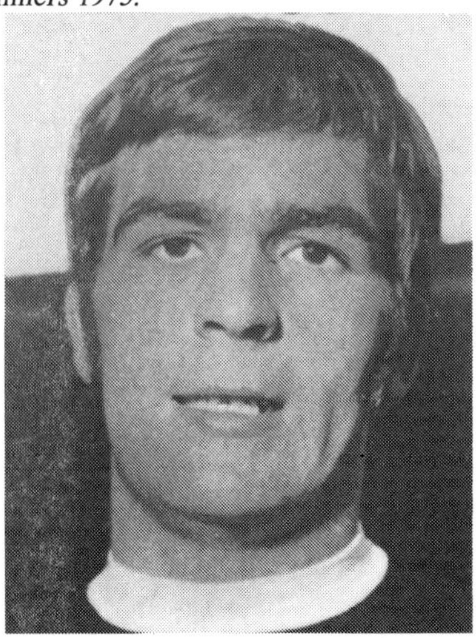

Ian Ross was a reserve at Anfield but one especially valued by manager Bill Shankly because of his ability as a marker. Ross filled seven positions for Liverpool, his best being midfield. He went on to skipper a re-emerging Aston Villa before making over 100 League appearances for Peterborough.

ROSS, James Daniel **1894-97**
Inside-right. 78 apps; 37 goals.
League debut: 13 September 1894.
Born: Edinburgh, 28 March 1866. Died: 12 June 1902.
5ft 6¾ins. 11st 8lbs.
Career: Edinburgh St Bernard's. Preston North End 1884. LIVERPOOL cs 1894. Burnley March 1897. Manchester City February 1899 to his death.
Club honours: Preston North End, Division One champions 1889, 1890. FA Cup winners 1889, runners-up 1888; Liverpool, Division Two champions 1896; Burnley, Division Two champions 1898.
Jimmy Ross was eulogized by the critics: 'clever as a monkey' and 'fast, brilliant and a deadly shot.' Playing in England undoubtedly cost him Scottish caps, as it did his brother, the celebrated Nick Ross. Jimmy captained Liverpool, won another Second Division medal at Burnley and almost gained a third with Manchester City. He was the first player to score six goals in a Football League match (6 October 1888).

ROWLEY, A(nthony) Arthur **1951-54**
Inside-left. 13 apps; 1 goal.
League debut: 23 August 1952.
Born: Liverpool, 9 May 1933.
5ft 6½ins. 10st 7lbs.
Career: Florence Melley Boys Club. LIVERPOOL May 1951. Wrexham November 1954. Crewe Alexandra February 1957. Tranmere Rovers September 1958. Burscough Rangers 1959.
Arthur Rowley's time at Anfield overlapped that of Welsh international Tony Rowley by a year. Arthur was a skilful little forward who played 88 games in the Third Division (15 goals) before entering non-League soccer.

ROWLEY, Antonio Camilio **1953-58**
Inside-right. 58 apps; 37 goals.
League debut: 21 August 1954.
Born: Porthcawl, Glamorgan, 19 September 1929.
6ft. 11st 7lbs.
Career: Wellington Town (Salop). Birmingham City January 1949. Stourbridge. LIVERPOOL October 1953. Tranmere Rovers March 1958 (£3,500).

Bangor City cs 1961. Northwich Victoria January 1962. Mossley September 1963.
International honours: Wales.
Of Italian extraction, as his christian names indicate, Tony Rowley failed to make a single senior appearance at Birmingham. He achieved an excellent scoring record at Anfield, despite never enjoying a prolonged run in the first team. He was said to lack class, but is one of the few players to have scored a hat-trick on their League debut.

RUDHAM, Kenneth Robert ('Doug') **1954-60**
Goalkeeper. 63 apps.
League debut: 20 November 1954.
Born: Johannesburg, 3 May 1926.
6ft. 12st.
Career: Johannesburg Rangers. LIVERPOOL amateur October 1954, professional August 1955. Johannesburg Ramblers May 1960.
International honours: South African Amateur.
Doug Rudham toured Britain with a South African national team in 1954, eventually signing forms for Liverpool just as Arthur Riley and Gordon Hodgson had done 30 years before. Rudham shared first-team duties with Dave Underwood and then understudied Tommy Younger and Bert Slater in turn.

RUSH, Ian James **1980-87 & 1988-**
Striker. 240 apps; 146 goals.
League debut: 13 December 1980.
Born: St Asaph, Flintshire, 20 October 1961.
6ft 2ins. 12st 6lbs.
Career: North Wales schools football. Chester apprentice, professional September 1979. LIVERPOOL April 1980 (£300,000, becoming Britain's most expensive teenager). Juventus (Turin) June 1987 (£3.2m, British record). LIVERPOOL August 1988 (£2.8m).
International honours: Wales. Wales Schoolboy. Wales Youth. Wales Under-21.
Club honours: Liverpool, European Cup winners 1984, runners-up 1985. Division One champions 1982, 1983, 1984, 1986. FA Cup winners 1986, 1989. Football League Cup winners 1981, 1982, 1983, 1984, runners-up 1987.
Ian Rush is the master striker whose speed and eye for the scoring chance have made him a major force in the Reds' many triumphs of the 1980s. After a quiet beginning at Anfield, he blossomed into an extremely dangerous striker in a hugely talented team. He signed for Juventus in 1986 but remained with Liverpool throughout the 1986-7 season. After one season in Italy, he looked ready to return to Britain and Everton were amongst the clubs reported to be bidding for him. Eventually, he returned to Anfield, to a hero's welcome. Although he struggled with injury for much of the season he scored two goals in the FA Cup Final after coming on as substitute.

RUSSELL, Colin **1977-82**
Forward. (1) app.
League debut: 2 May 1981.
Born: Liverpool, 21 January 1961.
5ft 7ins. 10st 7lbs.
Career: Junior football. LIVERPOOL apprentice, professional April 1978. Huddersfield Town September 1982 (£15,000). Stoke City, loan, March-May 1984. AFC Bournemouth August 1984 (£10,000). Doncaster Rovers July 1986 (£7,000). Scarborough, loan, October 1987).
Despite having made only one substitute appearance for the Reds' first team, Colin Russell still commanded a £15,000 fee when transferred to Huddersfield on the strength of his form in Liverpool's fine Central League team.

ST JOHN, Ian **1967-71**
Centre-forward/inside-left. 334 (2) apps; 95 goals.
League debut: 19 August 1961.
Born: Motherwell, 7 June 1938.
5ft 7½ins. 11st 10lbs.
Career: Motherwell Bridge Works FC.

Douglas Water Thistle. Motherwell FC August 1956. LIVERPOOL May 1961 (£37,500, then a Liverpool record). Coventry City August 1971, assistant manager December 1971-March 1972. Motherwell manager July 1973. Portsmouth manager September 1974-May 1977. Sheffield Wednesday coaching staff July 1978 to cs 1979.
International honours: Scotland. Scotland Under-23. Scottish League.
Club honours: Liverpool, European Cup-winners' Cup runners-up 1966. Division One champions 1964, 1966. Division Two champions 1962. FA Cup winners 1965.
Small in stature, Ian St John could nevertheless outjump taller opponents. He was an expert in close control and scored the fastest hat-trick in Scottish football (in two and a half minutes) on 15 August 1959. A qualified FA coach, St John turned his attention to television after leaving Sheffield Wednesday and is now well-known for his *The Saint and Greavsie Show* with his contemporary, Jimmy Greaves.

SALISBURY, William **1928-29**
Centre-forward. 16 apps; 2 goals.
League debut: 27 October 1928.
Born: Glasgow, 23 February 1899. Died: January 1965.
5ft 7ins. 11st 7lbs.
Career: St Anthony's, (Glasgow). Partick Thistle *c.*1919 to 1920. LIVERPOOL October 1928. Bangor (Irish League) August 1929.
Club honours: Partick Thistle, Scottish Cup winners 1921.
Bill Salisbury was signed for what was described as 'a four-figure fee'. He was essentially an outside-left, yet 13 of his 17 senior appearances for the Reds (16 League and one FA Cup) were at centre-forward. He had given Partick Thistle a decade of excellent service, playing in 256 Scottish League Division One matches and scoring 46 goals.

SAMBROOK, John Henry **1922-23**
Centre-forward. 2 apps.
League debut: 30 December 1922.
Born: Wednesfield, Wolverhampton, 10 March 1899. Died: 30 December 1973.
5ft 10ins. 10st 10lbs.
Career: Willenhall Town. Wolverhampton Wanderers 1919-20. LIVERPOOL late in 1922. Stockport County cs 1923. Southport cs 1924 to 1926.
Jack Sambrook did well at Southport, scoring 31 goals in 65 League games. In 1925, one commentator described him as 'a speedy, forceful player . . .he is one of those who introduces any amount of variety in his moves, is quick on the ball and knows his way round a defender.' He developed cartilage trouble and it is probable his playing career ended in 1926. He was the father of Ray Sambrook, the prominent Coventry and Manchester City winger of the 1950s.

SATTERTHWAITE, Charles Oliver 1899-1902
Inside-left. 46 apps; 12 goals.
League debut: 16 December 1899.
Born: Cockermouth, Cumberland, 1877.
Died: 25 May 1948.
5ft 10ins. 12st.
Career: Workington. Bury. Burton Swifts cs 1897. LIVERPOOL late in 1899. New Brompton cs 1902. West Ham United cs 1903. Woolwich Arsenal cs 1904 to 1910.
Club honours: Liverpool, Division One champions 1901.
Charlie Satterthwaite was a powerful inside man, renowned for his ferocious shooting. The story goes that on one occasion, playing for Woolwich Arsenal, his 25-yard drive hit the crossbar and rebounded to 'floor' the goalkeeper before finding its way into the back of the net. His younger brother, Joseph Norman Satterthwaite, was a professional with Woolwich Arsenal, Grimsby and New Brompton during the 1900s.

SAUL, Percy 1906-09
Right-/left-back. 75 apps; 1 goal.
League debut: 22 September 1906.
Born: Rotherham, 1881.
5ft 11ins. 12st 12lbs.
Career: Thornhill FC (West Yorks). Gainsborough Trinity cs 1901. Plymouth Argyle cs 1904. LIVERPOOL cs 1906. Coventry City cs 1909 to 1911. Rotherham County.
In his first season at Anfield, Percy Saul took over Alf West's position at right-back; in the next season, however, all his appearances were on the left. He was usually first choice with all his Football League and Southern League clubs.

SAUNDERS, Roy 1948-59
Right-half. 132 apps; 1 goal.
League debut: 7 February 1953.
Born: Salford, 4 September 1930.
5ft 6½ins. 10st 9lbs.
Career: Hull City amateur. LIVERPOOL professional May 1948. Swansea Town March 1959 (valued at £4,000 when transferred in part exchange for Des Palmer) to1966. Ammanford FC manager 1968. Swansea Town trainer 1971.

International honours: England Youth.
Club honours: Swansea, Welsh Cup winners 1961.
Roy Saunders was a purposeful wing-half, equally at home on the left flank. Small yet brave, he was fast and enterprising. He would have increased his appearances tally but for the presence of Phil Taylor, Bob Paisley and Geoff Twentyman. He made 95 League appearances for the Swans. Father of Dean Saunders, the Derby County and Wales striker.

SAVAGE, R(obert) Edward 1931-37
Right-half. 100 apps; 2 goals.
League debut: 26 September 1931.
Born: Louth, Lincs, 1912. Died: 30 January 1964.
5ft 11½ins. 12st 9lbs.
Career: Lincolnshire schools football.

Lincoln City 1928-9. LIVERPOOL May 1931. Manchester United December 1937. Wrexham November 1938 (wartime guest for Carlisle United, West Ham United, Chelsea, Fulham, Millwall, Southport and York City). Retired during the war.
Ted Savage forced his way into Lincoln's League side when he was only 17 and had made almost 100 Third Division North appearances by the time he joined the Reds. He was described as 'fast, resourceful, and a good judge in defence or attack'. He was latterly employed in the licensed trade.

SCOTT, Alan **1929-32**
Centre-forward. 3 apps; 2 goals.
League debut: 31 August 1929.
Born: Birkenhead, 1910.
5ft 9½ins. 10st 12lbs.
Career: Liverpool Pemblians. LIVERPOOL April 1929. Swindon Town June 1932. Gillingham June 1933 to 1934.
Merseysider Alan Scott was blooded when still a teenager and scored in two of his three First Division outings (at Blackburn on 27 December 1930 and at Old Trafford on 6 April 1931). He scored twice in 19 Third Division South matches for Swindon, for whom he also appeared at inside-right. He did not appear in the League for Gillingham.

SCOTT, Elisha **1912-34**
Goalkeeper. 430 apps.
League debut: 1 January 1913.
Born: Belfast, 24 August 1894. Died: 16 May 1959.
5ft 9ins. 10st 10lbs.
Career: Belfast Boys Brigade. Linfield. Broadway United (Belfast). LIVERPOOL late in 1912. Belfast Celtic player-manager June 1934. Retired as a player 1936 but continued as manager until after Celtic folded in 1949.
International honours: Ireland and Northern Ireland. Irish League.
Club honours: Belfast Celtic (wartime guest), Irish Cup winners 1918, runners-up 1917; Liverpool, Division One champions 1922, 1923.
Elisha Scott was amongst the greatest footballers ever produced by the British game. Lithe and cat-like, he possessed

superb judgment and was a master of his goal area. One contemporary writer summed him up: 'His piping Belfast brogue could be heard issuing instructions and sometimes imprecations.' Another writer said, 'He has the eye of an eagle, the swift movement of a panther . . .the clutch of a vice when gripping the ball.' He made the first of his 31 international appearances in 1920, the last in 1936 when he was nearly 42. In 1934, Everton offered £250 for his services but Liverpool refused after a wave of protest letters from their supporters.

SCOTT, J. **1910-15**
Left-half. 10 apps.
League debut: 8 April 1912.
Born: Stevenston, Ayrshire, *c.*1882.
5ft 9½ins. 11st 7lbs.
Career: Ardeer Thistle. LIVERPOOL 1910-15.
Scott was a Scottish junior brought to Anfield as a teenager. Described in the local Press as 'promising', following his opening run of League appearances early in 1912, he had a couple of outings in the first wartime season before drifting out of first-class football.

SCOTT, Thomas **1925-28**

Inside-forward. 17 apps; 4 goals.
League debut: 14 March 1925.
Born: Newcastle-upon-Tyne, 6 April 1904.
Died: 24 December 1979.
5ft 9¾ins. 12st 4lbs.
Career: Swifts FC (Tyneside). Pandon Temperance. Sunderland December 1922. Darlington cs 1924. LIVERPOOL February 1925. Bristol City October 1928. Preston North End June 1930. Norwich City June 1932. Exeter City October 1934. Hartlepools United during 1936-7 season to cs 1937.
Club honours: Norwich City, Division Three South champions 1934.
Tom Scott's main position was inside-right but he also turned out for the Reds at inside-left, centre-forward and outside-left. He was reckoned to be Norwich's 'cleverest' forward for years. Just previously, in 1931, a Preston scribe found him a 'vigorous, useful player though somewhat slow'. He was later a Liverpool licensee.

SEALEY, John A. **1963-66**

Inside-right. 1 app; 1 goal.
League debut: 26 April 1965.
Born: Wallasey, 27 December 1945.
5ft 11ins. 11st 10lbs.
Career: Warrington Town. LIVERPOOL December 1963. Chester June 1966. Wigan Athletic April 1968.
John Sealey was looked upon as a centre-forward but his lone League outing for the Reds was at inside-right, at Molineux on 26 April 1965 when he celebrated with a goal in the Reds' 3-1 victory. At Chester he appeared in four Fourth Division matches (plus a substitution) before his transfer to then non-League Wigan Athletic.

SHAFTO, John **1936-43**

Centre-forward. 17 apps; 6 goals.
League debut: 23 October 1937.
Born: Humshaugh, Northumberland, 8 November 1918. Died: 1978.
5ft 8½ins. 11st 12lbs.
Career: Hexham FC. LIVERPOOL November 1936 (wartime guest for Brighton & Hove Albion and Bradford

City). Did not resume in first-class football when peace returned.
Signed as a sturdy 18-year-old, John Shafto showed his paces while still a teenager, leading Liverpool's attack in promising style. At the outbreak of war he had scored seven goals in 20 League and FA Cup matches and would probably have become the regular centre-forward but for war's intervention.

SHANNON, Leslie **1943-49**

Centre-forward. 11 apps; 1 goal.
League debut: 17 April 1948.
Born: Liverpool, 12 March 1926.
5ft 7ins. 10st 4lbs.
Career: Merseyside junior football. LIVERPOOL amateur 1943, professional November 1944. Burnley November 1949 (around £6,000). Everton coach August 1959. Arsenal coach 1962, later assistant manager to May 1966. Bury manager July 1966 to cs 1967 and re-engaged two months later. Blackpool manager May 1969-October 1970. PAOK (Salonika) trainer-coach January 1971-April 1974. Iraklis manager. Olympiakos Piræus manager from 1976.
International honours: England 'B'.
Auburn-haired and terrier-like, Les

Shannon asked for a transfer in September 1949 because he had not secured a regular place. The Liverpool management thought he was too lightweight for a centre-forward. They were probably correct because, in the decade at Turf Moor, he played at left-half and inside-left (263 League appearances, 39 goals). Shannon was a fully qualified coach before leaving Burnley.

SHEARS, Albert Edward **1924-30**
Right-/Centre-half. 16 apps.
League debut: 10 April 1926.
Born: Newcastle-upon-Tyne, 12 May 1900.
Died: 1954.
5ft 8½ins. 11st 6lbs.
Career: Spen Black & White. Preston North End 1921-2. Doncaster Rovers 1923-4. Aberdare Athletic. LIVERPOOL 1924. Tranmere Rovers May 1930. Wigan Borough July 1931. Barnsley (trial) December 1931, was engaged but left May 1932.
Although in the mid- and late-1920s Bert Shears was regarded as a half-back, he also played in the forward line on occasions and did so for the Reds in three League games. Indeed, it seems that he should always have been a forward because a 1922 Lancashire football annual said 'he was the leading marksman in the (PNE) reserve team with 28 goals. . . .A player of considerable promise, speedy, and a capital shot.'

SHEEDY, Kevin M. **1978-82**
Midfield. 1 (2) app.
League debut: 14 February 1981.
Born: Builth Wells, 21 October 1959.
5ft 7ins. 9st 2lbs.
Career: Junior football. Hereford United apprentice, professional October 1976. LIVERPOOL July 1978 (£80,000). Everton May 1982 (£100,000).
International honours: Republic of Ireland. Republic of Ireland Under-21. Northern Ireland Youth.
Club honours: Everton, European Cup-winners' Cup winners 1985. Division One champions 1985, 1987. FA Cup runners-up 1985, 1986, 1989.
With the wealth of talent at Anfield, Kevin Sheedy did not get much of a chance to show what he could do in the top flight. That changed after he crossed Stanley Park and, notwithstanding troublesome injuries, he has enjoyed good times at Goodison. He must have grown in stature, too, because in 1987 his physique was recorded as 5ft 9in tall and 10st 11lb in weight. His craft and graceful presence have been major contributors to Everton's successes of the 1980s. He became famous for his 'educated' left foot, scoring goals from both dead ball and 'in play' situations.

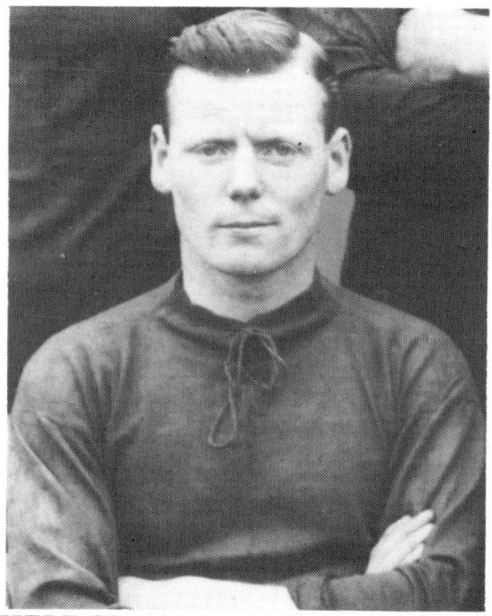

SHELDON, John **1913-22**
Outside-right. 129 apps; 17 goals.
League debut: 29 November 1913.
Born: Clay Cross near Chesterfield, 1888.
Died: 19 March 1941, aged 53.
5ft 6½ins. 10st.
Career: Nuneaton. Manchester United 1900s. LIVERPOOL November 1913. Retired through injury cs 1922.
Club honours: Liverpool, FA Cup runners-up 1914.
John Sheldon was a quick, lightweight forward who had the gift of being able to deliver pinpoint centres. At Old Trafford he had been starved of senior football because the incomparable Billy Meredith was in residence. His transfer to Liverpool changed things and he immediately stepped into the shoes of ageing Arthur Goddard.

SHEPHERD, J(ohn) William **1945-52**
Right-back. 53 apps.
League debut: 21 August 1948.
Born: Liverpool, 25 September 1920.
5ft 8½ins. 11st 1lb.
Career: Elm Park FC (Liverpool). LIVERPOOL December 1945. Wigan Athletic cs 1952.
Bill Shepherd made a good impression early in 1948 and missed only one League match in 1948-9. However, after playing in the first four games of the following season, he lost his place and appeared infrequently thereafter. His brother, Arthur, an inside-forward, was on Liverpool's books at the same time (no peacetime senior appearances) and afterwards played Third Division football with New Brighton.

SHIELD, John G. **1936**
Left-half. 1 app.
League debut: 11 April 1936.
Born: South Shields, 10 April 1915. Died: 1981.
Career: Durham University. Bishop Auckland FC (LIVERPOOL amateur seasons 1935-6 and 1936-7).
International honours: England Amateur.
Club honours: Bishop Auckland, FA Amateur Cup winners 1935.
John Shield was a top-class amateur said by the Liverpool Press to resemble Tom Bromilow in style. He certainly was stylish and brainy, although he was prone to be slow into the tackle and relied too much on a strong left foot. He was a teacher by profession.

SHIELDS, Samuel M. **1949-51**
Inside-right. 1 app.
League debut: 26 November 1949.
Born: Denny, Stirlings, 21 March 1929.
5ft 8ins. 11st 3lbs.
Career: Dunipace Juniors. Cowdenbeath September 1947. LIVERPOOL May 1949. Airdrieonians July 1951 (£700). Darlington June 1952. Horden Colliery cs 1953.
'Plays the Scottish type of football and is a brilliant schemer in addition to having a strong shot,' reported the 1949-50 Liverpool handbook on Sam Shields. He had to understudy Kevin Baron, Willie Fagan and Jack Balmer, however, and moved to Airdrie, where he was plagued by injuries. For Darlington he played 21 Third Division North games and scored two goals.

SHONE, Daniel **1915-28**
Centre-forward/inside-left. 76 apps; 23 goals.
League debut: 27 August 1921.
Born: Wirral, Cheshire, 27 April 1892. Died: 1974.
5ft 6¼ins. 11st 8lbs.
Career: Earle FC (Liverpool Zingari League). LIVERPOOL amateur *c.*1915. Grayson's (Garston) 1920-21. LIVERPOOL professional May 1921. West Ham United June 1928. Coventry City January 1929 to cs 1930.
Club honours: Liverpool, Division One champions 1922.
Danny Shone was a chunky forward, and possessor of a mighty left-foot shot. He was a subtle player who had a somewhat uneven career at Anfield, his League appearances reading (season-by-season) 15-1-15-42-3. Between 19 December 1925 and his West Ham debut on 25 August 1928, he did not make a single League appearance and was, indeed, a forgotten man at Anfield.

SIDLOW, Cyril **1946-52**
Goalkeeper. 149 apps.
League debut: 31 August 1946.
Born: Colwyn Bay, Denbighs, 26 November 1915.
6ft 1in. 13st 10lbs.
Career: Llandudno. Colwyn Bay FC. Wolverhampton Wanderers professional

May 1937 (wartime guest for Notts County, Wrexham, Darlington, Burnley and Hartlepools United.) LIVERPOOL February 1946 (£4,000). New Brighton August 1952.
International honours: Wales. Wales Amateur. Wales wartime.
Club honours: Liverpool, Division One champions 1947. FA Cup runners-up 1950.
A feature of Cyril Sidlow's game was his ability to clear the ball so accurately, whether throwing it or kicking it out of his hands. A Welsh junior international at 16, he was unsettled by Wolves' signing of Bert Williams, who went on to play for England. Sidlow made the move to Anfield and it proved beneficial to player and club.

SLATER, Robert ('Bert') 1959-62
Goalkeeper. 99 apps.
League debut: 22 August 1959.
Born: Musselburgh, Midlothian, 5 May 1936.
5ft 8½ins. 10st 12lbs.
Career: Airth Castle Rovers (Stirlings). Tranent Juniors. Falkirk 1953. LIVERPOOL June 1959 (exchange for Tommy Younger). Dundee July 1962. Watford May 1965, coach 1968 to 1975.
International honours: Scotland Under-23.
Club honours: Liverpool, Division Two champions 1962; Falkirk, Scottish Cup winners 1957; Dundee, Scottish Cup runners-up 1964.
Bert Slater was rather on the small side for a modern-day goalkeeper, but he was still a sound performer and remarkably consistent. After leaving football he worked for a firm involved in the construction and development of golf courses.

SLOAN, Donald 1908-09
Goalkeeper. 6 apps.
League debut: 10 October 1908.
Born: Rankinston, Ayr, 31 July 1883.
6ft 0½in. 14st 5lbs.
Career: Ayrshire junior football. Belfast Distillery 1903. Everton cs 1906. LIVERPOOL cs 1908. Belfast Distillery player-manager cs 1909.
Representative honours: Irish League.
Club honours: Belfast Distillery, Irish Cup winners 1905, 1910.
In August 1908, the *Athletic News* reported that Donald Sloan had been 'frequently in Everton's League side last season and never found wanting.' That was something of an exaggeration because Sloan played only four times for the Blues. He was, however, no mean performer and was unlucky that his career coincided with Will Scott at Goodison and Sam Hardy at Anfield. Sloan represented Ayrshire against Renfrewshire when only 17.

SMITH, Arthur 1937-39
Centre-forward. 1 app.
League debut: 16 October 1937.
Born: Buckie, Banffshire, 21 January (year unknown).
Career: Buckie Thistle. LIVERPOOL February 1937. Crewe Alexandra cs 1939.
Arthur Smith's only League game was against Wolves at Molineux when the Reds lost 2-0. Because of the war he made no League appearances for Crewe.

SMITH, James **1929-32**
Centre-forward. 61 apps; 38 goals.
League debut: 21 September 1929.
Born: Old Kilpatrick, Dunbartonshire, 1902. Died: 1975.
5ft 9½ins. 11st 10lbs.
Career: Dumbarton Harp. Clydebank *c.*1925. Rangers 1926. Ayr United May 1927. LIVERPOOL September 1929 (£5,500). Tunbridge Wells Rangers July 1932. Bristol Rovers May 1933. Newport County June 1935. Notts County June 1936. Dumbarton player-manager 1937 to the War.
Club honours: Ayr United, Scottish League Division Two champions 1928.
Jim Smith holds the British seasonal goalscoring record with a remarkable 66 in Ayr's runaway championship season of 1927-8. In all, including cup-ties and friendlies, the total was 72. He retained his goal touch with Liverpool and netted 24 in 59 Third Division South games. He later emigrated to the United States, settling at Bridgepoint, 60 miles from New York, and it was there he died.

SMITH, John T. **1951-54**
Centre-forward. 57 apps; 14 goals.
League debut: 29 September 1951.
Born: Birkenhead, 21 December 1927.
5ft 8¾ins. 11st 2lbs.
Career: Bromborough Pool, Cheshire. LIVERPOOL March 1951. Torquay United May 1954 (£1,500)-1959. Bromborough Pool cs 1961.
John Smith soon received his chance in the top flight and quickly established himself with 27 League outings in 1951-2, appearing in the same number the following campaign. He occasionally played at inside-forward for Liverpool. For Torquay he scored 16 goals in 65 Football League appearances.

SMITH, Sydney Warwick **1903-04**
Centre-forward. 2 apps; 1 goal.
League debut: 1 September 1903.
Born: Liverpool, 1875.
Career: Merseyside junior football. LIVERPOOL 1903. Southport Central April 1904.
Syd Smith was a well-known amateur in the Liverpool area around the turn of the century. He played in the first two League games of 1903-04 — both of which were lost — before giving way to another local product, John Carlin. (It may be remarked that Carlin's appearances in the following three matches also saw defeats.) Smith proved to be a good signing for Southport Central, scoring plenty of goals for the Lancashire Combination side.

SMITH, Thomas **1960-78**
Midfield/defender. 467 apps; 36 goals.
League debut: 8 May 1963.
Born: Liverpool, 5 April 1945.
5ft 10½ins. 13st.
Career: Liverpool Schools. LIVERPOOL groundstaff May 1960, professional April 1962. Swansea City August 1978, player-coach August 1979 to October 1979. Liverpool coach.
International honours: England. England Under-23. England Youth. Football League.
Club honours: Liverpool, European Cup winners 1977. European Cup-winners' Cup runners-up 1966. UEFA Cup winners 1973, 1976. Division One champions 1966, 1973, 1976, 1977. FA Cup winners 1965, 1974, runners-up 1971, 1977. Football League Cup runners-up 1978.

Tommy Smith was perhaps best known for his fierce tackles and no-nonsense approach, yet this was far from the whole story. He was a versatile footballer, starting his League career at inside-left and later moving to midfield and defence. He could play on either side of the field and was a skilful performer. His career was eventually ended by a knee injury and he spent some time coaching young players at Anfield before drifting out of the game.

SMYTH, Samuel **1952-55**
Centre-forward/inside-left. 45 apps; 20 goals.
League debut: 3 January 1953.
Born: Belfast, 25 February 1925.
5ft 11ins. 11st 2lbs.
Career: Dundela FC (Linfield amateur). Wolverhampton Wanderers professional July 1947. Stoke City September 1951 (£20,000). LIVERPOOL December 1952 (£12,000). Bangor January 1955 (£2,000, then a record for an Irish League club).
International honours: Northern Ireland. Northern Ireland amateur. Irish League.
Club honours: Wolverhampton Wanderers, FA Cup winners 1949.
Sam Smyth won his amateur and inter-League honours as a Linfield amateur, then signed as a professional for Dundela but did not appear for them before joining Wolves. He made a big name for himself at Molineux, playing inside-right, and the dazzling dribble that produced a goal in the 1949 Cup Final is a particular memory.

SOUNESS, Graeme James **1978-84**
Midfield. 246 (1) apps; 38 goals.
League debut: 14 January 1978.
Born: Edinburgh, 6 May 1953.
5ft 11ins. 12st 13lbs.
Career: Edinburgh Schools. Tottenham Hotspur apprentice April 1969, professional May 1970. Middlesbrough January 1973 (£30,000). LIVERPOOL January 1978 (£352,000, then Football League record). Sampdoria, Italy, June 1984 (£650,000). Rangers player-manager 1986. Retired May 1989. Rangers director.
International honours: Scotland. Scotland Under-23. Scotland Schoolboy. Scotland Youth.
Club honours: Middlesbrough, Division Two champions 1974; Liverpool, European Cup winners, 1978, 1981, 1984. Division One champions 1979, 1980, 1982, 1983, 1984. Football League Cup winners 1981 (first leg only), 1982, 1983, 1984; Rangers, Scottish League champions 1987. Scottish Cup runners-up 1989.
Graeme Souness is a leading, often controversial figure in modern football. He possesses plenty of skill — a fine distributor of the ball and a man with a powerful shot — but his over-robust approach has caused plenty of comment. He brought the championship back to Ibrox after nine years and his manoeuvres in the transfer market, particularly in taking English players north of the border, have meant that Rangers are seldom out of the headlines.

SOUTH, Alexander William **1954-56**
Centre-half. 6 apps; 1 goal.
League debut: 5 February 1955.
Born: Brighton, 7 July 1931.
5ft 11½ins. 11st 4lbs.
Career: Whitehawk Boys Club (Brighton). Brighton & Hove Albion amateur 1946, professional March 1949. LIVERPOOL December 1954 (£5,000). Halifax Town October 1956 (£2,500). Retired cs 1965. Halifax Town pools promoter.
Alex South established himself early in Brighton's first team after respresenting England against Wales in a Boys' Clubs international. He represented the RAF while on National Service. South was a real stalwart at Halifax and his 296 League appearances for them was a club record until 1974.

SPACKMAN, Nigel J. **1987-89**
Midfield. 39 (12) apps.
League debut: 28 February 1987.
Born: Romsey, Hants, 2 December 1960.
6ft 1in. 12st 4lbs.
Career: Andover Town. AFC Bournemouth May 1980. Chelsea June 1983 (£40,000). LIVERPOOL February 1987 (£400,000). Queen's Park Rangers February 1989 (£500,000 a QPR record).
Club honours: Chelsea, Division Two champions 1984; Liverpool, Division One champions 1988. FA Cup runners-up 1988. Football League Cup runners-up 1987.
Nigel Spackman is a strong midfielder, able to snuff out potential threats from 'name' opponents and feed a simple ball out of defence to his colleagues. He made his

name in Chelsea's surge to the 1983-4 Second Division title and was a first-teamer throughout his time at Stamford Bridge.

SPEAKMAN, James **1908-13**
Outside-right. 8 apps; 1 goal.
League debut: 9 October 1909.
Born: Huyton Quarry, Liverpool, 1888. Died 1962.
5ft 8½ins. 11st.
Career: Merseyside junior football. LIVERPOOL 1908 to 1913.
James Speakman was a speedy player and Arthur Goddard's understudy for some years. The *Athletic News* for 28 August 1909 remarked, 'he has a style that greatly resembles that of Goddard.' His brother, Sam, also played for Liverpool.

SPEAKMAN, Samuel **1912-20**
Right-/left-back. 25 apps.
League debut: 20 September 1913.
Born: Huyton Quarry, Liverpool, 9 August 1884. Died: 1934.
5ft 8½ins. 11st 4lbs.
Career: Colne FC (Lancashire Combination). LIVERPOOL early 1912. South Liverpool 1920.
Sam Speakman could play equally well in either full-back position and his League appearances in 1919-20 were at left-half. He made 31 wartime appearances for the Reds. His brother, James, was the club's reserve right winger.

SPICER, Edward W. **1937-53**
Left-back/wing-half. 158 apps; 2 goals.
League debut: 31 August 1946.
Born: Liverpool, 20 September 1922.

5ft 10ins. 12st 2lbs.
Career: Liverpool Schools. LIVERPOOL amateur 1937, professional October 1939. Retired through injury 1953.
International honours: England schoolboy.
Club honours: Liverpool, FA Cup runners-up 1950.
Eddie Spicer was strong on either flank, although he preferred the left. He twice suffered a broken leg, the second of which ended his career. Spicer made his early senior appearances at wing-half before settling at left-back in 1949-50. He served in the Royal Marines during World War Two.

STANIFORTH, Frederick Walter 1913-14
Outside-right. 3 apps.
League debut: 4 October 1913.
Born: Kilnhurst, Yorkshire, 1884. Died: 23 May 1955.
5ft 6½ins. 11st.
Career: Kilnhurst Town. Rotherham Main. Mexborough Town. Bristol City cs 1906. Grimsby Town cs 1911. LIVERPOOL May 1913 to 1914.
Club honours: Bristol City, FA Cup runners-up 1909.
Fred Staniforth's best spell was Bristol City's first five seasons in Division One, during which he made 135 League appearances and scored 14 goals. Short and sturdy, this clever winger created plenty of goals for his colleagues. His moderate tally of games for Liverpool is accounted for by the arrival of Jack Sheldon. Staniforth settled in Bristol after leaving the first-class game.

STAUNTON, Stephen 1986-
Defender. 17 (4) apps.
League debut:17 September 1988.
Born: Drogheda, Co Louth, 19 January 1969.
5ft 8ins. 11st 2lbs.
Career: Dundalk. LIVERPOOL August 1986. Bradford City (loan) November 1987-January 1988.
International honours: Republic of Ireland. Republic of Ireland Under-21.
Club honour: Liverpool, FA Cup winners 1989.
Steve Staunton has claims for consideration as 1988-9s discovery of the season. He had been blooded in League football during the loan period with Bradford City, getting his chance at Anfield because of the Reds' long autumnal injury list. His strong controlled performances enabled him to seize that chance. He made only three appearances for Dundalk before joining Liverpool. Prior to that he had starred in Gaelic football, becoming that game's youngest player to win a senior championship medal.

STEEL, William Gilbert 1931-5
Right-back. 120 apps.
League debut: 19 December 1931.
Born: Blantyre, Lanarkshire, 6 February 1908.
5ft 8ins. 11st 8lbs.
Career: Bridgton Waverley. St Johnstone 1926. LIVERPOOL September 1931 (after a month's trial). Birmingham March 1935 (£5,000). Derby County February 1939 to 1940. Airdrieonians trainer April 1950, manager April 1954. Third Lanark manager January 1963-June 1964.
Willie Steel was a resourceful back who gave excellent service wherever he went. He was an ever-present for three consecutive seasons with St Johnstone and, by the time war broke out, he had played 345 matches in the Scottish and English First Divisions. He later qualified as a masseur and assisted Scotland international teams around 1951. A former chairman of Airdrieonians reckoned Steel to be that club's best manager in his time as a director.

STEVENSON, General **1898-1900**
Right-back. 21 apps.
League debut: 26 November 1898.
Born: Burnley, 1877.
5ft 7½ins. 11st 10lbs.
Career: Hapton. Padiham. LIVERPOOL 1898. Barnsley cs 1900. Wellingborough cs 1902. Millwall Athletic May 1903. Retired September 1910. Later assisted non-League Accrington Stanley for about two years until 1913.
'Small, all heart . . .sturdy tackler and powerful kicker . . .style quiet, no rushing,' so a contemporary scribe described this Liverpool player with the unusual christian name. He proved extremely popular at Millwall, where he was skipper, and had two England trials during the mid-1900s. He retired in 1910 to take the licence of a Padiham public house. His son, Arthur, played for Wigan RLFC.

STEVENSON, William **1962-67**
Left-half. 188 apps; 15 goals.
League debut: 3 November 1962.
Born: Leith, Edinburgh, 26 October 1939.
5ft 11ins. 11st 13lbs.
Career: Edinburgh Schools. Edina Hearts. Dalkeith. Rangers 1956. LIVERPOOL October 1962 (£20,000). Stoke City December 1967 (£48,000). Tranmere Rovers July 1973 to 1974.
International honours: Scotland Schoolboy. Scottish League.
Club honours: Rangers, Scottish League champions 1959. Scottish Cup winners 1960; Liverpool, European Cup-winners' Cup runners-up 1966. Division One champions 1964, 1966. FA Cup winners 1965.
Willie Stevenson had gone to Australia, following Rangers' signing of Jim Baxter, but returned to Britain to resume his career with Liverpool. He was a class player with a biting tackle and excellent ball skills. He was capped as a schoolboy in three consecutive seasons.

STEWART, James Munro **1909-14**
Inside-right. 64 apps; 27 goals.
League debut: 4 September 1909.
Born: Dumbarton.
5ft 6½ins. 10st 10lbs.
Career: Junior football. Motherwell. LIVERPOOL April 1909. Hamilton Academical during 1913-14 season to 1920. Portsmouth training staff.
Jimmy Munro was a smart little inside-right, equally at home on the other flank, who could score goals. He was 'an acknowledged inside-left of ability,' according to the *Athletic News* of 28 August 1909.

STORER, Harry **1895-1901**
Goalkeeper. 106 apps.
League debut: 1 January 1896.

Born: Butterley, Ripley, Derbyshire, 24 July 1870. Died: 25 April 1908.
5ft 8½ins. 11st.
Career: Ripley Town. Derby Midland 1888. Gainsborough Trinity 1891. Loughborough Town 1892. Woolwich Arsenal May 1894. LIVERPOOL December 1895 to 1901.
Representative honours: Football League.
Club honours: Liverpool, Division Two champions 1896.
Shortly before his transfer to Liverpool, Harry Storer was described as a player 'with plenty of resource and no lack of pluck, he is always to be relied upon in goal, being clever alike with his hands and feet.' He played cricket for Derbyshire (six matches in 1895) and came from a sporting family. His son, Harry, played for Derby County and England at soccer and Derbyshire at cricket; his brother, William, played for Derby County, and for Derbyshire and England at cricket.

STORTON, Trevor G. 1972-74
Midfield. 5 apps.
League debut: 30 September 1972.
Born: Keighley, Yorks, 26 November 1949.
6ft 1in. 12st 4lbs.
Career: Junior football. Tranmere Rovers October 1967. LIVERPOOL July 1972 (£25,000). Chester July 1974 (£18,000) to March 1984.
Trevor Storton made well over 100 Football League appearances for Tranmere before joining Liverpool. For Chester, he played in 396 League games, only 12 short of their club record. His elder brother, Stan, played for Tranmere, Darlington and Bradford City and managed giant-killers Telford United.

STOTT, James 1893-94
Inside-left. 16 apps; 14 goals.
League debut: 2 September 1893.
Born: Darlington, 1870. Died: 8 October 1908.
5ft 10¼ins. 12st.
Career: South Bank. Middlesbrough. LIVERPOOL August 1893. Grimsby Town June 1894. Newcastle United June 1895 (£15). Middlesbrough cs 1899 to 1900.
Club honours: Liverpool, Division Two champions 1894.
Jimmy Stott's tremendous goalscoring record in his only Liverpool season was a major factor in the Reds winning promotion at the very first attempt. He also skippered Newcastle into Division One, although by then he had switched to left-half. He was fast, clever and a keen tackler. He was said to be something of a snappy dresser, wearing a frock coat and top-hat on Sundays. Latterly he was a Newcastle licensee.

STRONG, Geoffrey H. 1964-70
Utility player. 150 (5) apps; 29 goals.
League debut: 7 November 1964.
Born: Kirkheaton, Northumberland, 19 September 1937.
5ft 11ins. 11st 6lbs.
Career: Northumberland Schools. Stanley United (Northern League). Arsenal amateur November 1957, professional April 1958. LIVERPOOL November 1964 (£40,000). Coventry City August 1970 (around £30,000). Retired from first-class football 1973.
Club honours: Liverpool, Division One champions 1966. FA Cup winners 1965.
Geoff Strong appeared mostly at inside-left and left-back whilst on Liverpool's books but was versatile enough to play in most outfield positions. He was a real asset to Liverpool's first-team squad.

STUBBINS, Albert **1946-53**
Centre-forward. 161 apps; 75 goals.
League debut: 14 September 1946.
Born: Wallsend, 17 July 1919.
5ft 11ins. 11st 10lbs.
Career: Whitley & Monkseaton FC (Sunderland amateur). Newcastle United April 1937 (wartime guest for Sunderland). LIVERPOOL September 1946 (£12,500). Ashington September 1953. Retired 1954. Liverpool scout. USA national coach 1960.
Representative honours: Football League.
Club honours: Liverpool, Division One champions 1947. FA Cup runners-up 1950.
Albert Stubbins had a remarkable scoring record in wartime football with 237 goals in 199 matches for Newcastle. He was not simply a scoring 'machine', though, and had outstanding ball skills and the ability to control his forward-line. He spent his early years in the United States, returning to England when he was 12. He worked as a shipyard draughtsman before becoming a full-time footballer and after retiring he became a journalist in the North-East.

TAYLOR, Harold **1932-36**
Left-half/forward. 69 apps; 6 goals.
League debut: 5 November 1932.
Born: Hanley, Stoke-on-Trent, 1912.
5ft 8½ins. 11st 3lbs.
Career: Potteries schoolboy football. Stoke St Peter's. Stoke City amateur February 1929, professional June 1929. LIVERPOOL July 1932 to 1936.
Harold Taylor played in all five forward positions during his four years at Anfield, although he was mostly on the left flank. He won early acclaim as a Hanley schoolboy footballer and Stoke signed him when he was 17, giving him his League debut in 1929-30.

TAYLOR, Philip Henry **1936-54**
Right-half/inside-right. 314 apps; 34 goals.
League debut: 28 March 1936.
Born: Bristol, 18 September 1917.
5ft 9¾ins. 11st 2lbs.
Career: Bristol Schools. Bristol Rovers groundstaff cs 1932, professional 1935. LIVERPOOL March 1936 (about £5,000) (wartime guest for Bristol Rovers, Brighton & Hove Albion, Newcastle United and Leeds United). Retired July 1954. Liverpool coaching staff, acting manager May 1956, manager April 1957-November 1959.
International honours: England. England Schoolboy. England 'B'. Football League.
Club honours: Liverpool, Division One champions 1947. FA Cup runners-up 1950.
Phil Taylor, who skippered England Schoolboys, developed into a fine inside-forward at senior level before switching to become one of the classiest attacking half-backs of his day. He was a useful cricketer, making one first-class appearance for

Gloucestershire in 1938, and after leaving football he worked as a sales representative.

TENNANT, John Willie **1933-36**
Left-back. 39 apps.
League debut: 9 September 1933.
Born: Newcastle-upon-Tyne, 3 August 1907. Died: 1978.
5ft 8½ins. 11st 10lbs.
Career: Washington Colliery (Newcastle United Reserves). Stoke City in 1927-8. Torquay United cs 1932. LIVERPOOL May 1933. Bolton Wanderers January 1936. Stoke City November 1938 (wartime guest for Wrexham, Liverpool and Southport during World War Two). Did not resume in the first-class game when peace returned.

All Jack Tennant's League and Cup outings for Liverpool were at left-back, save one at right-back, but he proved a versatile player overall. He kept goal as a schoolboy, led Washington Colliery's attack (where he worked), played in almost every outfield position for Stoke Reserves and at full-back and inside-left for Torquay.

THOMPSON, Charles **1929-31**
Wing-half. 5 apps.
League debut: 21 April 1930.
Born: South Africa *c.*1909.
5ft 8½ins. 11st 5lbs.
Career: Wallsend (North-Eastern League). LIVERPOOL May 1929. Blackpool April 1931 to 1932.
Charlie Thompson created an impression in North-Eastern League football and at Liverpool proved a useful reserve for either wing-half position. He could also play at centre-half, a position in which he made his League debut. Thompson did not appear in Blackpool's senior side.

THOMPSON, Maxwell S. **1974-78**
Defender. 1 app.
League debut: 8 May 1974.
Born: Liverpool, 31 December 1956.
6ft 1in. 12st 10lbs.
Career: Junior football. LIVERPOOL apprentice, professional January 1974. Blackpool, loan, December 1977, signing permanently March 1978 (£80,000). Swansea City August 1981 (£20,000). AFC Bournemouth August 1983 (Port Vale, loan, November-December 1983) to February 1984.
Club honours: Swansea City, Welsh Cup winners 1982 (played in first leg).
Max Thompson was crowded out by the great talent at Anfield, but still attracted a substantial fee from Blackpool. He played 92 League games (plus seven substitutions) and scored six goals for the Seasiders; and made 25 appearances (plus one sub) and scored two goals for Swansea.

THOMPSON, Peter **1963-74**

Outside-left. 318 (4) apps; 41 goals.
League debut: 24 August 1963.
Born: Carlisle, 27 November 1942.
5ft 8ins. 11st 6lbs.
Career: Carlisle Schools. Preston North End groundstaff August 1958, professional November 1959. LIVERPOOL August 1963 (£37,000). Bolton Wanderers January 1974 (after six weeks on loan, £18,000). Retired March 1978.
International honours: England. England Under-23. England Schoolboy. Football League.
Club honours: Liverpool, European Cup-winners' Cup runners-up 1966. Division One champions 1964, 1966. FA Cup winners 1965, runners-up 1971 (sub).
Peter Thompson was a gifted individualist whose fast, tricky play delighted Anfield crowds for a decade. He had fine ball control and could centre accurately. Some newspapers liked to compare him to Tom Finney. His business interests included Blackpool caravan sites and the directorship of a garage business.

THOMPSON, Philip Bernard **1971-85**

Central defender. 337 (3) apps; 7 goals.
League debut: 3 April 1972 (sub).
Born: Kensington, Liverpool, 21 January 1954.
6ft. 11st 8lbs.
Career: Kirkby Schools (Liverpool). LIVERPOOL apprentice, professional February 1971. Sheffield United on loan December 1984, signing March 1985. Liverpool coaching staff July 1986.
International honours: England. England Under-23. England 'B'. England Youth.
Club honours: Liverpool, European Cup winners 1978, 1981. UEFA Cup winners 1976. Division One champions 1976, 1977, 1979, 1980, 1982. FA Cup winners 1974. Football League Cup winners 1981, 1982, runners-up 1978.
Phil Thompson looked a gangling figure, yet he possessed a hard tackle and was an authoritative player. Thompson, who captained the Reds for a time, used to stand on the Kop and support the club as a

youngster. He did not win a regular place until 1973-4, playing on the right side of defence before settling down at centre-back. He won 42 full England caps and it was the rise of Hansen and Lawrenson that finally saw the end of his Anfield career.

THOMSON, Robert **1962-65**
Right-back. 6 apps.
League debut: 20 April 1963.
Born: Menstrie, Clackmannanshire, 21 November 1939.
5ft 10ins. 11st 4½lbs.
Career: Sauchie FC. Partick Thistle 1957. LIVERPOOL December 1962 (£7,000). Luton Town August 1965 (£3,000) to 1967.
Bobby Thomson had shown promise with Partick Thistle Reserves before being signed by Liverpool a few weeks before Christmas 1962. He made 74 Fourth Division appearances for Luton before leaving the Football League scene.

TOMLEY, Frederick W. **1953-55**
Centre-half. 2 apps.
League debut: 12 March 1955.
Born: Liverpool, 11 July 1931.
6ft 2¼ins. 13st 13lbs.
Career: Litherland FC (Liverpool). LIVERPOOL September 1953. Chester July 1955-cs 1956.
Fred Tomley was a towering local product, one of five players to pull on the Reds' number-five shirt in season 1954-5. For Chester, he played only one Third Division North game and was given a free transfer at the end of the 1955-6 season.

TOSHACK, John Benjamin, OBE **1970-78**
Forward. 169 (3) apps; 74 goals.
League debut: 14 November 1970.
Born: Cardiff, 22 March 1949.
6ft. 11st 7lbs.
Career: Cardiff Schools. Cardiff City apprentice, professional March 1966. LIVERPOOL November 1970 (£110,000). Swansea City player-manager February 1978-October 1983 and December 1983-March 1984. Sporting Lisbon manager later in 1984 to May 1985. Real Sociedad (San Sebastian) manager later in 1985. Real Madrid manager 1989.

International honours: Wales. Wales Under-23. Wales Schoolboy.
Club honours: Cardiff City, Welsh Cup winners 1968, 1969, 1970; Liverpool, UEFA Cup winners 1973, 1976. Division One champions 1973, 1976, 1977. FA Cup winners 1974, runners-up 1971.
Even as a schoolboy, John Toshack was obviously destined for the big time and eventually became Cardiff's youngest-ever debutant. For Liverpool he developed a renowned partnership with Kevin Keegan, his perfectly placed flicked headers to the little man's feet bringing a rich goal harvest. Indeed, Tosh's heading ability was his greatest asset and he ranks amongst the greatest of modern players in the air. He has been highly successful as a manager, taking the Swans from the Fourth to the First Division in successive seasons and steering Real Sociedad to their first Spanish Cup win in 1987.

TOSSWILL, John Speare **1912-13**

Inside-right. 11 apps; 1 goal.
League debut: 4 September 1912.
Born: Eastbourne, 1890. Died: 28 September 1915.
5ft 11ins. 12st.
Career: Junior football. Queen's Park Rangers 1911-12. LIVERPOOL June 1912. Southend United cs 1913. Coventry City during season 1913-14.

'Comes with a good reputation,' wrote a Liverpool scribe on John Tosswill's signing. He was, however, quite inexperienced, with only three Southern League appearances to his name. In 1915 it was reported that he was serving as a Royal Engineers' despatch rider. Tosswill died at Brighton, aged only 24, after an operation.

TWENTYMAN, Geoffrey **1953-9**

Left-half. 170 apps; 18 goals.
League debut: 19 December 1953.
Born: Carlisle, 19 January 1930.
5ft 10¾ins. 12st 1lb.
Career: Swifts Rovers (Carlisle). Carlisle United amateur *c.*1945, professional February 1947. LIVERPOOL December 1953 (£10,000). Ballymena United player-manager March 1959. Carlisle United June 1963. Morecambe player-manager May 1964. Penrith FC manager-coach cs 1966. Liverpool chief scout August 1967.
Representative honours: Irish League.

Geoff Twentyman's reputation was made as a teenage centre-half and he was already a mature player when he arrived at Anfield, one month before his 24th birthday. He appeared mostly at left-half, Laurie Hughes still holding down the centre-half spot, but reverted to centre-half for Ballymena, the position from which he skippered the Irish League representative side.

UNDERWOOD, E(dmund) David **1953-56**

Goalkeeper. 45 apps.
League debut: 19 December 1953.
Born: St Pancras, London, 15 March 1928.
Died: January 1989.

6ft 1½ins. 13st 5lbs.
Career: Edgware Town. Queen's Park Rangers amateur September 1949, professional December 1949. Watford February 1952. LIVERPOOL December 1953 (£7,000). Watford July 1956 (£1,250). Dartford August 1957. Watford April 1960. Fulham July 1963. Dunstable Town cs 1965. Hastings United cs 1966.
Dave Underwood made his Liverpool debut on the same day as Geoff Twentyman, having signed the day before Twentyman. He had three spells with Watford, the last on a part-time basis as he was carrying on a haulage contractor's business.

UREN, Harold John **1907-12**
Outside-left. 43 apps; 2 goals.
League debut: 16 November 1907.
Born: Barton Regis, Bristol, 23 August 1885. Died: 7 April 1955.
5ft 9¾ins. 12st.
Career: Northern Nomads. Hoylake FC. LIVERPOOL amateur 1907, professional 1909. Everton February 1912 (in exchange for Billy Lacey and Tom Gracie). Wrexham 1913.
Club honours: Wrexham, Welsh Cup winners 1914.
Harold Uren was 'very tricky and a difficult man to dispossess,' according to a 1912 commentator. For a winger he was a hefty player but Everton must have valued him highly, exchanging him for Billy Lacey, already winner of ten Irish caps, and Tom Gracie, a future Scottish League 'cap'.

VAN DEN BERG, Harman H.C. **1937-40**
Outside-left. 22 apps; 4 goals.
League debut: 16 February 1938.
Born: Cape Town, South Africa.
5ft 10ins. 11st 6lbs.
Career: Peninsular FC (Cape Town). LIVERPOOL October 1937 to 1940. Retired during the war.
Chronologically the last of the Reds' many inter-war Springboks, Harman Van den Berg had a rangy build, was incisive and could score goals. In the last peacetime season he competed with Kinghorn for the job of succeeding Alf Hanson.

VENISON, Barry **1986-**
Left-back. 63 (3) apps.
League debut: 23 August 1986.
Born: Consett, County Durham, 16 August 1964.
5ft 10ins. 11st 9lbs.
Career: Stanley Schools. Sunderland apprentice, professional January 1982. LIVERPOOL July 1986 (£250,000).
International honours: England Youth. England Under-21.
Club honours: Sunderland, Football League Cup runners-up 1985; Liverpool, Division One champions 1988. FA Cup winners 1989. Football League Cup runners-up 1987.
Equally effective on the right, Barry Venison skippered Sunderland to a Wembley Cup final when he was only 20. He had over 170 League appearances for the Wearsiders under his belt on joining Liverpool 16 months later. A first-class defender, he suffered injury in 1987-8.

WADDLE, Alan R. **1973-77**
Centre-forward. 11 (5) apps; 1 goal.
League debut: 1 December 1973.
Born: Wallsend, 9 June 1954.
6ft 3ins. 12st 12lbs.
Career: Wallsend Boys Club. Halifax Town October 1971. LIVERPOOL June 1973 (£40,000, a Halifax record). Leicester City September 1977 (£45,000). Swansea City May 1978 (£20,000). Newport County December 1980 (£80,000, a Newport record). Mansfield Town August 1982. Hartlepool August 1983. Peterborough United October 1983 (£6,000). Swansea City early 1985-May 1986. Barry Town (part-time).
In recent times one of the game's travellers, Alan Waddle was a striker of impressive proportions, who was outstanding when the ball was in the air. Including substitutions, he made 289 League appearances and scored 76 goals. Cousin of Chris, the Spurs and England forward.

WADSWORTH, Harold **1918-24**
Outside-right/outside-left. 54 apps; 3 goals.
League debut: 4 October 1919.
Born: Bootle, 1 October 1898. Died: 2 November 1975.
5ft 6ins. 10st 2lbs.
Career: Bootle St Matthew's (Bootle League). Tranmere Rovers. LIVERPOOL 1918. Leicester City June 1924.

Nottingham Forest April 1927. Millwall June 1928 to 1932.
Club honours: Leicester City, Division Two champions 1925.
Harold Wadsworth was once summed up an 'extremely adroit tactician, as well as more than commonly fast, and with a trick of swerving when about to be tackled, which has baffled many an opponent'. Usually found at outside-left, he totalled 253 League games and 28 goals. Younger brother of Walter.

WADSWORTH, Walter **1912-26**
Centre-half. 217 apps; 7 goals.
League debut: 20 March 1915.
Born: Bootle, October 1890. Died: October 1951.

5ft 11ins. 11st 2lbs.
Career: Lingdale (West Cheshire League). Ormskirk. LIVERPOOL cs 1912. Bristol City May 1926. Flint Town player-manager June 1928. New Brighton January 1929. Oswestry Town September 1930.
Representative honours: Football League.
Club honours: Liverpool, Division One champions 1922, 1923; Bristol, City Division Three South champions 1927.
Known as 'Big Waddy', to identify him from brother, Harold, Walter Wadsworth joined Liverpool as a full-back but was well established as a pivot in wartime football, emerging as a vital part of the fine Liverpool side of the early 1920s.

WALKER, John **1898-1902**
Inside-right. 121 apps; 30 goals.
League debut: 3 September 1898.
Born: Coatbridge, 31 May 1874.
Career: Armadale. Heart of Midlothian 1893. LIVERPOOL April 1898 (£350 including Tom Robertson). Rangers cs 1902. Morton 1904-05.
International honours: Scotland. Scottish League.
Club honours: Hearts, Scottish League champions 1895, 1897. Scottish Cup winners 1896; Liverpool, Division One champions 1901; Rangers, Scottish Cup winners 1903, runners-up 1904.
John Walker fitted in admirably at Liverpool. Used chiefly at inside-right, he could play anywhere in the attack. He liked the occasional solo run and often surprised the opposition with his snap shooting. He played only a few games for Morton before a leg injury effectively ended his career.

WALL, T(homas) Peter **1966-70**
Left-back. 31 apps.
League debut: 16 March 1968.
Born: Westbury, Wilts, 13 September 1944.
5ft 9ins. 11st 8lbs.
Career: Junior football. Shrewsbury Town apprentice, professional September 1962. Wrexham November 1965 (£3,000). LIVERPOOL October 1966 (£26,000 including Stuart Mason). Crystal Palace May 1970 (£35,000). (Orient on loan December 1972-March 1973) to March 1978.
Together with Stuart Mason, Peter Wall was a member of an immensely promising young full-back pairing at Wrexham; Liverpool signed them both for a significant fee. Mason later returned to Wrexham without having played for the Reds' first team, but Wall had some useful runs in the League before joining Palace, for whom he made 177 League appearances (ten as subsitute) in eight years there.

WALLACE, Gordon H. **1961-67**
Inside-left. 19 (1) apps; 3 goals.
League debut: 27 October 1962.
Born: Lanark, 13 June 1944.
5ft 6½ins. 10st 13lbs.
Career: Lanarkshire schoolboy football. LIVERPOOL apprentice, professional July 1961. Crewe Alexandra October 1967 (£5,000) to 1972.
Gordon Wallace, an inside-left who could also play at inside-right and outside-left, made 94 League appearances (three as substitute) and scored 20 goals for Crewe. He attended Central School, Motherwell, which also produced Reds' star, Ian St John.

WALSH, James Arthur **1922-28**
Centre-/inside-forward. 68 apps; 24 goals.
League debut: 29 August 1923.
Born: Stockport, 15 May 1901. Died: 1971.
5ft 9ins. 11st 6lbs.
Career: Stockport junior football. Stockport County 1920 originally as an amateur. LIVERPOOL June 1922. Hull City June 1928 to 1931. Crewe Alexandra. Colwyn Bay August 1933.
Over half of Jim Walsh's League appearances for Liverpool were in season 1923-4, when he played in 37 games, all at centre-forward. However, perhaps his best position was inside-forward. In 1929-30, Hull successfully converted him to right-half. At that time he was summed up as 'keen in tackling and could play his forwards. A ready wit and a ready kick'. He toured Australia with the FA in 1925, playing three times against the Australian national team.

WALSH, Paul Anthony **1984-88**
Forward. 63 (14) apps; 25 goals.
League debut: 25 August 1984.
Born: Plumstead, London, 1 October 1962.
5ft 7ins. 10st 8lbs.
Career: Junior football. Charlton Athletic apprentice, professional October 1979. Luton Town July 1982 (£250,000 and another player). LIVERPOOL May 1984 (£700,000). Tottenham Hotspur February 1988 (£500,000).

International honours: England. England Under-21. England Youth.
Club honours: Liverpool, European Cup runners-up 1985. Division One champions 1986. Football League Cup runners-up 1987.
Paul Walsh is a gifted forward who was exceptionally unlucky with illness and injury while at Anfield. He suffered a cartilage injury, a hernia, damaged ankle ligaments and a broken wrist and his time on the sidelines totalled one year. He is a clever player with excellent dribbling skills and a telling burst of speed. He was voted 'Young Player of the Year' for 1984.

WARK, John **1984-88**
Midfield. 64 (6) apps; 28 goals.
League debut: 31 March 1984.
Born: Glasgow, 4 August 1957.
5ft 10ins. 11st 7lbs.
Career: Drumchapel Amateurs FC Youth Club. Ipswich Town amateur 1973, professional August 1974. LIVERPOOL March 1984 (£450,000). Ipswich Town January 1988 (£100,000).
International honours: Scotland. Scotland Under-21. Scotland Youth.
Club honours: Ipswich Town, UEFA Cup winners 1981. FA Cup winners 1978; Liverpool, European Cup runners-up 1985.
A leading member of the fine Ipswich team assembled by Bobby Robson in the 1970s, John Wark was signed by Liverpool to

compensate for Souness's impending transfer to Italy. He did well until sustaining a broken leg in March 1986. This practically ended his Anfield career. He is noted for strong runs from midfield that have brought him many goals. Wark was the PFA's 'Player of the Year' for 1981.

WATKINSON, William W. 1946-51
Outside-right. 24 apps; 2 goals.
League debut: 26 April 1947.
Born: Prescot, Lancashire, 16 March 1922.
5ft 9½ins. 11st 13lbs.
Career: Prescot Cables. LIVERPOOL February 1946. Accrington Stanley January 1951. Halifax Town September 1954. Prescot Cables August 1956.
Billy Watkinson was 'a strong type of

player, possessing a good shot,' according to the club's 1949 handbook. He was also an adaptable performer — he had been signed as a centre-forward, a position in which his useful physique was perhaps of more value. He led the attack during his Third Division North days at Accrington and Halifax. His career aggregate for those two clubs was 165 League games and 73 goals.

WATSON, Alexander F. 1984-
Defender. 3 (1) apps.
League debut: 5 March 1988.
Born: Liverpool, 6 April 1968.
6ft. 10st 12lbs.
Career: Junior football. LIVERPOOL apprentice, professional during 1984-5 season.
International honours: England Youth 1985, 1986.
Alex Watson was a promising young local product. In his first couple of League games he appeared in both full-back positions. Both games were in London, the first a win over Queen's Park Rangers and the other a draw at Chelsea. Brother of Dave Watson (Everton and England).

WELFARE, Henry 1912-14
Outside-right/outside-left. 4 apps; 1 goal.
League debut: 15 February 1913.
Born: Liverpool, 1888. Died: 1961.
5ft 11ins. 12st.
Career: St Helens Recreation. Southport Central cs 1911. Northern Nomads. LIVERPOOL amateur cs 1912-cs 1914. Corinthians (Rio de Janeiro). Fluminense (Rio de Janeiro).
Harry Welfare was a well-known amateur in the Merseyside area during the period prior to World War One. In the 1914 close season he emigrated to Brazil and became one of the best-known players with the Fluminense club when they won the Brazilian title three years running (1917-18-19). He spent most of his life in South America and died in Rio aged 72. He was nicknamed 'Celso' (apparently the local population could not get their tongues round the surname Welfare).

WEST, Alfred **1903-09 & 1910-11**
Right-back. 128 apps; 5 goals.
League debut: 7 November 1903.
Born: Nottingham, 15 December 1881.
5ft 7ins. 11st 9lbs.
Career: Ilkeston FC. Barnsley cs 1902. LIVERPOOL November 1903. Reading June 1909. LIVERPOOL cs 1910. Notts County July 1911-1915.
Club honours: Liverpool, Division One champions 1906; Notts County, Division Two champions 1914.
Alf West was a solid performer, equally capable on the left flank and it was as Notts County's left-back that he won his Second Division championship medal. He ended his League career on a high note, missing only two matches in the three seasons to 1914. In 1913, a local annual remarked that Alf was 'rarely showy, but never weak, has been simply invaluable to Notts. A clean, cool back and a favourite everywhere'.

WHEELER, John E. **1956-63**
Right-half. 164 apps; 21 goals.
League debut: 15 September 1956.
Born: Crosby, Liverpool, 26 July 1928.
5ft 9ins. 12st 2lbs.
Career: Carlton FC (Liverpool Combination). Tranmere Rovers amateur 1944, professional April 1946. Bolton Wanderers February 1951 (fee plus another player). LIVERPOOL September 1956 (about £9,000). New Brighton's player-manager May 1963 but did not take up

the post, later that close season becoming Bury's assistant trainer, head trainer cs 1967, trainer-assistant manager September 1969-September 1970.
International honours: England. England 'B'. Football League.
Club honours: Bolton Wanderers, FA Cup runners-up 1953.
John Wheeler also played inside-right with some flair. He had lots of stamina, a biting tackle and liked to attack. In an aggregate 454 Football League games he scored 48 goals. Wheeler captained the Reds for a spell.

WHELAN, Ronald A. 1979-
Midfield. 254 (10) apps; 42 goals.
League debut: 3 April 1981.
Born: Dublin, 25 September 1961.
5ft 9ins. 10st 13lbs.
Career: Dublin schools football. Home Farm. LIVERPOOL October 1979.
International honours: Republic of Ireland. Republic of Ireland Under-21. Republic of Ireland Youth. Republic of Ireland Schoolboy.
Club honours: Liverpool, European Cup winners 1984, runners-up 1985. Division One champions 1982, 1983, 1984, 1986, 1988. FA Cup winners 1986, 1989. Football League Cup winners 1982, 1983, 1984, runners-up 1987.
In former days, Ronnie Whelan would have been an attacking left-half. He is an eye-catching performer — fast, intelligent, an excellent distributor and scorer of spectacular goals. Ronnie is the son of the former Republic of Ireland international, Ron Whelan senior, who played for St Patrick's Athletic and Drogheda.

WHITE, Dick 1955-62
Centre-half. 203 apps.
League debut: 10 March 1956.
Born: Scunthorpe, 18 August 1931.
6ft. 11st 10lbs.
Career: Scunthorpe Sea Cadets. Brumby

Amateurs. Scunthorpe United 1949. LIVERPOOL November 1955. Doncaster Rovers May 1962 (about £4,000). Kettering Town player-manager April 1964.
Club honours: Liverpool, Division Two champions 1962.
Dick White went to Scunthorpe before that club entered the Football League and he was one of their early successes in the Third Division North. He continued that success with the Reds as a highly competent centre-half — cool, reliable and constructive. He moved to right-back when Ron Yeats arrived and occupied that position in the 1962 promotion side.

WHITE, W. 1901-02
Inside-right. 6 apps; 1 goal.
League debut: 14 September 1901.
Career: Queen's Park Rangers. LIVERPOOL cs 1901-1902.
White had been with QPR from their early days as a professional club and acquired Southern League experience with them. He could also play in the other forward positions and enjoyed a sensational debut for Liverpool, scoring in the second minute of a Merseyside derby at Goodison. The game ended 2-2. White's last senior appearance was a League match at Gigg Lane on 1 February 1902.

WHITEHEAD, J. 1894-6
Goalkeeper. 3 apps.
League debut: 27 April 1895.
Career: LIVERPOOL during 1894-5 to 1896.
Whitehead's first senior outing was in the 'Test match' of April 1895, which the Reds lost 1-0 to Bury, thus making a quick return to Division Two. He played in two League games the following season, a 5-1 win over Newcastle at Anfield and a 5-2 defeat at Newton Heath.

WHITEHURST, Albert John 1928-29
Centre-forward. 8 apps; 2 goals.
League debut: 25 August 1928.
Born: Fenton, Stoke-on-Trent, 22 June 1898. Died: 1976.
5ft 9½ins. 12st.
Career: Potteries junior football. Stoke 1920 to 1921. Rochdale cs 1923. LIVERPOOL May 1928. Bradford City February 1929. Tranmere Rovers June 1931-4.
Club honours: Bradford City, Division Three North champions 1929.
Bert Whitehurst joined the Reds following five excellent seasons with Rochdale, in which he scored 116 goals in 168 Northern Section appearances. This impressive total included 44 goals in 42 matches during 1926-7, when he headed the Division's scoring list. Whitehurst returned to the Third Division after only nine months at Anfield, in time to help assist Bradford City's successful promotion thrust by netting 24 goals in only 15 League outings. He played centre-half at Tranmere in the final part of his career.

WHITHAM, Jack 1970-74
Forward. 15 apps; 7 goals.
League debut: 12 September 1970.
Born: Burnley, 8 December 1946.
5ft 11½ins. 12st.
Career: Holy Trinity FC (Burnley Amateur League). Sheffield Wednesday November 1964, after a week's trial. LIVERPOOL April 1970 (£57,000). Cardiff City March 1974, after two months' loan. Reading July 1975 to 1976.
International honours: England Under-23.
Club honours: Cardiff City, Welsh Cup winners 1974.
Jack Whitham was a popular figure at Hillsborough because of goal-getting exploits — in all he scored 31 in 71 League and Cup games (including nine as substitute). The moderate appearances total for a five-and-a-half-year spell with the Owls is explained by the fact that he spent several periods on the injured list, his courageous style bringing its toll. With Liverpool, competition was fierce, his senior outings confined to his first two years at Anfield. After leaving football he returned to Sheffield and became a licensee.

WHITWORTH, George C. **1950-53**
Right-half. 9 apps.
League debut: 1 March 1952.
Born: Eckington, Derbyshire, 22 September 1927.
5ft 10ins. 11st 7lbs.
Career: Stanton Ironworks. LIVERPOOL February 1950-53.
Although listed as a full-back, all George Whitworth's League appearances were in the number-four shirt; and all were at the end of the 1951-2 season when he played in nine of the last 11 games, filling in for Phil Taylor.

WILKIE, Thomas **1895-99**
Left-back. 59 apps; 1 goal.
League debut: 7 September 1895.
Born: Edinburgh, 1876. Died: 8 January 1932.
Career: Junior football. Heart of Midlothian cs 1893. LIVERPOOL cs 1895. Portsmouth 1899-1904.
Club honours: Liverpool, Division Two champions 1896; Portsmouth, Southern League champions 1902.
One of Hearts' first professionals, Tom Wilkie was signed as a reserve. He showed excellent form for Liverpool and was a sound successor to Duncan McLean. Another good spell for Pompey followed, where his colleagues in the 1902 championship side included Tom Cleghorn and R.G. Marshall, both former Liverpudlians. Wilkie died in Perth, Australia.

WILKINSON, G(eorge) Barry **1953-60**
Wing-half. 78 apps.
League debut: 5 December 1953.
Born: Bishop Auckland, 16 June 1935.
5ft 10ins. 12st 10lbs.
Career: West Auckland. Bishop Auckland. LIVERPOOL amateur 1953, professional June 1954. Bangor City August 1960. Tranmere Rovers September 1963 (after a month's trial). Holyhead Town October 1964.
International honours: England Youth.
Club honours: Bishop Auckland, FA Amateur Cup runners-up 1954; Bangor City, Welsh Cup winners 1962, runners-up 1961.
Barry Wilkinson played in distinguished amateur company as a teenager and was only 18½ years old at the time of his League debut. He went on to make 16 First Division appearances that relegation season, in addition to gaining an FA Amateur Cup runners-up medal with Bishop Auckland. He could play on either flank and was always looking to be constructive.

WILLIAMS, R(obert) Brian **1945-53**
Utility player. 31 apps; 5 goals.
League debut: 12 March 1949.
Born: Liverpool, 4 October 1927.
5ft 6½ins. 12st.
Career: South Liverpool. LIVERPOOL amateur, professional August 1945. South Liverpool player-coach July 1953. Crewe Alexandra July 1954. Rhyl August 1958.
Brian Williams was equally at home at full-back, wing-half or inside-forward, although most of his Football League appearances for the Reds were at inside-left. He was well-known for his long throw-ins. Outside football he excelled at swimming and as a sprinter. He made 144 League appearances for Crewe, scoring five goals.

WILSON, Charles **1898-1905**
Wing-half. 84 apps; 3 goals.
League debut: 19 March 1898.
Born: Stockport.
5ft 10ins. 13st 7lbs.
Career: Junior football. LIVERPOOL 1897-8 to 1905. Remained with the club serving in scouting and coaching capacities. His last appointment was as head trainer from 1929 to his retirement in 1939.
Club honours: Liverpool, Division One champions 1901.
One of the Liverpool club's greatest servants, Charlie Wilson's Anfield connection lasted some 40 years. As a player he was used mostly at right-half but could also turn out at full-back, inside-forward and in the other half-back positions. A broken leg sustained in 1903 shortened his playing career.

WILSON, David C. **1967-68**
Outside-right. 1 app (sub).
League debut: 13 May 1967 (sub).
Born: Nelson, Lancashire, 24 December 1942.
5ft 8ins. 11st.
Career: Burnley Schools. Preston North End groundstaff, professional April 1960. LIVERPOOL February 1967 (£20,000). Preston North End May 1968 (£4,000) (Bradford City, loan, March 1972; Southport, loan, October 1973). Telford United April 1974.
International honours: England Under-23. England Schoolboy.
Club honours: Preston North End, Division Three champions 1971. FA Cup runners-up 1964.
Ian Callaghan's unyielding hold on the first-team outside-right position meant that David Wilson's Anfield career was unproductive. However, his spells at Preston took in a Cup Final, a championship medal and 281 Football League outings (including 14 as substitute). In the lower divisions he proved a fast winger and an excellent opportunist.

WILSON, D. **1899-1900**
Outside-right. 2 apps.
League debut: 2 December 1899.
Career: East Bontas. LIVERPOOL cs 1899 to 1900.
Wilson went to Anfield with another East Bontas player, full-back R. McNaven, who did not make any first-team appearances for Liverpool. Wilson twice deputized for Jack Cox, on successive Saturdays against Burnley and Preston North End.

WOAN, Donald **1950-51**
Outside-right. 2 apps.
League debut: 13 January 1951.
Born: Liverpool, 7 November 1927.
5ft 6¼ins. 11st 7lbs.
Career: Bootle FC. LIVERPOOL October 1950 (around £1,000). Leyton Orient November 1951 (in part exchange for Brian Jackson). Bradford City October 1952. Tranmere Rovers February 1954. Yeovil Town cs 1955.
Donald Woan was reported to be very popular at Orient, both with colleagues and supporters and fitted in there 'like a glove'. Woan, who could also play outside-left, was an older brother of, Alan, who was a well-known forward in the colours of Northampton Town, amongst other League clubs, during the 1950s.

WORGAN, A. **1893-95**
Centre-/inside-forward. 2 apps; 2 goals.
League debut: 3 March 1894.
Career: LIVERPOOL during 1893-4 to 1895.
Worgan made an impressive start, scoring two goals on his senior debut, a 3-1 home win over Burton Swifts. He had only one more outing, in a 2-2 home draw against Sheffield United on 6 October 1894. Those were the days of Malcolm McVean *et al*, and reserves found it hard to break into the big time as regular players.

WRIGHT, David **1930-34**
Centre-/inside-forward. 93 apps; 35 goals.
League debut: 12 April 1930.
Born: Kirkcaldy, 5 October 1905.
5ft 8ins. 11st 12lbs.
Career: Junior football. East Fife. Cowdenbeath 1926. Sunderland April 1927 (£8,000 including another player). LIVERPOOL March 1930. Hull City July 1934 (£1,000). Bradford May 1935 to 1936.
Prematurely balding David Wright looked much older than his years. A concise note on the player written in 1933, reads 'plays well anywhere. Never does anything haphazardly. Works out positions, and can hold a ball while he is doing that. Smart dribbler and a hard worker'. Wright once had a baker's business in his native Kirkcaldy.

WRIGHT, E(rnest) Victor **1934-37**
Centre-/inside-forward. 81 apps; 31 goals.
League debut: 17 March 1934.
Born: Walsall, 24 January 1909. Died 1964.
5ft 11½ins. 12st 9lbs.
Career: Bloxwich Strollers. Bristol City February 1929. Rotherham United June 1929. Sheffield Wednesday October 1930. Rotherham United February 1933. LIVERPOOL March 1934. Plymouth Argyle June 1937. Chelmsford City June 1938 (wartime guest player for Millwall, Crystal Palace and Walsall).
Vic Wright was a lively attacker who established a fine reputation in his two spells at Rotherham. Frank Johnston, a contemporary critic, wrote of him in 1935, 'He is a powerful shot and never wastes time fiddling for an opening, but seizes every advantage.' Wright was a nephew of the famous Aston Villa and England winger of the 1890s, Billy Athersmith.

YEATS, Ronald **1961-71**
Centre-half. 357 (1) apps; 13 goals.
League debut: 19 August 1961.
Born: Aberdeen, 15 November 1937.
6ft 2ins. 14st 5lbs.
Career: Aberdeen Lads' Club. Dundee United 1957. LIVERPOOL July 1961 (£22,000). Tranmere Rovers as player-assistant manager December 1971, player-manager April 1972-April 1974, manager to April 1975. Stalybridge Celtic as a player later in 1975. Barrow player-manager 1976 for a spell. Liverpool's chief scout 1986-7.
International honours: Scotland. Scotland Schoolboy.
Club honours: Liverpool, European Cup-winners' Cup runners-up 1966. Division One champions 1964, 1966. Division Two champions 1962. FA Cup winners 1965.
A major figure in every way, Ron Yeats' massive presence as captain and centre-half was of inestimable value for a decade. Naturally dominant in the air, he was also quick to recover and few forwards got the better of him, even though he was perhaps slow on the turn. Originally a slaughterman, he later had haulage and catering business interests on Merseyside.

YOUNGER, Thomas **1956-59**
Goalkeeper. 120 apps.
League debut: 18 August 1956.
Born: Edinburgh, 10 April 1930. Died: 13 January 1984.
6ft 1in. 14st 11lbs.
Career: Hutchison Vale. Hibernian 1948. LIVERPOOL June 1956 (£9,000). Falkirk player-manager June 1959 (in exchange for Bert Slater) to February 1960. Retired because of back trouble, but joined Stoke City July 1959. Leeds United September 1961 to October 1962. Leeds United scout. Toronto City coach. Hibernian PRO October 1969, later a Hibs' director.
International honours: Scotland. Scottish League.
Club honours: Hibernian, Scottish League champions 1951, 1952. Scottish Cup runners-up 1951.
Tommy Younger was a grand goalkeeper — dependable, quick, ever alert and a clean handler. He represented the BAOR XI when serving with the Royal Scots Greys in Germany. Latterly he was a successful businessman as a partner in a vending machine firm. Younger was a much-respected figure in the game and at the time of his death was President of the Scottish Football League.